JUDAISM AND
HUMAN RIGHTS

The B'nai B'rith Jewish Heritage Classics

Series Editors: DAVID PATTERSON · LILY EDELMAN

*Published in cooperation with the Commission
on Adult Jewish Education of B'nai B'rith*

JUDAISM AND HUMAN RIGHTS

Edited by MILTON R. KONVITZ

W · W · NORTON & COMPANY · INC · NEW YORK

To the memory of my brother
SOL A. KONVITZ

When Rabbi Joḥanan finished the Book of Job,
he said:

The end of man is death,
the end of cattle is to be slaughtered,
    all are doomed to die.
Blessed is he who is grown in the Torah,
and whose toil is in the Torah,
and who is giving pleasure to his Maker;
        and who has grown up with a good name,
        and with a good name departs from this world.

—Talmud, *Berakhot* 17a

Contents

Preface

A religion or a culture like Judaism, at least three thousand years old, cannot be expected to be all of one piece, homogeneous, self-contained, consistent, a neatly-constructed system of ideas. If Judaism were that, it would have died centuries ago and would be a subject of interest only to the historian and archeologist. Judaism has been a living force precisely because it is a teeming, thundering and clamoring phenomenon, full of contrary tendencies and inconsistencies.

Nor has Judaism ever been—in Egypt or Canaan, in Babylonia or Persia or Palestine, in Lithuania or Germany or America—a water-tight compartment. While containing what it itself has created, it has responded to outside forces and movements, and often its life was intertwined with the life of other religions and cultures. Notwithstanding obstructions and diversions and its own backwaters, Judaism has been a great river that has fed other streams and that itself has been fed by other streams.

To abstract from any such complex phenomenon as Judaism a single aspect such as human rights, and to present Judaism from this single perspective, is to run the risk of falsifying the subject. But it is a calculated risk which the philosophic or historical mind can hardly avoid. Only imagined religions or cultures are all of one piece and are as easily taken apart as put together. The authors of the essays here collected were all, I am sure, aware of the risks and dangers; but they sought truth, not as apologists but as scholars loyal to truth and the ideals of scholarship. More than this no one has a right to demand. There is no pretense in these papers that the Jewish people everywhere and throughout their long history without exception obeyed their own ideals of human

11

rights. The Hebrew Bible itself is an honest record of backsliding and waywardness. But it is also a record of the ideals of truth, justice, equality, goodness, and peace. Whether realized or not, the ideals remain as commandments, as human and historic forces. As Santayana rightly observed, "An ideal cannot wait for its realization to prove its validity."

In editing the essays for publication, I have sometimes changed the title of a paper in order to expose more clearly its subject. Authors have used different translations of the Bible, and their quotations from the Bible have been left undisturbed, except that the modern *you* has been substituted for *thou*. The Jewish authors speak of the Hebrew Bible or the Hebrew Scriptures, while the Christian writer speaks of the Old Testament; but the sophisticated reader easily adjusts to such discrepancies. Omissions have been indicated by the conventional three dots. Most footnotes have been omitted; the reader with a special interest can find them by turning to the original.

There were other essays I was tempted to include, but the exigencies of space compelled their exclusion. I hope that publication of this volume will stimulate scholars to make further explorations, so that in a few years there will be a need for at least one more volume on the subject.

I wish to express my gratitude to my friends Dr. David Patterson and Lily Edelman, editors of the Jewish Heritage Classics series, for their encouragement to prepare this volume. I wish to express my special thanks to the Hebrew University in Jerusalem—especially my friends Avraham Harman, president, and Professor Jacob Katz, rector—for affording me the opportunity, as visiting professor, to prepare this volume; and to my old and close friend Professor Julius Stone, of the Law Faculty at the University of Sydney, for more than I can say. I would also like to thank the Skillman Foundation of Detroit, Michigan, for their generous assistance given as a memorial to the late Rabbi Morris Adler.

Ithaca, New York   M. R. K.
December 8, 1971.

Introduction

There is no word or phrase for "human rights" in the Hebrew Scriptures or in other ancient Jewish texts. Nor is there in the Bible a word we would translate as "conscience." [1] Nor is there mention of due process of law. Yet, as the essays in this book make clear, the absence of these and related words and phrases does not mean the nonexistence of the ideals and values for which they stand or to which they point.

Take, as an example that comes readily to mind, the tantalizing incident of Abraham interceding for the cities of the plain, as it is related in Genesis:

> Then Abraham drew near before the Lord and said: "Will You indeed destroy the righteous with the wicked? Suppose there are fifty righteous within the city of Sodom; will You then destroy the place and not spare it for the fifty righteous who are in it? Far be it from You to do such a thing, to slay the righteous with the wicked, so that the righteous fare as the wicked! Far be it from You! Shall not the Judge of all the earth do right?" And the Lord said, "If I find at Sodom fifty righteous in the city, I will spare the whole place for their sake." Abraham answered, "Behold, I have taken upon myself to speak to the Lord, I who am but dust and ashes. Suppose five of the fifty of the righteous are lacking? Will You destroy the whole city for lack of five? . . . Suppose twenty are found there? . . . Suppose ten are found there?" He answered, "For the sake of ten I will not destroy it" (Genesis 18:22–34).

[1] In Genesis 20:5, the translation of the New English Bible uses the phrase "with a clear conscience" for the Hebrew, which says "in complete sincerity."

13

Abraham's appeal uses no abstraction like conscience, human rights, the right to life, personal responsibility and personal guilt rather than guilt by association; yet the story would have no significance unless these or such conceptions were presupposed or implied. The only explicit moral judgment in the passage is that provided in the rhetorical question: "Shall not the Judge of all the earth do right?" But what this rhetorical question implies is the conviction that, by some proper process, the innocent or virtuous must be separated from the guilty and sinful; that while it is right to punish the guilty, it is perverse to inflict undeserved suffering upon the innocent; that while the guilty may be spared on account of the innocent, it is wrong to subject innocent men to suffering when the guilty are punished. None of these propositions is stated, but what would be the point of the story were they not to be taken as presuppositions?

Or consider the famous incident of Naboth's vineyard (I Kings 21:1-24). Naboth owned a vineyard which Ahab, king of Israel, wanted. He offered to buy it for money or to exchange it for another vineyard, but Naboth said to the king: "The Lord forbid it me that I should give the inheritance of my fathers unto you." This refusal upset Ahab, and when the queen, Jezebel, learned of the incident, she procured two ruffians who testified at a trial of Naboth on false charges of blasphemy and sedition. After Naboth was convicted and executed, Jezebel told Ahab that Naboth was dead and that no obstacle now stood in the way of his taking possession of the vineyard.

As Ahab took possession of the murdered man's property, Elijah, the prophet, was sent by the Lord to say to him: "Thus says the Lord, Have you killed, and also taken possession? . . . Thus says the Lord, In the place where dogs licked the blood of Naboth shall dogs lick your blood, even yours. . . . And of Jezebel also spoke the Lord, saying, The dogs shall eat Jezebel by the wall of Jezreel."

There are no abstract principles or doctrines referred to by the record. There is no explicit statement regarding the guilt of the king and queen; there is no appeal to the Rule of Law, to the principle that the king himself is bound by the law and that he rules under God and the law; there is no explicit rejection of the claim that the king can do no wrong. The prophet asked rhetorically: "Have you killed, and also taken possession?" But not every killing is murder, and taking possession is not necessarily criminal. It is obvious that the ancient Hebraic mind did not tend to think in narrowly defined terms; it got along with very few legalisms, nor did it seem to need many abstract doctrines or principles. It had no need for the kind of thinking that went into Blackstone's *Commentaries,* nor for the formulations of the United Nations' Universal Declaration of Human Rights.[2] Yet the story of Naboth's vineyard and the condemnation of the king and queen of the Northern Kingdom would be without point if we could not read back into it modern conceptions of political theory, legal process, constitutional law, and fundamental human rights.

Erich Auerbach has written on this aspect of the Hebraic or Biblical mind and has contrasted it with the Homeric style. The latter leaves nothing in darkness or unexternalized; everything is made visible and palpable, and psychological processes leave nothing hidden or unexpressed; everything is brought to the foreground —thoughts are completely expressed, nothing is left in obscurity or unexpressed. The Biblical narrative, on the other hand, is fraught with unrevealed background, and character as well as story has many layers—layers of consciousness that may be in conflict and yet exist simultaneously. Much in a Biblical narrative is left dark and incomplete, meanings are concealed and mysterious, doctrines are unexpressed but incarnate. In the Hellenic style we have "externalized description, uniform illumination, uninterrupted connection, free expression, all events in the foreground, displaying unmistakable meaning." But in the Hebraic style we find instead: "certain parts brought into high relief, others left obscure, abruptness, suggestive influence of the unexpressed, 'background' quality, multiplicity of meanings and the need for interpretation, universal historical claims, development of the concept of the historically becoming, and preoccupation with the problematic."[3]

Greek philosophers agreed with Socrates that the unexamined life is not worth living; to them examination meant philosophical

[2] See Appendix B.

[3] Erich Auerbach, *Mimesis* (Garden City, N.Y.: Doubleday Anchor, 1957), p. 19.

analysis, as typified in the dialogues of Plato or a treatise by Aristotle. But the Hebraic mind simply assumed the existence of justice or the good—not as conceptions or abstractions or values, but as forces operative in the world and in human life and society. Justice did not need to be analyzed or examined; it needed only to be achieved or vindicated by the acts of men or nations. The Platonic philosophy of Forms or Ideas also projected Justice and the Good as metaphysical entities and forces, but the main drive of Plato's mind was toward the dialectic analysis which would expose the central role of these Forms. The essential differences were not substantive but methodological.[4]

Because of the nature of the Hebraic mind, the ancient and medieval Jewish scholars found it natural to follow the rabbinic maxim with respect to the study of Torah: "Turn it about, turn it about, for everything is in it." Indeed, it is precisely this quality of provocative openness that has sustained the Bible as a living book, that has made it possible for diverse men in different times and cultures—Philo of Alexandria, Akiba, Maimonides, Saadia Gaon, Samson Raphael Hirsch, Hermann Cohen, Martin Buber, and countless others—to take so much out of it or to read so much into it. Had the Hebrew Scriptures been written as a textbook of dogmatic theology, with all its terms clearly defined and all its assumptions and implications articulated, it could not have been an *aitz hayem,* a tree of life, productive and fruitful.

In their openness, the Hebrew Scriptures are like the fundamental provisions of the Bill of Rights of the United States Constitution, which contains no definitions of "religion," "press," "assembly," "an establishment of religion," the "free exercise" of "religion," "due process of law," "life," "liberty," "property," "privileges or immunities of citizens," or "the equal protection of the laws." These are all grand and sweeping generalities. But it is precisely because they are so open-ended that the Constitution has survived as a living, decisive force.

This quality of openness has been characteristic not only of the

4 See Milton R. Konvitz, "Law and Morals: In the Hebrew Scriptures, Plato, and Aristotle," *Conservative Judaism,* vol. 23, no. 44 (Winter 1969), pp. 67–71. Also published in Louis Finkelstein, ed., *Social Responsibility in an Age of Revolution* (New York: Jewish Theological Seminary, 1971).

ancient Hebraic mind but of the genius of Judaism generally—as the essays in this book bear witness. The fundamental liberties of man—as they are stated in the Bill of Rights or in the Universal Declaration of Human Rights—find their roots in the narratives and prophets of the Hebrew Scriptures and the teachings they have generated over the centuries.

This is not to claim that the Hebraic tradition is the only source of the liberties of man as they are known to us today. The tracing of ideas to their points of origin is a hazardous business. Besides, as the Bible itself teaches, the Creator did not make Israel the exclusive depository of all gifts and virtues. No one people was to have a monopoly on the qualities by which man is distinguished from the rest of creation. Long before the election of Israel, long before the covenant with Abraham, it was possible for man to be virtuous. Noah, we are told, was "a righteous man, blameless in his generation; Noah walked with God" (Genesis 6:9). No claim has been made that Job was a Jew, yet the Bible describes him as a man who was "blameless and upright, one who feared God, and turned away from evil" (Job 1:1). There is no ground, within the Jewish tradition itself, to make exaggerated claims: such claims would be violative of the spirit of universalism which is one of the most significant aspects of Judaism.

Furthermore, the Jewish tradition had its origin, but not its completion, three thousand or more years ago. The rabbinic conception of an oral revelation that interprets, supplements, and sustains the written revelation implies a never-ending process. Each generation and each scholar and teacher both receive and give. The tradition is thus both an inheritance and a creative opportunity. Is it any wonder, then, that the thoughts and teachings of the great rabbis reflect their own spirit and their own experience and milieu? The main stream of Judaism never tolerated a fundamentalistic position toward Torah: there was always the urgent, indispensable need for interpretation and inspiration; for creation as well as for reception and transmission. The result is that what is created is rooted in a past that is not wholly past, but a past that has an endless future—partly determined and closed, partly free and open.

This process involves a looking back and a looking forward at one and the same time, a use of memory and the intelligence simultaneously. This means an openness, but an openness guided by past experience, an openness that is canalized within banks, an openness that is not arbitrary but disciplined. This process not merely allows but invites the entry of "new" conceptions into the tradition. But the conceptions are new only in a relative sense, for they become immediately assimilated to an ancient system, where seemingly they have always existed but had not been seen or sufficiently noted: they are not inventions but discoveries— they had always been there, but no Columbus, no Maimonides or Hillel or Akiba, had taken the trouble to uncover them.

There are many examples of this process in this book. To cite one instance that will typify at least one aspect of its manifold ways, the Bible states: "When you make your neighbor a loan of any sort, you shall not go into his house to fetch his pledge. You shall stand outside, and the man to whom you make the loan shall bring the pledge out to you" (Deuteronomy 24:10–11). Today, thousands of years after this was written, we read this as a clear recognition of the "right of privacy." Are we reading a modern conception back into an ancient document? Yes and no. The conception was always "there," but it waited for us to uncover it. Adapting what was said by Molière's would-be gentleman, we may soberly say that the Hebrew Bible for nearly three thousand years has been speaking of the right of privacy without knowing it!—that is, without our knowing it. But then this is not essentially different from what has been the case with American constitutional law. The courts and legislatures today often speak of the right of privacy, but the right was first uncovered in the common law by Louis D. Brandeis and Samuel D. Warren in 1890, and was for the first time explicitly "found" in the United States Constitution by the Supreme Court in 1965.

This does not mean that in Judaism men are constantly fashioning and refashioning their faith to make it conform to their own image, to make it serve their own interests. This would be nothing short of idol-making and idolatry. Precisely the opposite is involved: in Judaism there is constant study, examination and re-examination of beliefs, values, historical events, narratives, myths, parables, proverbs, prophecy, and poetry, so that there may be no idols and no idolatries. There is a perpetual wrestling with and over every word, every name, every event, until it yields up its meaning. But then the meaning itself becomes a word, a name, an event, and the wrestling starts all over again. Interpretation thus is a transaction between an indeterminate past and an indeterminate present and future, and is grounded in the faith that somehow there is a conformity or harmony, howsoever subtle and delicate, between the past and the future and present. Thus the only real, the only radical heresy is fundamentalism, literalism—the belief that there is no room for interpretation, no role for the mind and spirit, that man is defined only by memory, that he receives but does not give, and that the Spirit that moved over the face of the waters no longer moves. For to deny the creative spirit of man is to deny the creative power of God, in whose image He made man. For Judaism, today is always the morning of the world. In the words of the morning service: "Daily He renews the work of creation." Man preeminently is renewed daily; and the Jew every day stands at Sinai, every day leaves Egypt and moves from slavery to freedom, from oppression to human rights.

Acknowledgments

Grateful acknowledgment is made for permission to reprint, in some cases in abridged form, the following:

Lord Acton, "The Bible and the Rule of Law," from *The History of Freedom and Other Essays*. London: The Macmillan Company, 1907. The passage is taken from Lord Acton's address to the Bridgnorth Institution in 1877.

Samuel Belkin, "Man Is a Tenant on Earth," from *In His Image*. New York: Abelard-Schuman, n.d.

Ben Zion Bokser, "Democratic Aspiration in Talmudic Judaism," from *Science, Philosophy and Religion, 2nd Symposium,* edited by Lyman Bryson and Louis Finkelstein. Conference on Science, Philosophy and Religion in Their Relation to Democratic Way of Life. New York: Harper & Row, 1942.

Louis Finkelstein, "Foundations of Democracy in the Scriptures and Talmud," from *Foundations of Democracy,* edited by F. Ernest Johnson. Institute for Religious and Social Studies, and New York: Harper & Row, 1947.

Henri Frankfort, "Kingship Under the Judgment of God," from *Kingship and the Gods*. Chicago: University of Chicago Press, 1948.

Eric G. Freudenstein, "Ecology and the Jewish Tradition," from *Judaism,* Fall 1970.

Robert Gordis, "Right of Dissent and Intellectual Liberty," from *Judaism for the Modern Age*. New York: Farrar, Straus & Cudahy, 1955.

Robert Gordis, "The Vision of Micah," from *Great Expressions of Human Rights,* edited by R. M. MacIver. Institute for Religious and Social Studies, and New York: Harper & Row, 1950.

Richard G. Hirsch, "There Shall Be No Poor," from a monograph of the same title. New York: Union of American Hebrew Congregations, 1965.

Samson Raphael Hirsch, "Do Not Destroy!" from *Horeb,* vol. II. New York: Soncino Press, 1962.

William A. Irwin, "A Common Humanity Under One God," from *The Old Testament: Keystone of Human Culture.* New York: Abelard-Schuman, 1952.

William A. Irwin, "The Rule of a Higher Law," from *The Intellectual Adventure of Ancient Man,* by Henri Frankfort et al. Chicago: University of Chicago Press, 1946.

Milton R. Konvitz, "Man's Dignity in God's World," from *Niv Hamidrashia.* Israel, 1971.

Milton R. Konvitz, "Many Are Called and Many Are Chosen," from *Judaism,* Winter 1955.

Milton R. Konvitz, "Judaism and the Democratic Ideal," from *The Jews: Their History, Culture, and Religion,* edited by Louis Finkelstein. New York: Harper & Row, 1949; 4th ed., 1971, Schocken Books.

Milton R. Konvitz, "The Good Life" (originally entitled "Judaism and the Pursuit of Happiness"), from *The Menorah Treasury,* edited by Leo Schwarz. Philadelphia: Jewish Publication Society of America, 1964.

Milton R. Konvitz, "Conscience and Civil Disobedience," published in 1971 in *Of Law and Man, Festschrift* for Justice Haim Cohn of Israel Supreme Court, edited by Shlomo Shoham, Tel Aviv University, and in Hebrew in a work on Jewish thought in the Diaspora, published by Brit Ivrit Olamit, Jerusalem. The essay was also the First Annual Horace M. Kallen Lecture at the Jewish Teachers Seminary-Herzliah, New York, in March 1971.

Norman Lamm, "The Right of Privacy," from *Judaism,* Summer 1967.

Moses Mendelssohn, "Freedom of Religion," from *Jerusalem,* translated and edited by Alfred Jospe. New York: Schocken Books, 1969.

Emanuel Rackman, "Judaism and Equality," from *Nomos IX: Equality,* edited by J. Roland Pennock and John W. Chapman. New York: Atherton Press, 1967.

PART I

Born Free and Equal

Editor's Note

"I lack nothing," wrote Franz Kafka, "except myself." From time without measure man has been desperately trying to fill that lack. It was the search for himself that compelled Thoreau to build his cabin in the woods at Walden Pond, for he was afraid, he said, that when he came to die, he might discover that he had not lived. What Thoreau meant, of course, was that his real self needed to live—the self, for example, that Socrates identified with his soul: that which made him a *self* and a *man*.

Much of the Hebrew Scriptures and of post-Biblical Judaism, in one way or another, expresses or implies this search—the search for that which, according to the Bible, is made in the "image of God." It is that real self that has dignity in the world that God has made. Since all such real selves were made by the same God —since all are the progeny of the same Adam and Eve—each self has the same dignity that all others have.

In this conception is rooted an ideal of equality: an ideal not granted by any constitution but found in the constitution of man himself. And all nations and races are of equal dignity. They may vary—as individual men do—in their gifts and talents; they may be "chosen" for different purposes, but this only means that they are "called" to perform different functions, to fulfill different obligations. Yet all remain members of the same—and the only— family of man.

"The foundation on which all [our constitutions] are built is the natural equality of man," Thomas Jefferson wrote to George Washington in 1784, "the denial of every preeminence but that annexed to legal office, and particularly the denial of preeminence by birth." This equality, Jefferson believed, was rooted in nature in the sense that nature's God ordained it; for men—as Jefferson put it in the Declaration of Independence—"are endowed by their Creator with certain inalienable rights"; and these rights are "inalienable" because they are part of the very composition of man himself, rights which all men have equally in order that they may enjoy equal dignity.

Man's Dignity in God's World

MILTON R. KONVITZ

"Son of man, stand upon your feet, and I will speak with you."
That is what the prophet Ezekiel heard from one who appeared
to him in the likeness of the glory of the Lord. In this stirring
passage in the Bible, God asks man to neither fall on his knees
nor grovel in the dust nor cringe in fear in the presence of His
glory. What the prophet heard was: "Son of man, stand upon
your feet!"

It was like that with the very first man and woman. Adam
and Eve hid themselves from the presence of the Lord among the
trees of the Garden of Eden as they heard the voice of God
calling: "Where are you?" God did not want Adam to hide; He
wanted to see and speak with him.

It was in similar fashion that God addressed Cain, who had
killed his brother in cold blood; and one of the most severe punishments inflicted on Cain was that thereafter the face of God was
to be hid from him—no longer would he be able to see God
face to face. And so it was with Abraham and the other patriarchs: they stood up to God almost as His equals; they argued
with Him on the basis of moral principles common to both. Even
Avimelekh, the unfortunate king of Gerar who brought Sarah into
his harem because Abraham had misrepresented her as his sister,
spoke up to God, not as a craven idiot, but as a man standing
on his feet, and he questioned God as to whether it was just
to slay innocent folk.

Man has dignity; he has a head on his shoulders and he walks

27

upright; he has a moral sense, he has intelligence, he uncovers
the secrets of the universe. He is a creature within the universe,
yet he is of a nature that transcends the universe, and so he is
at one and the same time the most noble thing in the universe
and more noble than the universe. "Even if the universe were to
crush him," the French philosopher Pascal said, "man would still
be nobler than what kills him because man knows that he dies;
but of its advantage over him the universe itself is unaware."

> When I look at Your heavens, the work of Your fingers,
>   the moon and the stars which You have established;
> What is man that You are mindful of him,
>   and the son of man that You do care for him?

> Yet You have made him little less than God,
>   and do crown him with glory and honor.
> You have given him dominion over the works of Your hands;
>   You have put all things under his feet . . .

In Psalm 8 one thus finds the essence of the Hebraic view of
the status of man in the universe. There is no belittling of man
in order to increase the glory or power of God. On the contrary,
God the Creator treats man—every son of Adam—as a partner
in the work of creation. Man is not merely a creature, he is also
a creator, a "little less than God." Man has no need to create
the moon and the stars, the sheep and the oxen, the birds of the
air and the fish of the sea; but the work of righteousness was
not finished in the first six days of creation; it was only begun
when God created Adam and Eve in His divine image.

In the creation of the kingdom of God on earth, man is indispensable. God will not coerce any son of man to walk in God's
ways, to keep His statutes and His ordinances and listen to His
voice. Man has the freedom to choose life or death, the blessing
or the curse; and throughout the Bible God pleads with man to
follow in the path of righteousness. Like a father who desperately
wants to see his wayward son straighten out, advising, remonstrat-
ing, crying, pleading, finally even threatening, yet knowing that
this child of His, man, has the freedom to do as he pleases. "If
what is commanded be not in the power of everyone," said Eras-

mus, "[then] all the numberless exhortations in the Scriptures, and
also all the promises, threatenings, expostulations, reproofs, as-
severations, benedictions, and maledictions, together with all the
forms of precepts, must of necessity stand useless." Once having
created man as a being possessing reason and free will, God will
do little without man. The son of man stands upon his feet to
listen as God speaks to him; but God speaks to man because He
is dependent upon him. God does not speak to cattle and birds
and fish, for they can do His bidding without hearing His voice;
but man, and man alone, is free, in a realm beyond cause and
effect, for he alone lives in the realm of good and evil. God could
have made the world so that there would be no evil in it, but
then there would be no good in it either. But the world, as Nich-
olas Berdyaev has said, "is full of wickedness and misery precisely
because it is based on freedom—yet that freedom constitutes the
whole dignity of man and of his world. Doubtless at the price
of its repudiation evil and suffering could be abolished, and the
world forced to be 'good' and 'happy'; but man would have lost
his likeness to God, which primarily resides in his freedom."

So it is that one could ask of God: "Where would You be,
Lord, what would You do if men gave judgments for bribes; if
men abhorred justice and perverted equity; if rich men were full
of violence, and everyman had wicked scales and a bag of deceit-
ful weights? What, Lord, would You do if men refused to see
beauty in Your handiwork, if parents refused to love their children and if neighbor refused to love neighbor? It is because of
my eyes and my ears and my heart that there is beauty in the
world, and compassion, and the love of a man for his wife and
their child. You, Lord, are dependent upon me to make and sustain a world worthy of reverence. If I did not salute the river before crossing it, if I did not venerate any person or thing, if I
did not reverence and love You, Lord, what, Lord, could You
do about it and where would You be?"

Just as God can and does say, "Son of man, stand upon your
feet, and I will speak with you," man, in turn, can say to God:
"Lord of the universe, listen to me, I am about to sing a lovely
song; look at me, for I am about to create a beautiful painting;
turn toward me, and You will see that in a moment there will be

love in the world, as I take this woman to be my wife; watch, Lord, as I increase justice in the world by lessening a poor man's misery; I am about to create mercy and loving-kindness as I operate on a patient, or go into a strange distant land to fight malaria or sleeping sickness; and once more, Lord, look at me as I land on the moon, and watch me as I discover stars that have not been in the heavens for thousands of years."

In God's dependence upon man we find the secret of the doctrine of election.[1] God was unknown in the world which He had made; men worshipped sticks and stones; they did nothing to enhance His glory; so God looked down upon the human scene and found some men with whom He made a bargain. He said to them that if they would spread His name and make known to the rest of mankind that there is one God and that He has one law of righteousness for all men everywhere, He would try to look after them in some special way. In its essence this election doctrine is an open admission by God that He is dependent upon man for His glory. But in disclosing to man that God depends on him for His glory, God in this act laid the basis for man's glory as well. The glory of one is the glory of the other. There would be no glory in human life if man could not feel that whatever he does, if his heart is directed toward God, he does in a way that is worthy of a being made in the image of God. It was this thought that Gerard Manley Hopkins expressed:

It is not only prayer that gives God glory but work. Smiting on an anvil, sawing a beam, whitewashing a wall, driving horses, sweeping, scouring, everything gives God some glory if being in His grace you do it as your duty. To go to communion worthily gives God great glory, but to take food in thankfulness and temperance gives Him glory too. To lift up the hands in prayer gives God glory, but a man with a dungfork in his hand, a woman with a sloppail, give Him glory too. He is so great that all things give Him glory if you mean they should.

In this passage Hopkins, a Roman Catholic priest-poet, echoed a famous saying of the Rabbis of the Talmud:

I am a creature of God and my neighbor is also His creature. My work is in the city and his is in the field. I rise early to my work

[1] For a discussion of the "chosen people," see pp. 75 ff.

and he rises early to his. He cannot excel in my work and I cannot excel in his. But perhaps you say, I do great things while he does small things. We have learned that it matters not whether a man does much or little, if only he directs his heart to heaven (*Berakhot* 17a).

In this connection one recalls an incident in the life of the late Chief Rabbi Kuk. Some persons complained to him that some of the Jewish pioneers in the Palestine farming cooperatives were not sufficiently religious, for they did not observe (at least not strictly) some of the rites and ceremonies of Judaism. Here is how the Chief Rabbi answered them: "Why should we say they are not religious? Is it not a religious act of great merit to convert a desert place into farmland and gardens? Is not such work a form of prayer?"

It is this polarity of God and man, as revealed in the Bible, with its consequent interdependence or partnership of God and man, which gives man his religious sense. Insofar as a man has this sense, he can feel that his life counts. Unless one's thoughts and feelings are rooted in this polarity, the human condition becomes the subject of a tale told by an idiot. For it is this polarity of God and man, the polarity of man as creature and creator, that alone can shatter the shroud of conventionality that our habits and customs spread over the world, so that we fail to respond quickly and warmly to the beauty of our days and nights, to the alternation of good and evil, justice and injustice; and so it is, as Rabindranath Tagore once said, that "on the day when the lotus bloomed, alas, my mind was straying, and I knew it not. My basket was empty and the flower remained unheeded." Days and years pass, and we do not keep ourselves in readiness for the plenitude that God offers but does not deliver. He will not live for us—each man must live his own life; each man must embrace experience with his own sense and mind and with his own freedom. Insofar as man is a creature, his hours and days are numbered, and his freedom is limited; insofar as man is a creator, he can, as the poet Shelley has said, become conscious of an infinite number of ideas in a minute and make that minute into eternity.

The great Ḥasidic Rabbi Bunam of Pzhysha once said: Everyone must have two pockets, so that he can reach into the one or the other as the need might arise. In his right pocket are the words: "For my sake was the world created"; and in his left pocket, the words: "I am earth and ashes."

Rabbi Bunam must have said this while recalling Abraham's standing before God and arguing with Him regarding the fate of the sinful cities of the plain. "Behold," said Abraham, "I have taken upon myself to speak to the Lord, I who am but earth and ashes. Suppose five of the fifty righteous are lacking? Will You destroy the whole city for lack of five?" Here in a brief flash is the Hebraic conception of the dignity of man: he who is but earth and ashes can speak to God, can even dare to argue with Him, because for his sake the earth was created.

Judaism and Equality

EMANUEL RACKMAN

Biblical Hebrew has no word for "equality." Nonetheless in the Book of Leviticus the Jews were told, "You shall have one law for the stranger and citizen alike; for I the Lord am your God" (Leviticus 24:22). Equality before the law, according to Judaism, was divinely ordained. By the same token Hebrew has many equivalents for "differentiate," and God Himself presumably ordained many of the differences—not only natural but also legal. Can such antithetical mandates be reconciled so that God's attribute of justice is not impugned and His role respected as "Judge of all the earth"? . . . Not easily, but the literature of Jewish law and theology reflects a continuing tension between the ideal of human equality and the many inequalities that result from differences for which the tradition holds the Creator Himself responsible. In the emerging dialectic, values other than equality play their part, as do the different functions assigned to human being in society as a whole.

. . . Judaism holds that God endows all humans with His image—the *Tzelem Elohim,* which Jewish philosophers in the Aristotelian tradition often equated with reason. The dogma was so basic in Judaism that the fundamental rationale for executing a murderer was that he destroyed a divine image. He killed, in a sense, God's likeness. "Whoso sheds man's blood, by man shall his blood be shed; for in the image of God made He man" (Genesis 9:6).

Judaism, however, also derives human likeness from the fact

33

that God had created only one man from whom all humanity is descended. No one could ever argue that he was superior in birth because of his genealogy. "Man was created alone. And why so? . . . That families might not quarrel with each other. Now, if at present, though but one was originally created, they quarrel, how much more if two had been created!" (Babylonian Talmud, *Sanhedrin* 38a.) That all men have only one progenitor, whereas animals were created by God in the plural number, was held to mean that all human beings are born equal. They enjoy this equality by virtue of the very fact that they were born, even if they never attain to the faculty of reason. This was the only source on which Thomas Paine could rely in his *Rights of Man* to support the dogma of the American Declaration of Independence that all men are created equal. And this dogma was basic in Judaism. . . .

Nonetheless, even as all men are born equal because they all descend from the one Adam, men do differ. "The creation of the first man *alone* was to show forth the greatness of the Supreme King of Kings, the Holy One, blessed be He. For if a man mints many coins from one mould, they are all alike, but the Holy One, blessed be He, fashioned all men in the mould of the first man, and not one resembles the other" (*ibid.*). Men differ in voice, appearance, and mind; men differ in sex and color; men differ ethnically and nationally. What is more, God Himself willed that they shall differ in language and geographic distribution. Within their national groupings, there are freemen and slaves, kings and subjects, priests, Levites, and prophets—and of all these differences the Bible takes note. To some it gives *de facto* recognition; to others even *de jure* recognition. Some differences it prescribes itself and it accords to the differentiated special duties and privileges. How can this be reconciled with the command to have one law for the citizen and the stranger? And how consonant is this proliferation of mankind with the prophetic protest, "Have we not all one father?"

To this very day the annals of Jewish history, the folios of Jewish law, and the apologetics of Jewish theologians reflect continuing concern with this dichotomy. . . . Too often the legal norms were ignored and the prophets inveighed against the oppressors; sometimes rabbis were progressive and at other times conservative and reactionary; communal leaders were often on the side of the status quo and often against it. As among all national and ethnic groups there were forces other than the law that precipitated or retarded the movement toward maximum social, economic, and political equality. Scriptures and Talmudic materials were quoted by all sides. Yet Jews have adequate cause for boasting that the ideal of equality suggested by the very first chapter of the Bible was fulfilled in their society to a greater extent than among the many peoples with whom they had contact in their millennial history, and today the collectives of the . . . State of Israel are not only living laboratories of the ideal's fullest fruition but also seats of very impressive philosophical discussion on the meaning of equality. Despite the absolutely equal sharing of goods in these collectives, there is growing concern that some members enjoy more prestige than others by virtue of their positions as decision-makers or of their greater ability to produce, think, or lead. Even this concern, this feeling of guilt, bespeaks an enduring preoccupation with an absolute ideal and the difficulty encountered in fulfilling it in practice.

Male and Female

From the seemingly divergent accounts in Genesis describing how God created Adam and Eve, one derives at least, first, that a man leaves his parents to cleave to his wife—wife in the singular. . . . While polygamy was practiced lawfully by many Jews, as it is in some oriental countries even today, monogamy appears to be the ideal. Second, women share the divine image; their lives, limbs, and property are to be accorded the same respect accorded those of men. Third, men and women have different functions. Judaism is, therefore, less receptive to the idea of a natural hierarchy but accepts the legitimacy of functional inequalities.

That a man might lawfully wed many women while a woman was bound to one husband at a time was a flouting of the ideal of equality. But Jewish law was committed to another value—the importance of the identity of the father in the case of offspring. Therefore, it could not countenance polyandry, which would result in children's uncertainty as to who their father was. To abolish polygamy was not easy, for most men resisted change. It required a considerable moral and social development that finally, in about the year 1000, culminated for occidental Jews in the ban of Rabbi Gershom against the practice. The Biblical ideal of man cleaving to one wife gave impetus to this moral and social development. Whenever it did discuss the polygamy of the patriarchs, some special reason for it was given: Abraham impregnated Hagar at Sarah's request; Jacob married two sisters because of his father-in-law's fraud and took two concubines at the request of the sisters. Kings were warned in it, moreover, not to enlarge their harems unduly. Especially noteworthy is the word used in the Bible to describe the relationship between two wives of the same man; it is *tzarah,* which also means "misfortune" and suggests that two wives of one husband can only bring grief to each other.

Yet, the advantage of the male over the female still predominates in the inequitous law of divorce. . . . Whereas males and females who had reached their legal majority were absolutely equal in consummating a marriage, they were not so in divorce.

Because the husband performs the formal act creating the marriage, the Law assumed that it is he who must give the order to write and deliver the bill of divorce. He who created the sacred bond must undo it. In Judaism, including the Kabbalah, the male is regarded as the active principle in the universe and the female as the passive principle. Therefore, in marriage and divorce it is he who must perform the legally operative acts.

Yet without the consent of the female, a marriage could not be consummated. But until the year 1000, her consent to the divorce was not required. The need for her consent was slower in coming because the Law assumed that it served no purpose to keep her wedded to a man who did not respect her. The Law sought only to provide for her maintenance after divorce.

Moreover, her right to sue for a divorce is suggested by the Talmud, not the Bible. The Law labored under a presumption that any woman would prefer a bad marriage to no marriage: "It is better to live with any other than alone." Yet virtual equality is now achieved and today where there is mutual consent, no court approval is required and no grounds for divorce need be offered.

If either spouse withholds consent, a court of competent jurisdiction is able to adjudicate and act against the will of either spouse.

Nonetheless an inequality, which begs for correction, persists. Because it is the husband who must give the order to write the bill of divorce, the court is still impotent to terminate the marriage when the husband is not subject to the jurisdiction of the court, when he is missing or insane, and especially in states in which rabbinic tribunals have no authority except such as the parties want to vest in them. Therefore, wives are often helpless in getting the necessary bill of divorce and without it cannot marry other men. In similar circumstances, however, men could remarry. They could, for example, deposit with a rabbinical court a bill of divorce for an insane wife. Because by Biblical law there is no objection to a man's being wedded to more than one woman at one time, a man can marry a second wife while his first is hospitalized. Or if a wife has disappeared, the husband can, again, deposit a bill of divorce with a rabbinical court. This inequity is very much the subject of discussion among modern rabbis who will have to promulgate new rules to solve a problem whose incidence is greater now, particularly in the areas of separation, due to the greater mobility of peoples and to the increase in and easier recognition of mental illness.

The extent to which the separate property of wives survived the creation of the marriage relationship was extraordinary. What a woman brought into the marriage as dowry became the husband's, but he was obligated, in the event that he predeceased or divorced her, to return the full amount he received. His liability in this connection was that of an insurer. The loss of the dowry because of acts of God or non-negligent management was no defense. What a woman acquired during her marriage by gift from friends or inheritance from relatives remained hers. Her right to separate property was well established. The husband became trustee of that property, taking the income for himself and conserving the corpus for her in the event of a divorce or his predeceasing her.

However, the one significant inequality was that she was not an heiress of her husband whereas he was her sole heir. She acquired from his estate her dowry, all separate property received by her during the marriage, and support until her remarriage. However, if she predeceased her husband, he took all of her estate to the exclusion even of the issue of the marriage.

In rights of inheritance generally males had the advantage. It would appear that the advantage enjoyed by males was due to the central importance, in the wealth of the community, of land, which the men were expected to cultivate and defend. The role of woman was truly domestic; she was to serve spouse and off-spring. The rest of the family's economy was the responsibility of the man. Thus differences in function may have contributed to the advantage of males.

But the husband had no special privileges with regard to the life and limb of his wife. He could not kill her even if he apprehended her in the commission of adultery. He was also responsible for torts committed against her person not excluding torts committed in the course of coitus.

Offspring

Jewish law limited the right of the father to disinherit his children—or, for that matter, any of the heirs entitled to the succession. In his lifetime the father could dispose of his property as he chose. But even a written document altering the Biblical pattern of inheritance was a nullity. The Oral Law did permit him to alter the disposition among his sons, or among his daughters if he had no sons. He could prefer one to the others. Yet the Rabbis frowned on such behavior; their rationale was based on the religious value of penitence. One had no right to disinherit a child in anger or resentment because the child might repent, or the child's offspring might prove worthy of the estate. Saints are often born to parents who are villains.

The rights of issue were so vested that it did not matter whether the children were born in or out of wedlock, or whether they were even legitimate. A child was deemed illegitimate only in the rarest situation when proof was incontrovertible that he was born of an adulterous or incestuous relationship—and to prove this was almost impossible. The child born out of wedlock was legitimate even if there was no subsequent marriage between its parents. And these children were heirs. They were not subjected to the indignity of proving that they were entitled to take a share of their father's estate so long as their paternity was either generally known or admitted by the father in his lifetime. Moreover, if an illegitimate son, and *a fortiori* one born out of wedlock who was not illegitimate, was the first issue of the father, he was entitled to all the rights of primogeniture.

The rights of the first-born were generally prescribed. The Bible had said that they were entitled to a double portion. Did that mean two-thirds of the estate in every case, or two portions of the estate after it was divided by the number of sons plus one? The latter interpretation was upheld. The Biblical verse was strictly construed in this respect, as it was with every other problem that arose.

The first-born took his double portion only of such property that the deceased actually possessed at the time of his death. Claims of the deceased were not to be included. In addition, the first-born had to prove beyond the shadow of a doubt that he was the father's first-born. If a stillborn preceded him, he forfeited his special position. He must also have been born before his father died—he did not acquire special privileges as a foetus, and thus could not take more than his twin brother born moments after him. Moreover, he must have been born naturally from the womb and not by a Caesarean operation. This was strict construction of a verse, proscribing a right which the Oral Law deemed anomalous and inconsistent with the ideal of equality.

Perhaps the institution of primogeniture should have been abolished altogether rather than only radically proscribed. Certainly the narratives in . . . Genesis reveal how much grief resulted from the deeply entrenched preference for the first-born— for example, the rivalry between Ishmael and Isaac, Esau and Jacob, Reuben and Joseph. The Midrash so dwells upon these rivalries that one wonders whether some of Adler's psychoanalytic theories did not derive from it. But the Rabbis did not abolish the institution. The Bible had approved of it even if it did curtail its benefits, and the Rabbis were not prepared to abolish it altogether as they might well have done. Perhaps they regarded the first-born as the bearer of special social, economic, and educational responsibilities in the family. The first-born had been the family priests until the tribe of Levi replaced them as religious functionaries. As the eldest in the family, they were also expected to provide leadership after the father's death and even during his lifetime. Perhaps as Philo suggested, the first-born was owed a debt of gratitude by the father. After all, he made the father a father. Therefore, some special consideration was accorded him in the distribution of the estate. But to that extent the ideal of equality remains compromised.

If Rabbis frown upon a Biblical law but refrain from nullifying it, is their thought to be regarded as deontological and Kantian rather than as teleological and utilitarian? It would be more accurate to say that it was all of these: The Law was theocentric —divine in origin and with creative achievement ever oriented to the fulfillment of God's will. Never to lose sight of this commitment, the Law had its suprarational mandates not readily explicable in terms of human values and interests. Every branch of the Law had them. But the Law was given to people, who alone were responsible for its development. The Bible itself appeals to man to comprehend the justice-content of the Law. It also bids him to live by the Law, not to perish because of it. Thus suprarational norms remain the Law's theocentric roots and prevent it from becoming altogether positive in character. But rabbinic creativity had to be mindful too of ends and utility.

Slaves and Slavery

Jewish law distinguished between slaves who were Jews and slaves who were non-Jews, usually called Canaanite slaves. Their legal status was not the same, and the inequality derived from religious values that conflicted with the value of equality.

The abolition of the ownership of one Jew by a fellow Jew was accomplished centuries ago. Those who heard on Mount Sinai that all Jews were God's servants were not to become further indentured to coreligionists who shared with them a common bondage to the same Master! But what is most significant about

this result is that it represented the achievement of Jewish jurisprudence—that very legalism of the Pharisees which became the
butt of Christian criticism.

No one became a slave for failure to pay a debt. The sale was
permitted only for failure to pay for one's theft. Furthermore, a
man could be sold only if he failed to pay the principal amount
due on the theft. If he could pay the principal but not the double
or quadruple or quintuple damages due, he could not be sold
into slavery. Nor could he be sold as a punishment for false witness. The Bible said "theft" and theft alone it shall be!

Having become a slave, the person kept a status virtually like
that of a freeman. He could not be disgraced by a sale at public
auction. The work he could do for his master was not to be
difficult or degrading. Wherever possible, he was to continue in his
former education. He was also to enjoy the same food, clothing
and shelter as his master.

His life and limb were as protected as the life and limb of any
freeman. The master was as liable for homicide or mayhem as if
the slave were an equal. The slave's wife and children were not
sold with him, as was the custom in most other contemporaneous
cultures. As a matter of fact, the master was obliged to support
the slave's dependents.

The slave could acquire property and redeem himself to freedom. At most his bondage would last six years and out of any
property he acquired he could pay for any part of his unexpired
term. According to Maimonides, his wife could engage in gainful
employment. None of her earnings belonged to her husband's
master, even while the master remained responsible for her and
her children's maintenance. If the slave were ill for any part of
his term—up to one-half thereof—he did not have to serve any
extended period to compensate for the time of his indisposition.

He could sue and be sued. He was also competent as a witness.
In one respect only was his legal status different from that of a
freeman. The master could compel him to take a Canaanitish slave
woman as a wife. The progeny would belong to the master, for the
status of the progeny was that of their mother. In an age when
polygamy was quite prevalent, this was not a serious invasion of
personal rights.

Even in those isolated instances where the master was permitted to cause the Jewish male slave to mate with a non-Jewish female slave—the only instance justifying the contention that the master owned the very body of the slave—the moral standards of a monogamous relationship were applicable. Promiscuous relationships were prohibited. The institution of slavery was never to place in jeopardy the lofty moral ideals of the Law.

To demonstrate the high value set upon freedom, a slave who refused to become free had his ear pierced with an awl. Unlike the Hammurabi code, which prescribed this penalty for a runaway slave, Jewish law prescribed it for the slave who did not avail himself of an opportunity to become free.

When the slave's term expired, the master was to give him a gift —severance pay. Talmudic jurists fixed the amount instead of relying upon the master's generosity. Moreover, they exempted the gift from execution by the slave's creditors to insure the slave of the wherewithal for a new start in life.

With this kind of legal development, it was to be expected that one would hardly ever want to become a master of a Jewish slave. And thus by a rigid legalism slavery was abolished—a result sermons and homilies could hardly achieve.

A Jewish girl could become a slave only if her father sold her into bondage prior to her reaching puberty. The sale, however, was less a sale than a betrothal, for she was automatically emancipated upon reaching puberty unless her master or her master's son wed her. If the master or his son did wed her, she had the status of a wife with all the privileges thereunto appertaining. Moreover, her consent to the betrothal was required.

In all other respects her legal status was that of the male Hebrew slave. And neither the male nor the female could be resold by the master to another.

The Oral Law did not permit even a non-Jew to be enslaved without giving him sufficient status as a Jew to insure the protection of his life and limb and his partial participation in the religious life of the family and community. As such, he had a higher status than even a free Gentile. If the non-Jew was brought with the express proviso that he should not be converted to Judaism, then he had to acquiesce at least in the observance of the seven Noahide laws.

It would appear, however, that non-Jewish slaves preferred Jewish owners. As a consequence of their becoming members of a Jewish household, pursuant to the performance of the appropriate rituals, they could not be killed with impunity. There was no difference whatever in the law of homicide, whether willful or accidental, as to whether the victim was a Jewish freeman or a non-Jewish slave. Torts committed against the non-Jewish slave by persons other than the master were actionable. Though the recovery was the master's, the injuring of slaves was deterred by the very fact that a tort against him was actionable. And the master himself did not escape with impunity for his own torts against his non-Jewish slave. Emancipation of the slave might be the consequence of the master's tort. Under certain circumstances the master would even pay the death penalty for having killed his slave, although the Law also sought to protect his disciplinary authority. If a master refused to feed his non-Jewish slave (presumably as a disciplinary measure), the community performed this obligation for the slave as it performed it for the poor generally. The Rabbis even penalized a Jewish master for selling his slave to a non-Jew who would not respect the non-Jewish slave's right to observe Sabbaths and festivals. The master was compelled to repurchase the slave though the cost of the repurchase might be ten times the amount of the original sale. Moreover, the master could not sell a non-Jewish slave even to a Jew residing outside the territorial limits of the land of Israel. Such a sale automatically emancipated the slave.

True, the Law frowned upon the emancipation of the non-Jewish slave. Such emancipation would give the non-Jewish slave the status of a full-fledged Jew, and the Law did not encourage this way of increasing the Jewish population. The Law abhorred the less stringent sexual code prevailing among non-Jews. Many authorities even observed that the non-Jewish slave would prefer slavery, with its license for promiscuity, to freedom as a Jew with its stern limitations on sexual relationships. Not having been reared in a milieu stressing the high moral standards the Law imposed, the non-Jewish slave was not to be catapulted into a free society that would make him unhappy or that he would feel constrained to corrupt. Nonetheless, the Rabbis ruled that if by emancipation a moral purpose was achieved, or a *mitzvah* (a religious goal) was fulfilled, one might violate the injunction against freeing the non-Jewish slave. If, for example, a non-Jewish female slave has been promiscuous with the people at large, the Law urged her master to free her in the hope that she might marry and establish a monogamous relationship with a husband, infidelity to whom would be less probable because of the threat of the death penalty.

Society and State

In the liberal tradition equality is stressed as a means to freedom and inequalities are often justified when they promote freedom. In the Jewish tradition equality is not principally a means but rather a fulfillment of all men's "creatureliness" under God, the only Master. Despite inescapable functional inequalities, equality was achieved within the family and household. It had to be achieved also within society and state. Indeed, equality must be achieved for the sake of order as well.

According to Maimonides, society requires a ruler "who gauges the actions of the individuals, perfecting that which is deficient and reducing that which is excessive and who prescribes actions and moral habits for all of them to practice always in the same way, until the natural diversity is hidden by the many points of conventional accord, and so the society becomes well-ordered."

Yet shall the goals of equality and order negate the possibility of differences, in intellectual and moral excellence or in economic productivity, which freedom makes possible? Freedom is also a means to serve God better and improve His earth and its inhabitants. The Law certainly cherished the value of freedom, but equality was to be safeguarded by many principles.

Judaism was committed to the general principle that all are equal in the eyes of the Law. This applied to kings as it did to commoners.

With respect to racial differentiation, Judaism always was, and still is, color blind. Males and females, except as previously indicated, were equal in all matters civil and criminal. Women could not be judges or witnesses because this was inconsistent with their primary household roles. This did not mean that their credibility was impugned. With respect to all matters in which strictly formal testimony was not required, they could impart information to religious functionaries and would be believed. It was in a trial that might lead to a capital or corporal punishment, or in the creation of a new personal status such as marriage or divorce, or in an action in tort or contract, that they suffered exclusion. Indeed, there were matters in which they might be the only or most readily available witnesses and the Law had to make exceptions and admit their testimony. A classic example is a tort action for an assault committed in the women's section of a synagogue where no men could possibly be present. Moreover, they could act as judges in a civil action if the parties consented. Thus their exclusion from participation in the judicial function was not a reflection on their inferiority—although many Rabbis were unchivalrous enough so to hold—but rather on the need for keeping women unseen that men might be more chaste.

Paradoxically, the one great exception to the principle were persons who had achieved greater intellectual and moral excellence. They were held accountable to stricter standards in tort and contract. "A distinguished person is different." More is expected of him, says the Talmud.

In their earliest history Jews maintained the idea that leadership was the responsibility of merit rather than the prerogative of a class or family. In the religious sphere one tribe did ultimately become responsible for the performance of specified rituals, and in the political sphere one family acquired an indefeasible right to kingship. However, this situation did not long endure and all of the most important opportunities for leadership in temporal and spiritual matters became available to all equally. Even Moses divided the temporal and spiritual authority between Joshua, of the tribe of Ephraim, and Aaron, his brother, of the tribe of Levi. The "Judges" were recruited from all ranks to deliver the people from oppressive invaders, and they founded no dynasties.

The prophets especially championed the ideal of equality, denouncing as they did the exploitation of the poor by the rich and disregard of the Law, which sought to achieve economic equality by such institutions as the Jubilee with its redistribution of the land every fifty years. The prophets also gave the world the messianic vision of an age when there would be universal peace and justice and nature itself would become perfect. The Rabbis, who succeeded the prophets as the "Law's doctors," were also recruited from all ranks and even from among converts to Judaism. The requirement that they take no remuneration for their services made their labor one of love with the result that as a group they wielded more authority over the people than did priests or kings whose limited authority was hereditary. Thus the Jewish community ever enjoyed the circulation of the intellectual and moral elite and there never was a bar to the emergence of new leadership.

The most effective safeguard against the evils of any kind of monopoly on spiritual or temporal authority was the fact that Judaism was an exoteric rather than an esoteric religion; the law was promulgated, taught, and interpreted by all. "Would that every man in the camp of Israel were a prophet," exclaimed Moses.

In this instance, equality advanced the cause of freedom.

Despite the unequivocal establishment by the Bible of a hereditary priesthood, the virtual obliteration of the difference between clergy and laity was achieved almost two thousand years ago. This was a giant step in the direction of social equality.

The priests and Levites of whom the Bible speaks were the only persons in the Jewish community who had special status by virtue of their birth. Even long before the destruction of the central shrine in Jerusalem, their claim to hegemony over the spiritual lives of the people was successfully challenged by prophets and rabbis who came from all classes of society. In the year 70 they lost their special roles and rabbis became the guardians and exponents of the Law. And a rabbi never had any special sacerdotal power. He is nothing more than a layman who has more knowledge of Judaism than most people and can, therefore, offer them religious guidance. He does not even conduct religious services except as a layman might.

How the Bible created the anomaly of a hereditary priesthood in the face of so much concern for equality is itself a revelation of its commitment to the ideal that men shall not crave power over their fellows. Students of political theory are well aware of the discussions from Plato to the present about citizens' avoidance of civic responsibility. The best people often choose not to hold political office. Particularly with regard to the performance of sacred tasks in God's shrine, one may expect that the truly pious and devout will shy away, deeming themselves unworthy in thought and deed of any special role in the public service of God. Failure to decline is itself proof of the lack of the humility necessary for the purpose. Therefore, one must be drafted and only one who is drafted can qualify. Thus one never chooses to be a priest or Levite. One has the obligation thrust upon him, and this is the only way it could possibly be unless the temple was to be staffed by people driven by ambition to rise above their brethren.

The tradition regards Moses himself as a drafted leader. When Aaron, his brother, was asked to be the High Priest, he too hesitated. Moses had to order him to serve. Moses also had to seize the Levites forcibly and ordain them keepers of the shrine. And because they were drafted, it did not mean that they were rewarded. On the other hand, they were told of the greater hazards that would be theirs because of their service of the Lord. They would have to fulfill prescriptions meticulously and risk punishment for sins of omission or commission. Furthermore, they were given no share of the Promised Land. Fear, perhaps, of the extensive land holdings of the Egyptian priesthood—whom even Joseph could not expropriate—may have been behind the Law's denial to the priests and Levites of any territory in Canaan. The Law even hedged their statutory gifts and taxes with so many conditions and restrictions that their delivery was in effect voluntary. A Jew was required to set the tithe gifts aside, thus learning the discipline of self-denial, but if he chose to let them rot, there was no one to stop him.

The Rabbis' role in classical Judaism was determined primarily by a long-felt need to prevent the surrogates of God from exploiting their position for personal aggrandizement. All the safeguards proved inadequate to stop the priests and Levites from abusing their election to serve God. The prophets had to denounce them for aligning themselves with the rich against the poor and the Pharisees had to denounce them for their usurpation of political power as well. The Rabbis ruled that no one might derive a profit by his pursuit of Torah. Rabbis were to be volunteers. If they did perform services for another, they could lawfully be compensated only for time lost from their non-rabbinic vocations (no fewer than one hundred named in the Talmud were artisans). Indeed the Rabbis were not clergymen. The measure of their authority was based principally on the confidence of the community of believers.

The Law assured equality of status to all non-Jews who embraced the creed and practice of Judaism. Although there were some minor restrictions, one can generalize that all converts enjoyed the same privileges and were subject to the same duties as Jews. Yet, whereas their legal status was one of equality, socially they were often subjected to discrimination and suspicion. By the same token many rabbis held them in higher esteem than those who were born Jewish, but not always did these rabbis prevail against popular prejudice. Notwithstanding the prejudice, several important rulings reveal that the kinship of Jews with each other is not the kinship of blood but the kinship of a common faith. This is shown by the fact that in prayer the convert, no differently from the priest who can trace his male lineage to Aaron the High Priest, addresses God as "the God of our fathers." The patriarchs Abraham, Isaac, and Jacob, are his progenitors too. Moreover, the convert speaks of the land of Israel as the land given to his forbears in a special rite connected with the Pentecost festival.

Social and Political Equality

Jewish society was like all other societies in that social inequality did exist, even though the Law regarded all persons as equal. Yet generally the tradition was no respecter of wealth and the only aristocracy recognized was that based on piety and scholarship. And those so recognized rarely received special privilege or power unless a majority in the community—and this was true especially in the Middle Ages—elected them to comprise the "Seven Good Men of the City" who handled the affairs of the public.

A considerable amount of self-government prevailed in the medieval Jewish communities and by the twelfth century their form of government was democratic.

"The Seven Good Men of the City" were presumed to have been elected by a majority of male constituents and exercised authority because Jewish law recognized that a majority could properly create authority. Yet their powers were circumscribed. On many matters they had to conduct referenda, referring decisions to majority vote of all the male inhabitants of the city. On the other matters they had to obtain unanimous approval. On matters involving taxation and property it was often held that only a majority of taxpayers or property-holders could make decisions. Interestingly enough, if women were among the taxpayers or property-holders, they too were entitled to vote.

If only taxpayers and property-holders were to vote on matters pertaining to taxation or to the use and distribution of property, then the achievement of economic equality under such a system would appear to have been an impossibility. The expropriated would have no political means for improving their status. Paradoxically enough, it was precisely through a non-democratic institution that they achieved amelioration of their lot. The Bet-Din—constituted of the duly recognized doctors of the law—had virtually unlimited power to legislate as well as adjudicate matters affecting property. They could impose taxes and coerce the rich to support the poor as well as all public agencies and institutions. They also adjudicated occasional claims that the "Seven Good Men of the City" had exceeded their authority.

Thus whereas there was no clear distinction between legislative and judicial functions, there was a diffusion of power and a mixed form of government created by the people. Their choice of members of the Bet-Din was limited because the persons chosen had to qualify as scholars. However, once chosen, they had broad power and in patriarchal fashion could protect rich and poor and balance equities. The "Seven Good Men of the City" had more limited power, but anyone could qualify for that position.

The democratic experience of Jews in their own self-governing communities from the Middle Ages virtually up to World War II in Eastern and Central Europe predetermined their total acceptance of universal suffrage in the . . . State of Israel. Its legislature has the broadest governmental power comparable only to that of a king, who was anointed by the prophets. The latter, however, was subject to the Law and the sovereignty of God. According to Judaism, all the people, not just a majority, are denied the right to violate the basic norms of God's revealed will. Modern Israel's legislature is not now so limited. Yet it does represent the full blossoming of the seed of political equality—"one person, one vote"—contained in the medieval sources.

Economic Equality

It is doubtful whether the Levitical law of the Jubilee, which provided for a major redistribution of the promised land every fifty years, was ever implemented. However, the elimination of poverty was a Biblical injunction. It appears that a poor person even had a legal right to demand support from the community. But before modern times there were no significant experiments with total economic equality such as prevail in Israel's collectives. The Law itself is very respectful of the institution of private ownership of property. Limited the right to such ownership was—much more so than in modern capitalist states. Yet no measures were ever taken to limit incomes or restrict acquisitions. Consequently Jewish communities always had their very rich and very poor. They differed from other communities only insofar as they cultivated and maintained a high degree of responsibility for all their constituents. Jewish historians even maintain that one cause for the failure of Christendom to win more converts among Jews, aside from the suffering and humiliation inflicted on them, is that Jews within their own communities felt more secure than they might have felt outside ghetto walls that their basic needs would be fulfilled. Jews remembered that their exile was predicted by the prophets as a consequence of the exploitation of the poor by the rich; for social and economic inequalities, which were the root of all evil, were to be eradicated in the messianic era. Augustine regarded inequality as punishment for sin. Judaism, by contrast, regarded the continuance of inequality as sin and the cause for God's anger and national disaster.

Economic equality was the goal. Economic freedom was great. But it was weighted heavily with responsibility.

The Bible denies Jews the right to give interest to, or to take it from, Jews. To Gentiles Jews were permitted to pay interest and consequently they could also take it. Plato, in his *Laws,* suggested the same dichotomy for Athenians and "barbarians." Apparently, within the family, so to speak, free loans were to be the rule. Or it may be that a particular type of economy was to be promoted for the in-group while the out-group could engage in other economic activities, usually more peripheral ones.

During the Middle Ages the inequality became virtually academic because legal fictions were developed and Jews paid interest to fellow Jews as readily as they did to non-Jews and vice versa. Contemporary Israel has as yet done nothing to revive the Biblical prohibition, and modern capitalism is as entrenched there as in most of the Christian world.

The greatest tension between the ideal of equality and the imperative need for inequality is in the area of taxation. To justify the imposition of higher rates on the rich than on the poor, moderns have invented the notion of the equality of burden.

Jewish law also exacted more from those more able to pay. But in one instance the system of taxation so sustained the ideal of equality that few, if any, other rules of law gave the ideal comparable popularity and esteem. For the support of the temple, all Jews—rich or poor—gave the same half-shekel. This poll tax became one of the most cherished of all practices of Judaism. Vis-à-vis the central shrine, all were equal.

Theodor Herzl, founder of the Zionist movement at the turn of the century, evoked popular support for his cause by reviving the institution. Commitment to the belief that the solution of the Jewish problem was the establishment of a Jewish state was evidenced by the purchase of a "shekel"—cheap enough for all Jews, no matter how depressed their lot. Fulfillment of his ob-

jective required substantial gifts from affluent persons and an unequal burden on donors. Yet membership in the movement was
based on a nominal gift, equal for all. The new state in the
imagination of many Jews replaced the central shrine of yester-
year and the revival of a time-honored practice gave impetus to
the ideal of equality set forth in the Bible's first chapter.

Pagans and Gentiles

In no area of Jewish law is the tension between antithetical
ideas comparable to that which exists between Judaism's theological notion that all men are possessed of the divine image and
its strict, sometimes seemingly inhumane, attitude toward pagans
and Gentiles. The literature on the subject is so confusing and the
views of the authorities so disparate that only a few guidelines
can be indicated.

First, the "chosenness" of the Jewish people—no matter how
understood or expounded by prophets and philosophers—never
furnished a foundation for a legal norm. The basic norm of the
legal order was simply that pagans were "outlaws," for they had
not accepted the seven Noahide laws regarded as essential for
a society with a minimal morality. They would constitute no threat
to Jewish settlements or communities unless they resided among
Jews, and, therefore, when Jews conquered and occupied the
promised land, they had to get rid of these pagans or compel them
to submit to the seven Noahide laws whereupon their status was
changed to that of resident aliens with considerable protection by
Jewish law. Pagan nations or tribes that created no problem for
the Jewish people were not to be attacked, exterminated, or even
coerced to change their way of life. Indeed, the prophets had
stressed the equality of all nations, and one prophet was even
forced to go to the Assyrians to deliver God's message to them.
God may have chosen the Jewish people (for whatever reason
or mission one can glean from the sources), but He is the Father
not only of all creatures as individuals but also of all nations and
ethnic groups, and He judges all of them continuously, especially
in the messianic age.

Even pagans who were outlaws could bring offerings to God in the central shrine in Jerusalem. Their divine image was the warrant for this privilege and gifts that they made to the building itself in perpetuity were never to be altered. In this respect they enjoyed an even greater assurance of the perpetuity of their donations than did Jews. Moreover, Jews were obliged to deport themselves so honorably vis-à-vis even pagans that pagans might exclaim, "Blessed is the Lord of Israel."

Yet Jewish law often "recognized" the rules of law prevailing among pagans. For example, their rights of inheritance were repected as were their claims to property personal and real. Jewish law even established special forms for their acquisition of title. In the law of tort there was even the notion of reciprocity—whatever wrongful acts non-Jewish courts regarded as actionable when committed by non-Jews against Jews, Jewish courts regarded as actionable when committed by Jews against non-Jews. This is a far cry from justice but it makes for some degree of equality.

Persons or peoples, however, who had accepted the seven Noahide laws were deemed civilized and it is to them that the Bible refers when it orders Jews to love the stranger.

But Jewish law itself—the Written and Oral Law—was given by God to the Jewish people for the governance of Jews. This made the Law "personal" rather than "territorial." And it applied to Jews no matter where they lived. It was to receive and obey this law that they were chosen, whether for the purpose of being a light or a blessing unto the nations, or bearing testimony to the perpetuity of their personal relationship with God, or helping to establish His kingdom on earth. As a law for a Jewish society, it had only peripheral concern with those whose "personal" law was different. It did provide for rules of warfare when such war was forced on Jews or sought by them. In no instance was the massacre of the enemy justified if the enemy chose to live in peace and accept the seven laws of Noah.

Perhaps the mood of Jewish law can best be understood in the light of the dilemma of modern liberals in the United States who are torn between a respect for human life—even the lives of Chinese Communists—and their anxiety that the free world has to reckon with leaders who have little respect for the rule of law within or without their borders. In such a situation one must be ambivalent. To respect life may require inaction. But to insure the survival of cherished values may require wholesale slaughter. This was the dilemma of Jewish law vis-à-vis those who would not abide by the seven laws of Noah, and the Law did not move as rapidly or as dramatically in the direction of the equality of pagans with Jews as it did in the direction of the equality of resident aliens.

So committed is the Jewish tradition to the equality of the non-Jew who leads a righteous life that it accords to him the coveted title of Ḥasid and assures him salvation just as it is vouchsafed to righteous Jews themselves. Maimonides distinguishes between a righteous non-Jew who pursues righteousness because it is the will of God and a righteous non-Jew whose pursuit of eternal values and moral deportment is derived from reason and natural law. The latter he calls a *Ḥakham,* a wise man; the title Ḥasid is reserved for those who are also God-fearing. But whatever the title, the conclusion is that Jews did not feel impelled to convert non-Jews to Judaism. Commitment to Judaism was not the condition prerequisite for salvation for anyone but Jews. Non-Jews could achieve it by righteous living alone. And Judaism today is still fully committed to this view.

Freedom of belief thus emerged from the recognition of universal equality. The freedom of Jews, however, was more limited. Whereas they enjoyed a considerable measure of latitude in connection with dogma and doctrine, they were held strictly to the fulfillment of the Law. By observance of the commandments they were to play a special role in God's vision of human history.

Since God had created all men equal, their natural inequality can only be justified with reference to His service, which means the fulfillment of the very equality God had willed. Freedom does not serve primarily the purpose of man's self-fulfillment, as in the writings of John Stuart Mill, but rather God's purpose—that justice and righteousness shall reign on earth. In Judaic thought, therefore, freedom is more the means and equality more the end.

A Common Humanity
under One God

WILLIAM A. IRWIN

Thus says the Lord,
   For three transgressions of Damascus
     and for four I will not turn back its punishment,
   because they have threshed Gilead with threshing sleds of iron;
   but I will send fire into the house of Hazael
     and it shall devour the palaces of Ben-Hadad.

                                 (Amos 1:3–4)

And thus in reiterated phraseology the prophet moves round, as in the swing of a scythe of destiny, from Damascus to Gaza, to Tyre, to Edom and Ammon and Moab, before coming at length to his own people. It is the accepted critical view that the list has been somewhat expanded since Amos' day; but the reduction so demanded does not affect the basic significance of the passage.

Two things stand out for present consideration. Note how the accepted limitations of the thought of the prophet's time have been ignored or transcended. Here is no little national god minding his own business strictly behind the borders or at most the military outreach of his own people. Indeed, one may speculate on the absurdity of Amos' position, as it must have seemed to his contemporaries, and most of all to the foreign lands here so boldly castigated by this peasant spokesman of a petty deity. What had the God of Israel to do with Damascus, the power that for a hundred years had wasted and ravaged His land, had enslaved and despoiled and brutally maltreated His people, while He looked on impotent? How well the "practical" men of the time might scoff! But indifferent to all alleged lack of realism and logic, Amos swept on round Israel's land with words of rebuke for all these neighbor and enemy countries.

Here, then, is our first observation: the "national god" concept is for Israel broken and discarded. The God of Israel is a being who has powers and responsibilities and authority over all the lands of Israel's neighbors. We must admit notable exceptions from the list. There is nothing here about Egypt, not a word of Assyria or of Urartu, whichever seemed to Amos' day the dominant power. The list concerns only the principalities round about Israel. But the prophet has gone too far to stop here; he has set out on a line of thought that has no proper boundaries short of attributing to Yahweh universal rule. And, indeed, in further oracles of his book Amos introduces some nameless nation of his age in a role of divine judgment that implies the Lord's dominion far out also into the midst of the great powers of the time.

But this in itself could be of little more significance than the oriental trends toward monotheism. . . . Monotheism in itself may be no more than despotism in religion. The great achievement of Israel was not primarily that she asserted the oneness of the world and of God, but rather the character of the God so affirmed. Amos' thought goes beyond a mere implication of the supremacy of his God. The Lord's coming punishment of Israel's neighbors is for moral reasons. Damascus and Ammon have practiced barbarities in war; Tyre and Gaza have inhumanly sold whole peoples into slavery; and so the indictment runs on. Now, all these practices were standard, accepted conduct in the eighth century B.C. Once more the scoffer might have found occasion to jeer: this common peasant getting himself excited over what everyone was doing! The independence of Amos' thinking here evidenced is of less importance for us, however, than his moral judgment. The nations are condemned for the depravity of their morals. And here is the point: they are so condemned in the name of the God of Israel! It is His righteousness, be it observed, not His might or His glory or any other of the divine qualities prized in the time, which provides the ground of His supremacy. Here we see the meaning of that phrase so commonly employed in the study of Hebrew history: Israel's monotheism was an ethical monotheism.

Those who sat in the history classes of the late James H. Breasted will recall his treatment of the alleged solar monotheism of Egypt of the fourteenth century B.C. He pointed out that it came as the culmination of a century of Egyptian imperialism. In his phrase, this "monotheism was imperialism in religion." The Egyptian sun-worshiper leaving his narrow valley found the same sun shining not only in the hills of Palestine and Syria but also in the upper valley of the Nile beyond the traditional limits of Egypt; and so he was impelled to conclude that there was but one sun, hence, sun-god. It appears to be a comparable process that we see working itself out, first in the mind of Amos, and then becoming the accepted faith of all the prophets and later of the nation. The standards of decency and honor and human compassion which were valid and prized among individuals in the little communities of Palestine did not cease their high demands when one stepped over the boundary into Syria or Philistia; but there alike men were human, with human needs and, consequently, with human standards. Amos would have denied emphatically the light assertion of Kipling's nostalgic old soldier that "east of Suez" there "ain't no Ten Commandments." Indeed, in one famous passage which again witnesses the incredible vigor of thought of this simple peasant, Amos does more than imply, he asserts in unmistakable language the common human bond among diverse and remote races.

> Are you not as the Ethiopians to me,
>   O children of Israel, says the Lord;
> Did I not bring up Israel from the land of Egypt;
> and the Philistines from Caphtor, and the Syrians from Kir?
>   (Amos 9:7)

The Negroes of central Africa, and Israel's two traditional enemies, the Philistines on one side and the Syrians on the other, as human beings stood on the same footing as the "chosen people" themselves. The passage is a valuable commentary on the judgments found in chapters 1 and 2 of the Book of Amos, for it might be claimed that some at least of these are partisan in their motivation—that Amos thunders his denunciations because his own people were the sufferers. But even in that list of divine judgments there are some that cannot be disposed of so lightly; and this utterance about God's care of the Philistines and Syrians serves to corroborate what one may deduce there. The basis of Amos' moral thinking is a sense of common humanity.

And this, it will be observed, is carried over into the concept of the nature of God: God utters His judgments upon cruelty and inhumanity. Now this is a line of thought that was to receive notable development in the course of time and to provide one of the distinctive aspects of the Hebrew outlook on the world. Notwithstanding the passages we have mentioned and others not less worthy of remark, Amos appears in the record we have of him somewhat as a stern moralist. He is a prophet of impending doom; he utters the judgments of God upon a careless and selfish people. Only at one or two points do his pronouncements leave room for argument that at heart he cherished a deep hope for the reformation and salvation of his people.

But when we move on to his immediate successor, if not younger contemporary, all is changed. Though Hosea was not less concerned with the ruin that social selfishness was bringing upon the nation, yet his mood is emotional rather than judicial. He is a man of deep affection and tender motivation. It is he who has left for us that striking and charming picture of God as a loving Father leading His people as though holding the hand of a toddling infant in its first uncertain steps:

> I taught Ephraim to walk;
> I took them in my arms; . . .
> with human bonds I drew them,
> with cords of love. . . .
> How shall I give you up, Ephraim;
> how shall I let you go, Israel?
> My heart turns within Me;
> all My tenderness is kindled.
> I will not perform My fierce anger,

> I will not turn about to destroy Ephraim;
> For I am God and not man.
>
> (Hosea 11:3–4, 8–9)

We recall too the famous passage with which the Book of Jonah closes. The ill-tempered prophet wanted the great city destroyed just to "save his face" as a predictor; but the Lord rebuked him. "Should I not have compassion on Nineveh, that great city, in which are more than a hundred and twenty thousand people who do not know their right hands from their left; and also many cattle?" (Jonah 4:11). One thinks as well of the words:

> Like as a father pities his children,
>   so the Lord pities them that fear Him.
> For He knows our frame;
>   He remembers that we are dust.
>
> (Psalms 103:13–14)

And the corollary and complement of all is represented by an equally famous passage, "You shall love the Lord your God with all your heart and with all your soul and with all your might" (Deuteronomy 6:5). Here we see what may well be adjudged the culmination of Israel's monotheistic achievement: the one God of the universe is a God of righteousness, but still more He is a God of love: "His tender mercies are over all His works" (Psalms 145:9). The significance of this in the long sequel of history a moment's thought will suffice to show. And the revolutionary nature of Israel's discovery becomes evident by study of the great religions of Egypt and Babylonia, dominant through Israel's world, as well as of those of the lesser peoples of the time. All of them alike, to the question of the attitude of the gods toward mankind would have responded that while these could at times be most beneficent, their relation with man was on the whole little better than one of indifference. They had their own concerns, and only by special effort could they be induced to turn aside to the troublesome interruptions of mundane affairs.

Here, we have come upon an aspect of the third of the great persistent human questions. . . . It is said that a religious thinker of the past generation, when asked what inquiry he would make of the Sphinx if assured that it would answer truly just a single question, replied, "Is the Universe friendly to me?" It was a profound insight; for man's most poignant question throughout all ages has been "What is my place in a world of immense and seemingly callous might?" And Israel's great attainment was the vision that we may walk this earth with the confident tread of a son in his father's house.

Much time has been expended upon detailing the attributes of Israel's God; He was Creator, Sustainer, the Source of all good, a God who spoke, who revealed Himself, a God of judgment who brought just punishment upon the wicked, but also a God of forgiveness, a redeemer God—and so on. It is all quite good; and useful for those for whom it is useful. Yet all is comprised in the simple points we have suggested. For Israel, God was the ultimate reality, He was all power (though that is very different from the concept of omnipotence of later centuries), and He was good— not a being concerned with selfish interests, but His character was grace and love.

Implicit in monotheism is a movement toward transcendence. And in Israel's monotheism it was inevitable. A God such as envisaged by Israel must be exalted in divine quality far above puny man, above this earth, and above all that is of the earth and earthy. A pregnant symbol of the many expressions of this throughout the Old Testament is the great vision of Isaiah; he "saw the Lord seated upon a throne high and lifted up, and His train filled the temple. Above Him were the seraphim . . . and one cried to another and said, Holy, Holy, Holy is the Lord of hosts, the whole earth is full of His glory. And the foundations of the threshold shook at the voice of Him who cried and the house was filled with smoke" (Isaiah 6:1–4). Israel's characteristic thought of God was that He was awful in holiness, terrible in righteousness. And on this side of the vast gulf in quality that separated him from the divine stood man, frail, mortal and sinful, whose best righteousnesses were, in the light of that pure countenance, "but as filthy rags." This will make clear one reason why Israel abhorred apotheosis, whether of the king or of any other;

for the Hebrew thinkers, God was in heaven, and man below. This provides also the basis of their concept of sin. . . .

Such, then, was the Hebrew view of the nature of the world. At its center there sat enthroned a Being of unutterable greatness and holiness, who was at once its creator and sustainer. But Israel never went the distance of abstracting this One into a cold and remote absolute. It is of the very essence of Hebrew thought that God is a person. The I-Thou relation in which primitive man saw his natural environment was maintained—no, rather, was sublimated—in Israel's faith: the world was to be understood in terms of personality. Its center and essence was not blind force or some sort of cold, inert reality, but a personal God. And for them personality meant the sort of concept that they, and we, in turn, apply to human nature. . . .

. . . Creative skepticism was at home in this profoundly religious people. Here is the seeming paradox that a people, freely recognized as supremely *the* religious people of the ancient world, at the same time were without a peer in the power and scope of their critical intellectualism. But indeed it is not paradoxical, for religion that is not criticized quickly deteriorates into mere superstition. It was only by virtue of their skeptical mood that the Hebrew thinkers were able to attain a view of the world that still shapes our outlook.

This critical mood is well manifested in Israel's attitude toward the pagan gods and their symbols. Although deeply dependent on the mythology of their contemporaries, the Hebrew thinkers yet came to repudiate the reality of the symbols in which these clothed the physical reality of the world. We know very little of the story, doubtless of protracted question and debate, that lies back of Israel's attainment of this uniqueness in the ancient world. There is some reason to believe that it rests ultimately in a deep moral conviction. The religions of Canaan, ornate as they were with divine symbols in public worship and private shrines, were in large measure characterized by the features of so-called nature worship. And everyone knows what this has inevitably entailed. Canaanite worship of the forces of life meant public immorality as a sacred rite and commonly of a disgusting depravity.

It is true that Israel in considerable measure gave herself for a time to this as the accepted means of securing the increase of the fields and of flocks and herds; we recall the reiterated complaint that they "forgot the Lord their God and went after the Baals and Ashtoreth." Yet there were, even in early times, and increasingly with the passing of the centuries, men who stood aloof and condemned the thing for the depravity that it was. It is such moral revulsion that speaks in the prophetic warnings and denunciations where we commonly meet the scathing summary of this whole system of religion: "On every high hill and under every green tree you prostrated yourself as a harlot" (Jeremiah 2:20). It was apparently, then, a deep ethical motivation that at length found expression in the dogma now familiar but in its cultural environment of astonishing radicalism: "You shall not make any graven image nor any likeness of anything that is in the heavens above or in the earth beneath or in the waters that are under the earth: you shall not bow down to them nor serve them" (Exodus 20:4–5). And, be it observed, the passage runs on, "For the Lord your God is a jealous God." All was gathered up in Israel's theological uniqueness and in her consciousness of that uniqueness. The righteousness and holiness of God imposed upon the Israelite an exacting standard of action and thought and, in turn, revealed the depravity of pagan religion, however pompous or ancient.

Such is the mood that finds notable expression in a term somewhat widely employed for the pagan gods. In a number of cases we are told that they are "nothingnesses"—so we render the contemptuous word; but indeed it has common use as a normal term for foreign images: all alike, the gods and their symbols were nothing at all. It is now believed that the Hebrew word is an adaptation of a foreign one meaning god; and so we see how the Hebrew mind operated in relation to this matter: from foreign god to nothingness—they were intimately one and the same! However, what was here only implicit in a word was fully developed by the great prophet of the Exile, whom, for lack of better information, we call Second Isaiah. And such is the depth of the Hebrew conviction that he applies it to the most august gods of his time. With biting wit that might do credit to Lucian, he laughs the great gods of Babylon out of countenance. . . .

Yet all such thought might well seem no more than a sort of sublimated national bigotry. The crucial question is whether Israel's thinkers could apply the same rigid standards of criticism to their own inherited dogmas, in particular to those of the nature, attributes, and activity of Yahweh Himself. Their intellectual attainment will be realized only when we admit fully, as the evidence demands, that Hebrew religion achieved freedom from an idolatry (to use a common term) similar to that of the rest of the ancient East—Yahweh was, through the earlier period of the nation's life in Palestine, worshiped in physical form, just as Marduk or Ammon or any of the rest of them in their lands. It argues much, then, of the intellectual vigor and independence of generations of unknown Hebrew thinkers that still far back in the nation's history the invisibility of Yahweh had become a dogma of the orthodox religion. In full repudiation of the power and mystic realism of symbols, a writer in Deuteronomy argues that even in the personal presence of their God, manifest in the great theophany on Sinai, no physical form was apparent, but only an invisible presence felt in power and in religious perception:

> The Lord spoke to you out of the midst of the fire: you heard the voice of words, but you saw no form; only you heard a voice. And He declared unto you His covenant, which He commanded you to perform. . . . Take therefore good heed unto youselves; for you saw no manner of form on the day that the Lord spoke unto you in Horeb out of the midst of the fire; lest you corrupt yourselves, and make a graven image in the form of any figure, the likeness of male or female . . . and lest you lift up your eyes to heaven and when you see the sun and the moon and the stars, even the whole host of heaven, you be drawn away and worship them and serve them, which the Lord your God has allotted to all the peoples under the whole heaven (Deuteronomy 4:12–19).

How characteristic of Israel's religion this feature became is so well known to us that its force is in danger of being blunted. But, for the contemporary world, it was heresy of the first order, such, in fact, as to set the Hebrews off as a *peculiar* people in a sense quite different from what their own thinkers boasted. An aspect of this is portrayed by a dramatic incident of a later time.

When Pompey in 63 B.C. stormed Jerusalem, he forced his way into the Holy of Holies, much to the horror of the Jews, in order to see for himself what was the inmost secret of this unusual religion. And there he found—we all know what: nothing but an empty room! The perplexity of this leader from the image-ridden West, standing in the presence of a mystery that still evaded him, is a true symbol of Israel's place in the ancient world: a place that might well be equally unique in the modern, save for our debt to Israel herself. . . .

A significant contribution to this line of thought came about through the experience of the deported Jews in the Babylonian captivity. Carried off from Jerusalem, which they had in their provincialism supposed to be one of the great cities of the world, and planted in the plain of Babylonia not far from the great imperial city itself, the exiles, when the first pangs of homesickness had passed, began to realize wonders and achievements of Babylonian civilization such as shamed their poor rustic culture. And, as time went on, the more open-minded learned of the pomp and magnificence of the religion of their captors and the might of supreme Marduk, before whom, by the accepted test of arms, Yahweh's puny strength had but mocked His people's need. A mood of disillusionment, it would seem, set in and carried many of the Jews far along the road of assimilation and denial of their religious heritage. It was a larger world into which they had come.

From imperial Babylon lines of close communication led out eastward into Iran, of which the first captives had scarcely even heard, and westward through Asia Minor to the Greek world. In the city itself merchants and governmental officials from the far ends of the known world might be met day by day. How petty and remote Judah and all for which it stood must have seemed to the ostensibly liberal-minded. And as a climax of all this impact of foreign culture that was slowly eating the vitals out of the Jewish faith was the fact that at just this time the Babylonian study of the heavens was attaining the status of a real science. Before the astonished Jews there was unfolded a world of immensity, of wonder, and of regularity such as to render ludicrous the traditional claim that Yahweh, God of the tiny land of Palestine, had made not alone the sun and moon but the host of the stars also.

Here we meet, certainly not the first interrelation of science and religion (for that reaches back into the very beginnings of man's thought about the world), but one of the earliest clashes of the two, in a form much like what has been familiar right to our own day. Indeed, these very considerations arose within our own times relevant to recent disclosures of astronomy. But how could they be met in the sixth century B.C.? Did the Jews abandon their faith for the new-found false messiah, science? Certainly not the best of them! Did they retire into intellectual isolation and refuse to admit the findings of science? Did they satisfy themselves with re-affirmation of ancient dogmas? Not at all. It is again an index of their intellectual vitality that instead they met the problem with high courage, recognized the validity of the new knowledge and its destructive implications, and then, embracing the facts, rebuilt their faith on a new and better basis into a greater religion than it was before.

Fortunate it was that there lived among these perplexed people the great poet-thinker Second Isaiah. He realized that the difficulty was inherent, not in the character of Yahweh, but in the unworthy thought of Him which his people held. Seizing boldly on the very findings of science which were sweeping more tender-minded Jews off their feet, he claimed that, far from nullifying faith in Israel's God, these were but evidences of His greatness and of His reality. For God was Maker and Master of the physical universe. "Lift up your eyes on high and see who has created these things, that bring out their host by number; He calls them all by name, great in might and strong in power, not one is lacking" (Isaiah 40:26).

However, already familiar elements of the cosmological argument also received fresh and vigorous handling by Second Isaiah. It was not merely the enlarged world of his time that impinged on his consciousness with fresh conviction, but in a mood very much like that of the philosophic scientists of today he adduced the consideration that the ordered world declares its origin in a universal mind.

> Who has measured the waters in the hollow of His hand,
>   and has meted out the heaven with the span,
>   and comprehended the dust of the earth in a measure,

and weighed the mountains in scales
and the hills in a balance?
Who directed the spirit of the Lord? . . .
With whom took He counsel? . . .
Who . . . taught Him knowledge
and showed Him the way of understanding?

(Isaiah 40: 12–14)

This was evidently a real contribution to Israel's thinking, for in a later age the wisdom writers turn frequently to it as a favorite theme, and in particular it serves as the basis of the lengthy dissertation upon the transcendent intelligence of the divine that is put into the mouth of the Lord in the latter part of the Book of Job:

Where were you when I laid the foundations of the earth?
Declare if you have intelligence.
Who determined its measures?—if you possess knowledge.
Whereupon were its foundations fastened?
Or who laid its cornerstone? . . .
Have you commanded the morning since your days began,
and caused the dayspring to know its place? . . .
Where is the way to the dwelling of light?
And as for darkness, where is its place? . . .
Can you bind the cluster of the Pleiades or loose the bands of
Orion? . . .
Know you the time when the wild goats of the rock bring forth?
Or can you number the months that they fulfil?

(Job 38:4–39:2)

And so this lengthy survey of the complex interaction of animate and inanimate creation runs on. It will be noted that, in part, this is a mere disparagement of human knowledge: that the world contains much more than mortal mind can compass. But basic to the discussion is that it treats of the wonders of the infinite intelligence which not alone established these wonders but holds them in their proper relations.

It is important to realize that Second Isaiah wrote with conscious recognition of the problem of apologetics; he took up the issue specifically and of set purpose. It is a sort of undertone running through his poems. He treats it relevant to the claims of the great contemporary pagan gods; but this does not alter the point of prime interest, namely, that he was answering the question "How can man know rationally that God exists and that He is the sort of being which Jewish tradition claims Him to be?" To this end his favorite device is to picture a cosmic assize in which Yahweh is at once Plaintiff and Judge; He advances His arguments and introduces His witnesses and then challenges the defendants to make out their case. But at this point only silence ensues; and the decision goes to Yahweh, not by default, but by the demonstration of the complete powerlessness and inanity of the others. And Yahweh's argument, in addition to what we have already noted, is that He has been operative in history and still is the vital force in the affairs of men. Notwithstanding certain new features which were introduced into this consideration, it is important to recognize that Second Isaiah is here but applying an opinion that was very old among Israelite thinkers. It had received notable expression by Isaiah a hundred and fifty years before in his bold claim that the God of Israel was using the Assyrians for His great purposes. But it was not uniquely his; for it is the theme running throughout the Old Testament. The Hebrew thinkers, with a penetration that might have spared some later thought its worst blunders, recognized that the meaning of the world can be understood, if at all, only in the light of, and by inclusion of, human life, which is its highest expression. For them "the proper study of mankind was man."

This is peculiarly the field of investigation of the wise men. They were primarily students of human life from the ethical and metaphysical point of view. In their age-long investigation, carried on by successive generations of scholars, history and society provided facilities in a sense comparable with those offered in modern scientific experimentation. It is scarcely an exaggeration to claim that they were empirical, though admittedly the method had not yet come to self-consciousness and hence could easily fall below scientific strictness or give way to traditional dogma. Nonetheless, their activity is in itself demonstration of the keen intellectualism of ancient Israel and the distance this people had gone in methods of sound thinking. The wise men sought to evolve codes of conduct that might conduce to the accepted ideal of the good life, but as well they saw everything taking its place in a continuing stream of action and history which was leading on to determined results in the divine purpose. . . .

We took occasion to note that Amos' thought of the universality of God was in some way dependent on his sense of a common human standard of right and wrong. It is clear, then, that in this was one of the fruitful sources of Israel's convictions as to the being and nature of God. The universality of the human regard for those higher qualities which the Hebrew gathered up in the concept of righteousness found rational explanation best in a cosmic origin which some modern thinkers describe as a Process; but, for the Hebrew mind, that Process was personal. In the unceasing human striving from the good to the better, in the contempt of the base and mean, in the universal homage to the true and noble and unselfish, there was, for Israel's thought, . . . a profound mystery that compelled speculation to venture beyond the immediate and tangible, out into the region of cause and nature and being. Israel's thinkers concluded that here is the ultimate revelation of the character of God: He is righteousness and truth.

In addition to the argument from the wonders and the apparent intelligence of the world, and from the course of human history, past and future, as he believed it might be calculated, Second Isaiah had one other consideration which is presented with such brevity that there is danger of reading into it perhaps more than he meant. In his favorite figure of a great court scene, he has the Lord in several passages say of Israel, "You are my witnesses." . . . The context in some measure may suggest that he is thinking of Israel as the recipient of God's bounty and His notable interventions in her history, of which now she could testify. Yet though this may be uppermost in the passages, the further concept cannot be absent that Israel can testify out of her whole knowledge of God. However that may be in these passages, it is certain that such consideration came to have force in Jewish thought. A psalmist exclaims, "O taste and see that the Lord is good"; again:

> The judgments of the Lord are true
> and righteous altogether
> More to be desired are they than gold,
> yea than much fine gold
> Sweeter also than honey
> and the droppings of the honeycomb.
>
>   (Psalms 19:9–10)

> O how I love your law; it is my meditation all the day.
>
>   (Psalms 119:97)

And this is but the merest sample of the immense bulk of such utterances that one might excerpt from the Psalms and other poetry of the Old Testament. The devout Israelite felt and knew that in his experience of his God he had a treasure of the rarest quality. And in this, finally, it would appear, he found the proof of the reality and the goodness of the Person whom his traditional faith postulated as the center and meaning of the physical universe. It is apparent that the question of the validity of such thinking comes into consideration. Did the Hebrew ever go behind his processes of observation and thought to question their finality? But this question we can take up more effectively as part of Israel's whole understanding of human life.

It is said that, for the ancient Hebrew, there were three realities: God, man, and the world. The remark is, however, less profound than it may appear; for what more is there? And how could he have taken account of less, being the person that he was? But, in any case, it is now time to turn to the second of these entities.

Israel was fully aware of that most critical question of all man's thought—the problem that man is to himself. The Hebrew thinkers meditated upon this strange two-legged creature that struts about in such a pompous mood, arrogantly rivaling the gods yet knowing full well that he is much less than divine, conscious of his close relation with the beasts but refusing to be a brute, and always—even in his proudest moments—haunted with a sense of insufficiency and with the knowledge that the nemesis which dogs his every footstep will ultimately overtake him. And what, then, of all he has hoped and done? In itself such thinking is not remarkable, for even primitive man had early learned to ask questions about his origin and nature. But the uniqueness of Israel's thought is in the elevation of its conclusions, an answer to the problem of man that even in this modern day some regard as superior to much of recent thought as well as to the aberration which Greek speculation fastened upon Western culture.

The consciousness of the problem was widely diffused among Hebrew thinkers, if we may judge from frequent allusion and formal discussion. One of the notable passages of more extensive treatment is Psalm 90, which in majestic wording sketches the agelessness of the world, and the eternity of the divine, by contrast with which man is transient, frail, and fallible:

> Before the mountains were brought forth
>   or ever You had formed the earth and the world,
> even from everlasting to everlasting You are, O God. . . .
> A thousand years in Your sight
>   are but as yesterday when it is past,
>   and as a watch in the night.
>
> (Psalms 90:2–4)

But as for man:

> You carry them away as with a flood; they are as a sleep;
>   in the morning they are like grass that grows up:
> in the morning it grows up and flourishes,
>   in the evening it is cut down and withers. . . .
> You have set our iniquities before You,
>   our secret sins in the light of Your countenance. . . .
> We spend our years as a sigh. . . .
>
> (Psalms 90:5–9)

One influence that stimulated Israel's interest in the problem was the obvious similarity that exists between man and the beasts. We are told that in his three thousand proverbs Solomon "spoke of birds and of beasts and of creeping things" (I Kings 4:32–33). But this had been a very old interest in the Orient, where fables

of plants and animals of the sort familiar to the modern world
under the title *Aesop's Fables* had long been employed in teaching and speculation about the nature of man. The well-known
fable of Jotham in chapter 9 of Judges is the clearest illustration
of this that we possess from Israel, but certain passages in the
Book of Proverbs, some prophetic figures, and, most of all, this
clear statement in the account of Solomon's career demonstate
that the Hebrew thinkers recognized our kinship with the lower
animals. But then what? Is man nothing but a more intelligent
brute? In view of the freedom of Israel's skeptical thought, it is
not surprising that the question found answer in the affirmative.
Nor shall we think it remarkable that our familiar acquaintance,
Ecclesiastes, is the one to voice this with frankness. He states his
conclusion:

> I said in my heart in regard to the sons of men that, since God
> has created them and He sees that they are in their nature but
> beasts, the fate of the sons of men and the fate of beasts is one: as
> this dies, so dies that; they have all the same spirit, and man has no
> superiority above the beasts, for all is futile. . . . Who knows
> whether the spirit of man goes upward, and the spirit of the beast
> goes down into the earth? (Ecclesiastes 3:18–21)

There we have frank and complete repudiation of man's higher
claims. Our life, just like that of the animals, is told in purely
biological terms. And when death overtakes us, nothing has happened but biological and then chemical dissolution. But the very
terms of Ecclesiastes' pessimism reveal that the consensus of Hebrew thought was against him. He is clearly at pains to criticize
and repudiate an accepted belief.

Similar is the mood of the "friends" in the Book of Job, although their traditional piety is far from the radicalism of Ecclesiastes. But at least it is apparent that they too assign man a
lowly place. Bildad, indeed, alludes to "man that is a maggot,
and the son of man that is a worm" (Job 25:6). And Eliphaz, in
a comparable utterance, stresses the frailty and transience of
human life:

> . . . them that dwell in houses of clay,
> whose foundation is in the dust,

who are crushed before the moth!
Betwixt morning and evening they are destroyed;
    they perish forever without any regarding it.
Is not their tent-cord plucked up within them?
They die, and that without wisdom.

(Job 4:19–21)

But we must beware of deducing a like inference from the con-
trite confession of a psalmist:

But I am a worm and no man,
    a reproach of men and despised of the people.

(Psalms 22:6)

It means, indeed, just the opposite of the view of Job's friends.
For it is clear that it is the writer himself who, as a worm, is
less than human—so he claims. The characteristic belief of Israel,
indeed, finds nowhere more challenging formulation than in the
Psalter, and most notably in the Eighth Psalm . . .

What is man that thou are mindful of him,
    and the son of man that thou visitest him?
For thou hast made him a little lower than the angels,
    and hast crowned him with glory and honor.

(Psalms 8:4–6)

But the word here rendered "angels" is 'elohim, the familiar and
regular term for God. And nowhere does it certainly mean angels.
There is no evidence whatever that would support the action of
the seventeenth-century translators at this point; it rests only on
dogmatic presuppositions which precluded their rising to the bold-
ness of the Hebrew concept. The passage says as clearly as may
be: "You have made him a little lower than God"! [1] The essential
meaning of the passage, as well as its astonishing character, is
very little altered if we should admit, in accordance with some
recent thought, that "man" is here the half-mythical, primeval
man.

In few regards is the uniqueness of Hebrew thought more evi-

[1] See editor's analysis of this passage, p. 28.

dent than in this concept of the basic character of human life. Indeed to this day (not merely until the time of King James' translators), we have but inadequately approached the majesty of the conception that man is in his nature but "a little lower than God." And such a view was propounded by a people who had no less painful cause than our own generation to know the depraved possibilities of the human heart, and who, on the other hand, maintained an unrivaled faith in a transcendent God. But yet the paradox—for them, man is but "a little lower" and "crowned with glory and honor." Here is none of the contamination of flesh, of the essential badness of matter, of the evil of the world and all that it signifies: ideas which we have erroneously fathered upon the Orient, and which in turn have distorted our religious thinking for two millennia. But they are Greek and not Hebrew, traceable not to Moses but to Plato! True, the Hebrew would grant the terms of our familiar hymn, "Frail children of dust, and feeble as frail"; but in that feebleness there was no taint of worthlessness. On the contrary, man is of exalted origin; and his destiny, by implication, is likewise one of majesty. Echoing the words of the creation story, our psalmist goes on: "You made him to have dominion over the works of Your hands; You have put all things under his feet" (Psalms 8:6).

It is, indeed, in the accounts of the Creation that we find the basic and almost complete statement of the Hebrew answer to the problem of man. God made him in his own image. Or, in another narrative, he was shaped by divine hands from dust of the earth, and then God blew into his nostrils the breath of life, and man became a living being. There is at once both man's earthy and his divine nature. But the important thing to emphasize is that our mention of such antithesis is un-Hebraic. For Israel it was a single and consistent idea. God had made the world also; and on all that He made, step by step, He pronounced the judgment that it was good. The world, like man, came fresh from the hands of the Creator, trailing clouds of glory. Such was Hebrew and Jewish thought throughout. However bad the troubles that might fall, however thick the gloom, yet Israel's basic conviction was that the world was permeated with its divine origin and high purpose. . . .

We have mentioned the universalism of Second Isaiah. Dreamer as this poet was, he could well picture glowing ideals which the practical men of affairs might struggle toward only as time and circumstance would permit. The truth of his vision and the greatness of his achievement are not disparaged when it is recognized that his dreams were impossible of realization in that time. They were the seed of the future, which in fact did produce bounteous harvest. But their time of fruitage was not in his day. Still, initiated by his utterances, there ensued . . . a notable mood of universalism in Jewish thought from which there are numerous passages of broad humanitarianism in the latter chapters of the Book of Isaiah and in the Minor Prophets. The length to which these thinkers went may well surprise us. They seem frankly to have abandoned all claims of Jewish privilege, holding only for a faithful loyalty to Israel's God. In every nation, they believed, there were those who served the Lord, and His name was honored throughout the world. The foreigner, also, who joined himself to the Lord to minister to Him and to love His name would come to the Temple in Jerusalem with all the rights of native-born Jews and there would rejoice in worship in the house that would be called a house of prayer for all peoples. This movement seems to have been most powerful in the sixth and fifth centuries. Then the success of the reform of Ezra changed the aspect of Jewish thought, but not its essence; for the ideals of this expansive period lived on to moderate the stringency of ritual particularism and to offer promise of wider vision when the destined moment should arrive.

Many Are Called and
Many Are Chosen

MILTON R. KONVITZ

Years ago as I studied the ancient Greek civilization, especially
Greek philosophy and drama, I began to wonder about the meaning and validity of the claim that Jews are the "chosen people":
that God elected the Jews to be his "peculiar treasure," that Israel
was chosen from among the families of the earth [1]—no greater
claim of spiritual distinction could possibly be made by any people. Yet here I was discovering that Jeremiah and Solon were near
contemporaries; that Ezekiel lived only about a century before
Socrates; that at the time Ezra was attempting the restoration in
Judea, Aristotle was teaching in the Lyceum.

The question came to me with startling and shattering force:
Could it possibly be that the Lord of the universe, the Creator of
light and darkness, the God who brings and takes life, that He
who has created and sustained all things, the heavens and the
earth and all the host of them—that the Creator of the universe
and the Lord of history could possibly say: "And I will establish
My covenant between Me and you" (Genesis 17:7)?

Suppose the ancient Greeks had made the claim of election,
would not then the Jews have cause to wonder how God could
love with a special love the people of Homer, Hesiod, Solon,
Pericles, Socrates, Plato, Aristotle, Aeschylus, Sophocles, Eurip-
ides, Aristophanes, Phidias, Heraclitus, Euclid, Democritus, Py-

[1] "You only have I known" (Amos 3:2).

75

thagoras, Herodotus, and Thucydides, and not love *with an equal love* the people of Abraham, Moses, Joshua, David, Solomon, Isaiah, Jeremiah, Ezekiel, Hosea, Micah, Amos, and Jonah? Did the Jews give their great spiritual treasure to the world under a special providence, while the Greeks worked and created without God seeing or hearing? True it is that the life of Western man would seem empty if the Jewish heritage were suddenly withdrawn from him, if there were a "brain-washing" and the Bible were cast out from his mind and heart. But would not his life become impoverished, if not barren, if the Greek heritage were eradicated from his consciousness?

These questions disturbed me greatly, and, I must confess, they still do. And some years later, when I began to study the literature of Christianity, the election problem began to disturb me from another standpoint. . . . From the point of view of the man who attempted to think and live as a Christian, he who tried to live a holy life in "the imitation of Christ"—say a Saint Francis of Assisi, an Albert Schweitzer, a Tolstoy, or a humble carpenter or cobbler—a Christian Bontshe Schweig—the rejection of Jesus by his own people must seem to have been, as John C. Bennett expresses it, "strangely providential." For this meant that Jesus "belonged to no national group"; no race or nation or class could lay special claim to him; he belonged "to all who received him, who believed on his name," for to all such persons "he gave power to become children of God."

Could it be, I asked myself, that God had no hand in all this; that God, as it were, looked the other way as Saul of Tarsus became Paul, the bearer, in some way, of the name of the Living God to Cyprus and Salamis and Galatia and Lystra and countless other places, remote and near, where men had not heard that name before? Is it possible that the Righteous Ruler of the universe—not a local deity, a mere tribal god—could have dropped an iron curtain before His mind's eye so that He would know what Jonah did, but not what Paul did? Could the Lord of whom we say "Blessed are You, O Lord our God, King of the Universe, who opens the eyes of the blind" have been indifferent when the eyes of blind barbarians were opened to a vision of His kingdom and power and glory?

And then my perplexity was compounded even more when I learned how radically pluralistic must be the man who adhered to the philosophy of democracy. For this philosophy starts from the premise that nature and nature's God had created all men equal; that every man anywhere and any time is made in the image of God; that God is equally solicitous for the welfare of every race, nation, and tribe—that all people and all men have their place in the sun; that God wants variety and differences, for otherwise He would have made a different kind of world. When it was asked, "From which part of the earth's surface did God gather the dust from which He made the first man?" Rabbi Meir answered, "From every part of the habitable earth was the dust taken for the formation of Adam," so that men everywhere are brothers—yet different one from the other. Had God wanted uniformity He could have made Adam of an unmixed dust. Then each man would resemble every other man, even as one coin resembles all other coins struck from the same die.

Finally, there was the problem of squaring the doctrine of the election of Israel with a world view of history. As long as one's interest in history is limited to the Biblical period, it may be possible to look upon all recorded events as revolving about Israel. God could then use Ethiopia or Assyria as actors in an Israel-centered drama. In such a world, America, Siam, Japan, China, and India do not exist. But can one be so parochial-minded as to believe that the Jewish people are today at the center of events as these happen before God? Does God see the sun rise and set primarily for the sake of His people, Israel? Is Communist China, e.g., significant only as it serves God's purpose for the role and destiny of Israel? To believe this today is to make of God, the Creator and Ruler of the universe, a mere means to Israel's ends; and even though these ends may be posited by God and not by Israel, this view reduces the moral power of God to that of a tribal deity with imperialistic pretensions. To believe in such a God is to blaspheme; for it means making Israel greater than God Himself, even as the folk imagination has at times made God subject to His Torah—a captive of His own creature.

How does one solve these problems?

The early Christians, who were also Jews, thought that they

solved the problem through interpreting the covenant with Israel in such a way as to make possible a "new covenant." In chapter 9 of the *Epistle to the Romans,* Paul gives what has become the classical Christian position. God chose Abraham, but not for the personal aggrandizement of Abraham; rather, he was chosen so that in him and in his seed all families of the earth may be blessed. The covenant was not handed down to Ishmael, the first-born son of Abraham, but to Isaac; not to Esau, who was equally with Jacob seed of Isaac, but only to Jacob. At Sinai, Israel was again chosen, but not because it deserved any special favor and not for itself, but as a means of blessing to the other nations. Israel as a nation, as a collectivity, failed to be the blessing, but here and there were individuals who lived up to the promise of "all that the Lord has spoken we will do." Such persons were the "remnant," of whom the great prophets spoke, and it was the remnant who bore the covenant; they were the kernel, and the rest were the husk—"for they are not all Israel that are of Israel." [2] Election, then, is not a virtue that is attached to a nation or group; it is personal. God chose Israel, true enough; but the individual Jew must choose God, or the covenant is not effective. Election becomes, thus, a matter of inner conviction, personal faith or commitment. This inward faith, after Paul, is built on Christ; and the Church, as a voluntary congregation of believers, is the "new Israel," bound to God by the "new covenant." Everyone, without regard to race or nation or class or language, Greek or Jew, bound or free, may elect himself into the "new Israel" and become bound by the "new covenant." Self-election, by the grace of God, displaces, in the Christian view, election by God, by the grace of God; and each believer becomes a "vessel of election" to bear Christ's name to the Gentiles.

This view leaves the Jew standing outside the covenant, old or new, for the old covenant no longer, since the coming of Christ, obtains, and the Jew's stiff-neckedness excludes him from the "new covenant." But each Jew can by his own will choose to become a member of the "new Israel," and it is the mission of Christians to bring this about.

But the Christian claim of election does not, for the Christian,

[2] Epistle to Romans, ch. 9.

solve the problems that we have stated: (1) Before the Christian era, were the Jews alone the "chosen people"? Were the Greeks, e.g., not, in some significant sense, also chosen by God? (2) Does God love only the Christian saint? Does God not have a special love for saints and good, decent people wherever He may find them, within or without a designated church? Is there no salvation for the righteous Jew, Hindu, Moslem, or "humanist"? (3) In a world of "united nations," in which a man is a man "for a' that," and the equal of every other man, can it be maintained that God has "elected" only those who are members of the Christian church? And, by the way, which church is the true Christian church? For even among those who profess to be Christians there are rival claimants for the covenant and the election. The democratic challenge thus faces the Christian in a two-fold way; (a) In relation to other Christian denominations, and (b) in relation to the whole non-Christian world. (4) Does God manipulate history, in some sense or other, so that His elect will ever remain at its center? Is there a special providence that looks after His chosen church?

Paul thought he was solving the problem of the covenant by his Janus-faced interpretation of the election doctrine, which makes it look two ways—the old way and the new. It is no solution, however; it only aggravates the quarrel between Jew and Christian over who enjoys the election and the covenant. Each now claims to be *the* Israel, *the* people of *the* covenant. The substitution of a church for a nation-church does not eradicate or even lessen the "scandal" of the doctrine of election.

The Rabbis themselves were to a degree aware of this problem. They satisfied themselves by emphasizing that Israel was elected not for honor but for service. Israel was called upon to be a holy nation, a kingdom of priests. It was no life of ease and luxury to which they were called. To live by the word of God may mean living on a morsel of bread; and to have honor in the eyes of God may mean to have shame in the eyes of men. The Jews were elected to be servants to God and not to be rulers of men; the election offers no privileges, it only imposes duties. The only crown that Israel can wear is "the crown of a good name" as Isriel lives in a way that sanctifies the Name, and Israel can do this only if all its deeds are done for the sake of heaven. The life lived in accordance with the Torah is a hard life—no other people "allowed" itself to be chosen for this covenanted way of life.

This interpretation removes the possibility of Israel claiming to be a *Herrenvolk*. It removes from the election any taint of conscious race superiority or national arrogance. It leaves, however, the mission of Israel at the center of the universe. Not the messenger, but the message, is to be honored; the world exists not for the sake of Israel but for the sake of the holy life to which Israel is dedicated. But insofar as the message must be borne by a messenger, insofar as the holy life must be lived by people of flesh and blood and bone, Israel significantly stands at the center of creation. A man is elected President of a country not so that he may live in an Executive Mansion and exercise the prerogatives of rulership; no, he is elected for service—he must work harder, worry more, and often suffer more—e.g., Abraham Lincoln and Woodrow Wilson—than most men. He is elected for service—that is what Israel says of its own election; but how can one possibly escape from concluding that pre-eminent dignity and honor must enwrap him whom God has chosen for a mission? He who is chosen may be "despised and rejected of men," but before God he has the riches of royal glory and the splendor and pomp of majesty; and "if God be for us, who can be against us?" (Romans 8:31)—or rather if God be for us, what does it matter if all others are against us?

The rabbinic interpretation of election is, however, a necessary one, for it puts the emphasis where it belongs—on service and not on prerogatives. If the President were elected for anything other than service, he would be unbearable; the election concept would then be totally discredited. It is the same with the election of Israel. The doctrine can be saved only by the interpretation made by the Rabbis—an interpretation entirely in the spirit of the Bible: Israel was elected to live up to its promise "to do and to obey" "all that the Lord has spoken."

But the rabbinical interpretation, though a necessary one, is insufficient, for it leaves our questions unanswered: the unity of God, Creator and Ruler of the universe, and the election of any one people, even if the election is for service, are inconsistent one with the other.

Saadia Gaon, it seems to me, was also troubled by this problem. The passage in Deuteronomy, "For the portion of the Lord is His people, Jacob the lot of His inheritance," provided him with a text around which he wove an extremely significant homily. "As regards [the matter of] *possession*," says Saadia, "inasmuch as all creatures are God's creation and handiwork, it is not seemly for us to say that He possesses one thing [Israel] to the exclusion of another, nor that He possesses the one [Israel] to a greater and the other to a lesser degree. If we, nevertheless, see the Scriptures assert that a certain people [Israel] is His peculiar property and His possession and His portion and inheritance . . . that is done merely as a means of conferring honor and distinction. For, as appears to us, every man's portion and lot are precious to Him. Nay, the Scriptures even go so far as to declare God, too, figuratively to be the lot of the pious and their portion, as they do in their statement: 'O Lord, the portion of mine inheritance and of my cup.' This is, therefore, also an expression of special devotion and esteem." Furthermore, says R. Saadia, Scripture speaks of "the God of Abraham, of Isaac, and of Jacob." Is He not the God of all men, of all creation? Yet the Scriptural designation of God as the God of Israel "is entirely in order," says Saadia, "since God is the Master of all." When Scripture, then, says "God of Abraham" or "God of Israel" it merely intends to use "an expression of His esteem and high regard." [3]

In other words, . . . the election of Israel by no means implies the rejection of the rest of mankind, no more than saying "God of Abraham" means that God is not the God of Terah, Abraham's idol-worshipping father. Israel was chosen by God for a special purpose, and Scripture is the record, in part, of Israel's mission. It is, therefore, proper *in this context,* to speak of Israel as God's "peculiar treasure" or "possession." In other contexts, other people may be equally God's "peculiar treasure." God is the God of all mankind, and "the worth of each man and his lot are equally precious before Him." All men are equally His crea-

[3] Saadia Gaon, *Book of Beliefs and Opinions,* Treatise 2, Ch. XI.

tures; God does not possess one people or one man to a greater and the other people or the other man to a lesser degree. Israel is conscious of the fact that God delivered them from Egypt. But God also delivered the Philistines from Caphtor and the Syrians from Kir. There is nothing that can keep the Philistines from saying: "I will sing to the Lord, for He has triumphed gloriously; the horse and his rider He has thrown into the sea" (Exodus 15:1). Had the Philistines seen "the great work which the Lord did" against Caphtor, they, too, would have sung of their deliverance in the manner of Moses. So, too, the Syrians, and the Persians, and the Egyptians, and the Greeks: God possesses them all and equally, and each, in one context or another, is God's "peculiar treasure." Damascus is punished "because they threshed Gilead with threshing instruments of iron" (Amos 1:5, 6). Gaza is punished because "they carried away captive the whole people to deliver them up to Edom"; and Nineveh might have been punished had its people not listened to Jonah. God is the Lord of all history; had the history of Egypt or Greece been written from the standpoint of God, each of them would have had a Bible. They lacked, however, the consciousness of their dependence upon God, and so their Bibles remain unwritten—the deliverance of the Philistines from Caphtor and of the Syrians from Kir remains unsung. Just as *every man* can say to God: "My Father," so *every people* can say: "Our God, and God of our fathers." The only requisite is the consciousness of one's relation to God—a relation which makes every man and every people God's "peculiar treasure," His "chosen people." God's covenants may be oral as well as written, implied as well as expressed. God had a mission for the Greeks, just as he had for Israel; and perhaps God has a mission for America, "the new nation," as Emerson said: "to liberate, to abolish kingcraft, priestcraft, caste, monopoly; to pull down the gallows, to burn up the bloody statute book, to take in the immigrant, to open the doors of the sea and the fields of the earth. . . ."

This concept of a multiple election was . . . partially seen by the great Saadia. It was also, in a limited way, projected by the Renaissance French theologian, mystic and orientalist, Guillaume

Postel, who argued that the Moslems had come into a covenant with God, for everywhere they were waging war on all idolators and temples of idols, and bringing to men a knowledge and love of God.

But it remained for Justice Louis D. Brandeis to state clearly this concept. . . . Here is his full statement on this topic:

> I should think it presumptuous for any people in this century to assert that it alone had a mission for all peoples, but that none of the other peoples had any mission for it. Every people, it is becoming more and more evident, has its own character. And insofar as it has a character of its own it has a mission. For it has that elusive something, its essence, which the other peoples do not have and of which they may stand in need. But all other peoples should have those elusive somethings, of some of which the Jewish people certainly stand in need. In the realm of things material one people may be a solitary benefactor and not a beneficiary. In the realm of the spirit there is no such solitary philanthropist. Here all peoples give and take, some more and some less, each giving what it has, and if it is wise it takes what it needs.
>
> The experience of the Jewish people is unique. It is Jewish. Consequently the Jews have much to contribute toward the solution of the problems that perplex and confound all men. As a comparatively small people the Jewish people may be in a position to do better than bigger peoples. Palestine, when the Jews constitute the majority there, may, because of its very smallness, serve as a laboratory for some far-reaching experiments in democracy and social justice. But let us not forget that there are other small peoples who have in recent decades performed miracles in soil reclamation, in the rebuilding of their lands and peoples, and in advancing popular education and democratic ideals. Nor can we as Americans forget what our country has already done for the world and what it may yet do. The Pilgrim Fathers, in their day, and many of our most representative men since then, all conceived of America as God's gift to humanity. President Wilson spoke with deep conviction of America's mission. Perhaps Mr. Wilson had learned to speak this way because he was a constant reader of the Bible. Well then, let us teach all peoples that they are all chosen, and that each has a mission for all. I should prefer such an effort to that of boasting of our election.

And at another time Justice Brandeis said: "If the Greeks and Romans had been favorably disposed toward the Jews and there had been understanding and sympathy on both sides, the Rabbis would have recognized the immense contributions those two peoples made to the advancement of civilization, and might not perhaps have rejected the possibility of their having been 'chosen' in some way."

Israel requires—as does every people—the doctrine of election; but there is nothing in the genius of Judaism that makes impossible or undesirable a belief that other peoples, too, have been chosen, only we are not God and we do not know all His ways, His plans, His thoughts. Yet we know enough to believe that God is, in some significant sense, the Lord of all history, and so no one people can rightly claim to be at the center of all history, especially if the mission of this people is to serve all others—a means to an end cannot be the center of all history. Perhaps there is no one center; perhaps God sees many centers; or maybe the center is yet to be made, when it will no longer be necessary—when God's righteous rule will prevail throughout the world in the Kingdom which is yet to come; for then only will it be seen by all that "there are varieties of gifts but the same Spirit" (I Corinthians 12:4). Then will it be clear that Walt Whitman spoke as a prophet when he said that there are "unnumbered supremes" and "that one does not countervail another." As in the legend of Saladin and the three rings, each people will be able to say that it has the true inheritance, God's true law and commandments—and God will sustain the claims of each.

My election is not negated or diminished when I know that others, too, have been elected by God; nor are our differences wiped out. On the contrary, as we recognize each other's quality of chosenness, we see that our right to be different—our right to be differently gifted—is rooted in the very nature of things as God created them.

PART II

The Rule of Law

PART II

The Rule of L

Editor's Note

There are those who say that man and society are corrupted and degraded by law, that love, benevolence, should suffice as a guide for conduct and for the building of a good social order. This extreme position is sometimes an expression of Christian antinomianism—and also an expression of philosophical anarchism. As an instance of the latter, one may cite Proudhon, who wrote: "I will have no laws. I will acknowledge none. I protest against every law which an authority calling itself necessary imposes upon my free will." This philosopher of anarchism could have cited in support of his position passages in the New Testament by Paul, John, and Timothy, along with writings by Kropotkin, Tolstoy, Bakunin, and William Godwin.

Judaism finds ample room for love. After all, the original source of the Love Commandment, it should never be forgotten, is Leviticus 19: "You shall love your neighbor as yourself: I am the Lord." But Judaism has never understood this to mean absolute unselfishness. There is also the commandment, repeated countless times, to do justice, to pursue justice, to seek righteousness. This means that man cannot always be trusted to do spontaneously what is right, what is just, what is the loving thing to do. Subjectivity can have as many measures as there are men. The law, therefore, comes in, as Justice Holmes said, as "the witness and external deposit of our moral life," so that the history of law "is the history of the moral development of man."

Western society bears out the genius of Judaism, which has placed great stress on law and the ideal of life under law. Perhaps no book in history has served as much as the Hebrew Bible to teach the significance of law and a legal order. In the Biblical conception, no one is above the law. There is no conception of a dictatorship—even of a "benevolent" dictatorship—in the Bible. When the king rules, he must rule within and under the law, and the law made him a servant and not a master of the people. When Solomon died and Rehoboam made it clear that he would not be a servant to the people, ten of the tribes revolted and set up their own kingdom of Israel. The theory of divine right of kings—that the sovereign is not responsible to the governed and that he is outside the legal order that obtains in his nation—is to be found in the views of King James I and his son Charles I, in the views of Louis XIV, and in Asiatic countries. But it is not to be found in the Hebrew Scriptures, which provide one law for citizen and sojourner, strong and weak, king and commoner.

The Bible
and the Rule of Law

LORD ACTON

By liberty I mean the assurance that every man shall be protected in doing what he believes his duty against the influence of authority and majorities, custom and opinion. The State is competent to assign duties and draw the line between good and evil only in its immediate sphere. Beyond the limits of things necessary for its well-being, it can only give indirect help to fight the battle of life by promoting the influences which prevail against temptation—religion, education, and the distribution of wealth. In ancient times the State absorbed authorities not its own, and intruded on the domain of personal freedom. In the Middle Ages it possessed too little authority, and suffered others to intrude. Modern states fall habitually into both excesses.

The most certain test by which we judge whether a country is really free is the amount of security enjoyed by minorities. Liberty, by this definition, is the essential condition and guardian of religion; and it is in the history of the "chosen people," accordingly, that the first illustrations of my subject are obtained. The government of the Israelites was a federation, held together by no political authority, but by the unity of race and faith, and founded, not on physical force, but on a voluntary covenant. The principle of self-government was carried out not only in each tribe, but in every group of at least 120 families; and there was neither privilege of rank nor inequality before the law. Monarchy was so alien to the primitive spirit of the community that it was resisted by Samuel in that momentous protestation and warning which all the kingdoms of Asia and many of the kingdoms of Europe have unceasingly confirmed. The throne was erected on a compact; and the king was deprived of the right of legislation among a people that recognized no lawgiver but God, whose highest aim in politics was to restore the original purity of the constitution, and to make its government conform to the ideal type that was hallowed by the sanctions of heaven. The inspired men who rose in unfailing succession to prophesy against the usurper and the tyrant constantly proclaimed that the laws, which were divine, were paramount over sinful rulers, and appealed from the established authorities, from the king, the priests, and the princes of the people, to the healing forces that slept in the uncorrupted consciences of the masses.

Thus the example of the Hebrew nation laid down the parallel lines on which all freedom has been won—the doctrine of national tradition and the doctrine of the higher law; the principle that a constitution grows from a root, by process of development, and not of essential change; and the principle that all political authorities must be tested and reformed according to a code which was not made by man. . . .

The conflict between liberty under divine authority and the abolutism of human authorities ended disastrously. In the year 622 a supreme effort was made at Jerusalem to reform and preserve the State. The High Priest produced from the temple of Jehovah the book of the deserted and forgotten law, and both king and people bound themselves by solemn oaths to observe it. But that early example of limited monarchy and of the supremacy of law neither lasted nor spread; and the forces by which freedom has conquered must be sought elsewhere. In the very year 586, in which the flood of Asiatic despotism closed over the city which had been, and was destined again to be, the sanctuary of freedom in the East, a new home was prepared for it in the West, where, guarded by the sea and the mountains, and by valiant hearts, that stately plant was reared under whose shade we dwell, and which is extending its invincible arms so slowly and yet so surely over the civilized world.

According to a famous saying of the most famous authoress of the Continent, liberty is ancient, and it is despotism that is new. It has been the pride of recent historians to vindicate the truth of that maxim. . . .

Kingship under the
Judgment of God

HENRI FRANKFORT

Our knowledge of Hittite, Syrian, and Persian kingship is so incomplete that we cannot pass beyond generalities. But we know more about the Hebrew monarchy. This was also based upon descent but possessed a peculiar character of its own . . . for the Hebrews, though in the Near East, were only partly of it. Much is made nowadays of Canaanite and other Near Eastern elements in Hebrew culture, and a phenomenon like Solomon's kingship conforms indeed to the type of glorified native chieftainship. . . . But it should be plain that the borrowed features in Hebrew culture, and those which have foreign analogies, are least significant. In the case of kingship they are externalities, the less important since they did not affect the basic oddness of the Hebrew institution. If kingship counted in Egypt as a function of the gods, and in Mesopotamia as a divinely ordained political order, the Hebrews knew that they had introduced it on their own initiative, in imitation of others and under the strain of an emergency. When Ammonite oppression was added to the Philistine menace, the people said: "Nay; but we will have a king over us; that we also may be like all the nations; and that our king may judge us, and go out before us, and fight our battles" (I Samuel 8:19–20).

If the Hebrews, like the Mesopotamians, remembered a kingless period, they never thought that "kingship descended from

92

heaven." Hence the Hebrew king did not become a necessary bond between the people and the divine powers. On the contrary, it was in the kingless period that the people had been singled out by Yahweh and that they had been bound, as a whole, by the covenant of Sinai. It was said in the Law: "You are the children of the Lord your God: . . . and the Lord has chosen you to be a peculiar people unto himself, above all the nations that are upon earth" (Deuteronomy 14:1–2). Moses said to Pharaoh: "Thus says the Lord, Israel is My son, even My first-born: and I say unto you, Let My son go, that he may serve Me" (Exodus 4:22–23). For the service of God was part of the covenant, which the people must keep even though it imposes a moral obligation which man's inadequacy makes forever incapable of fulfillment: "Now therefore, if you will obey My voice indeed, and keep My covenant, then you shall be a peculiar treasure unto Me above all people: for all earth is Mine: And you shall be unto Me a kingdom of priests and a holy nation (Exodus 19:5–6).

The conviction of the Hebrews that they were a "chosen people" is the one permanent, as it is the most significant, feature in their history. The tenacity of the Hebrew struggle for existence in the sordid turmoil of the Levant was rooted in the consciousness of their election. This animated the leaders of the people, whether they were kings like David and Hezekiah, or prophets opposing kings in whom belief in the unique destiny of Israel had been compromised. But this intimate relationship between the Hebrew people and their God ignored the existence of an earthly ruler altogether. Hebrew tradition, vigorously defended by the great prophets and the post-Exilic leaders, recognized as the formative phase of Hebrew culture the sojourn in the desert when Moses, the man of God, led the people and gave them the Law. Kingship never achieved a standing equal to that of institutions which were claimed—rightly or wrongly—to have originated during the Exodus and the desert wandering.

The antecedents of Saul's kingship were known. The settlement in Canaan left the tribal divisions intact, and the Book of Judges shows the varying ranges of power to which individual chieftains might aspire. Avimelekh made himself king after he "slew his brethren, the sons of Jerubbaal, being threescore and ten persons"

(Judges 9:5). His power was founded on force, was challenged by Jotham, and was in turn destroyed by force: "And when the men of Israel saw that Avimelekh was dead, they departed every man unto his place" (Judges 9:55).

The tribesmen recognized the bond of blood alone, and it was exceedingly difficult to envisage a loyalty surpassing the scope of kinship. Nevertheless, when the separate tribes were threatened with extinction or enslavement, Saul was made king over all. Samuel anointed Saul, thereby expressing Yahweh's approval of the initiative of the people who had in any case sought advice from the seer. But royalty received little sanctity from this involvement. It is true that David shrank from buying personal immunity at the price of laying hands "upon the Lord's anointed" (I Samuel 24:10); but such scruples are perhaps more revealing of David's character than of the esteem in which kingship was held among the Hebrews. And the tragic sequel of Saul's history proves how little Yahweh's initial approval protected office and officeholder. In fact, once kingship had been established, it conformed to the tribal laws which treat relatives as one, for better or for worse. Saul's "house" was exterminated by David (II Samuel 21) on Yahweh's orders. . . . It is very significant that in actual fact the Davidian dynasty was never dethroned in Judah. But David belonged to Judah; and when Solomon died and his son Rehoboam was ill-advised and refused to alleviate the burdens imposed by Solomon's splendor, ten of the tribes refused to acknowledge him: "So when all Israel saw that the king hearkened not unto them, the people answered the king saying, What portion have we in David? neither have we an inheritance in the son of Jesse: to your tents O Israel: now see to your own house, David" (I Kings 12:16). No voice was raised to decry the rejection of David's grandson as an impious act. On the contrary, even David, Yahweh's favorite, had been confirmed in his rulership by the elders of all the tribes who, in accepting him, began by acknowledging their consanguinity: "Then came all the tribes of Israel to David unto Hebron, and spake, saying, Behold we are your bone and your flesh. . . . So all the elders of Israel came to the king to Hebron; and King David made a league with them in

Hebron before the Lord: and they anointed David king of Israel" (II Samuel 5:1,3).

In the light of Egyptian, and even Mesopotamian, kingship, that of the Hebrews lacks sanctity. The relation between the Hebrew monarch and his people was as nearly secular as is possible in a society wherein religion is a living force. The unparalleled feature in this situation is the independence, the almost complete separation, of the bonds which existed between Yahweh and the Hebrew people, on the one hand, and between Yahweh and the House of David, on the other. Yahweh's covenant with the people antedated kingship. His covenant with David concerned the king and his descendants, but not the people. Through Nathan, Yahweh promised David: "I will set up your seed after you. . . . I will be his father, and he shall be My son. If he commits iniquity, I will chasten him with the rod of men, and with the stripes of the children of men: But My mercy shall not depart from him, as I took it from Saul, whom I put away before you. And your house and your kingdom shall be established for ever before you: your throne shall be established for ever" (II Samuel 7:12–16).

Only in later times, when this promise was made the foundation of messianic expectations, did the people claim a share in it. As it was made, it was as simple and direct a pledge to David as the earlier divine promises had been to the patriarchs (e.g., Genesis 15:18–21). It committed Yahweh solely to maintain the greatness of the House of David. It can be argued that this implied the greatness of the Hebrew people, or at least of Judah; but the conclusion is not inevitable.

Nowhere else in the Near East do we find this dissociation of a people from its leader in relation to the divine; with the Hebrews we find parallelism while everywhere else we find coincidence. In the meager information about Hebrew ritual it has been attempted to find indications that the king fulfilled a function not unlike that of contemporary rulers. But even if we take an exceptional and apparently simple phrase, "[Solomon] sat on the throne of the Lord as king, instead of David, his father" (I Chronicles 29:23), we need only compare this with the corresponding phrases "throne of Horus" or "throne of Atum" to realize that the Hebrew expression can only mean "throne favored by the Lord," or something similar. The phrase confirms what the account of Saul's elevation and David's scruples showed in the first place—namely, that there is interplay between the king's person and sanctity, as there was a connection between the king's fate and the national destiny. But these relations were not the nerve center of the monarchy, as they were in Egypt and Mesopotamia, but rather crosscurrents due to the religious orientation of Hebrew society; and their secondary nature stands out most clearly when we consider the functions of the Hebrew king.

The Hebrew king normally functioned in the profane sphere, not in the sacred sphere. He was the arbiter in disputes and the leader in war. He was emphatically not the leader in the cult. The king created the conditions which made a given form of worship possible: David's power allowed him to bring the Ark to Jerusalem; Solomon's riches enabled him to build the Temple; Jeroboam, Ahab, Manasseh, and others had idols made, and arranged for "groves" and "high places" for the cult of the gods of fertility. But the king played little part in the cult. He did not, as a rule, sacrifice; that was the task of the priests. He did not interpret the divine will; that, again, was the task of the priests, who cast lots for an oracle. Moreover, the divine intentions were sometimes made known in a more dramatic way when prophets—men possessed—cried, "Thus says the Lord." These prophets were often in open conflict with the king precisely because the secular character of the king entitled them to censor him.

The predominant accusation of the prophets against the kings was faithlessness to Yahweh, a "seduction" of His "chosen people" (e.g., II Kings 21:9–11) so that they followed the ways of the Gentiles. Said the prophet Jehu in the name of Yahweh to Baasha, king of Israel: "Forasmuch as I exalted you out of the dust, and made you prince over My people Israel; and you have walked in the way of Jeroboam, and have made My people Israel to sin, to provoke Me to anger with their sins" (I Kings 16:2). Such accusations recur with monotonous regularity throughout the Books of Kings. Most rulers "did evil in the sight of the Lord"; and we cannot discuss Hebrew kingship without considering this evil which seems attached to it. If the kings seduced the people, we must admit, in the light of the Egyptian and Mesopotamian evidence, that they offered the people something eminently desirable.

The keeping of Yahweh's covenant meant relinquishing a great deal. It meant, in a word, sacrificing the greatest good ancient Near Eastern religion could bestow—the harmonious integration of man's life with the life of nature. The Biblical accounts stress the orgiastic joys of the Canaanite cult of natural powers; we must remember that this cult also offered the serene awareness of being at one with the universe. In this experience ancient oriental religion rewarded its devotees with the peace of fulfillment. But the boon was available only for those who believed that the divine was immanent in nature, and Hebrew religion precisely rejected this doctrine. The absolute transcendence of God is the foundation of Hebrew religious thought. God is absolute, unqualified, ineffable, transcending every phenomenon, the one and only cause of all existence. God, moreover, is holy, which means that all values are ultimately His. Consequently, every concrete phenomenon is devaluated. . . . This austere transcendentalism of Hebrew thought . . . denied the greatest values and the most cherished potentialities of contemporary creeds. . . . Here we must point out that it bereft kingship of a function which it exercised all through the Near East, where its principal task lay in the maintenance of the harmony with the gods in nature.

And so we observe—now for the third time—the inner logic and consistency of ancient Near Eastern thought. We have described the peculiar nature of Hebrew kingship, starting from its relation to the people and their past; it would have appeared with the same characteristics if we had taken our stand on Hebrew theology. The transcendentalism of Hebrew religion prevented kingship from assuming the profound significance which it possessed in Egypt and Mesopotamia. It excluded, in particular, the king's being instrumental in the integration of society and nature. It denied the possibility of such an integration. It protested vehemently—in the persons of the great prophets—that attempts by king and people to experience that integration were incompatible with their avowed faithfulness to Yahweh. To Hebrew thought nature appeared void of divinity, and it was worse

than futile to seek a harmony with created life when only obedience to the will of the Creator could bring peace and salvation.
God was not in sun and stars, rain and wind; they were His creatures and served Him (Deuteronomy 4:19; Psalms 19). Every
alleviation of the stern belief in God's transcendence was corruption. In Hebrew religion—and in Hebrew religion alone—the
ancient bond between man and nature was destroyed. Those who
served Yahweh must forego the richness, the fulfillment, and the
consolation of a life which moves in tune with the great rhythms
of earth and sky. There were no festivals to celebrate it. No act of
the king could promote it. Man remained outside nature, exploiting it for a livelihood, offering its first-fruits as a sacrifice to
Yahweh, using its imagery for the expression of His moods; but
never sharing its mysterious life, never an actor in the perennial
cosmic pageant in which the sun is made "to rise on the evil and
on the good" and the rain is sent "on the just and the unjust."

Kingship, too, was not, for the Hebrews, anchored in the
cosmos. Except by way of contrast, it has no place in a "study
of ancient Near Eastern religion as an integration of society and
nature." The Hebrew king, like every other Hebrew, stood under
the judgment of God in an alien world, which—as the dying
David knew (II Samuel 23:3–4)—seems friendly only on those
rare occasions when man proves not inadequate: "He that rules
over men must be just, ruling in the fear of God. And he shall
be as the light of the morning, when the sun rises, even a morning
without clouds; as the tender grass, springing out of the earth by
clear shining after rain."

The Rule of a Higher Law

WILLIAM A. IRWIN

What Israel's original concept of government may have been, it is difficult to say. The earliest rule by the elders of the community and the essentially democratic freedom inherited from nomad society would seem to imply a respect for inherited custom and some more or less crude sense of justice. Certainly the traditions that are presented in the Old Testament as the early history of the nation reveal a sense of law beyond and supreme above mere individual whim. But the validity of such representation is precisely our problem. It carries some plausibility. But, on the other hand, the older strata in the Book of Judges, which are among our earliest genuinely historic sources for Hebrew society, provide disturbing considerations. A later writer generalizes about the period that "there was no king in Israel; every man did that which was right in his own eyes" (Judges 21:25; cf. 18:1, 19:1), an explanation which, in its context, means nothing but social anarchy. And certainly the conduct of the Danites at Laish, their treatment of Micah, and the whole incident of the Levite's concubine and its sequel (Judges 18–21) speak eloquently of a complete lack of moral restraint. The standard of conduct was desire, and the means to attain one's ends was physical, then political, power. The life of the strong was the happy life, since it was one of realized desire. The folk tale of Samson, whatever else it may originally have been intended to teach, certainly expresses an ideal of the time; he was such a one as the writer wished he might have been: able to buffet and toss about his foes, to make

99

sport of their retribution and plots, to take what he would, and consort with harlots at his desire. Such was a real life for a man! And there clearly we have the "natural law" of the time of the Judges: it was the law of the jungle.

We may not suppose that these heroes themselves critically evaluated and, with ethical self-consciousness, chose such courses. But Israel's thought on the problem certainly dates far back into an early period, for even in these stories, notably those of Samson and of Avimelekh, judgment is passed upon their principals' conduct. But it was in a later age that thinkers set this sort of "natural law" over against principles of equity and voiced their condemnation. Yet for the time of the Judges we may with confidence assert the prevalent thought was that might constituted the one socially valid norm, qualified only by the restraining magical powers of the oath . . . and certain established usages, such as blood revenge, and also possibly some tribal and family custom. We may still refuse to accept this view in its completeness; doubtless our understanding of the beginnings of Israel's religion compels the postulation of better ideals even through this rough period. But the evidence is such that we must then conclude that they were an esoteric concept practically impotent for society as a whole.

Nor can we trace the causes and the course of evolution of a public sense of law but only point out a few relevant facts. Israel inherited the law of the Canaanites, and her life among their relatively cultured communities must have exerted a moderating influence upon primitive violence. The kingship, too, in spite of the obloquy it receives from certain Biblical writers, clearly entailed a national law that all must recognize. Such is the implication of the comment on the period of the Judges just now quoted; such, too, is the impression we derive from glimpses of David's judicial administration. It is significant, also, that in this period we find voiced a strong sense of the restraining power of social practice and norms: "It is not so done in Israel" (II Samuel 13:12).

Yet it must be recognized that the supremacy of positive law was deeply imbedded in Israel's concept of the monarchy. Since the kingship was historically a projection of the rule of the Judges, it was inevitable that an ideal of the finality of power should carry over into the conduct of the kings. Such is the summary of royal prerogatives attributed to Samuel when the people proposed a monarchy; he warned, "the king . . . will take your sons and appoint them to himself for his chariots and to be his horsemen, and they shall run before his chariots. . . . He will take your daughters to be perfumers and cooks and bakers. He will take your fields and your vineyards and your olive yards, the best of them, and give them to his servants" (I Samuel 8:11–12). The passage,[1] it is recognized, is late, but its evidence for the character of the Hebrew monarchy is not less reliable, for this is how we see it actually working itself out. The oriental ideal of the absolute monarch who "could do no wrong" invaded Israel's court in the days of David, if, indeed, it was not already manifest under Saul; it became supreme through Solomon's reign; it was the impelling principle in Rehoboam's folly at Shekhem. And though it suffered a solemn check in the revolt of the northern tribes, yet even these devotees of freedom soon found themselves under a ruling class even more irresponsible than that in Jerusalem. We need here cite only the Naboth incident (I Kings, chap. 21) and recall the social oppression against which the prophets of the eighth century spoke to realize that Israel, north and south alike, gave itself officially to the theory that power is irresponsible, since it is the ultimate source of law. . . .

Two incidents of the period of the kings are highly significant of thought in the time. They are the Bath-sheba and the Naboth episodes. In their highhanded indifference to human rights and in their bold arrogation of absolute royal authority, they are intimately related. But both are highly important also as steps in the rise of Israel's sense of a higher law, for in both a prophet intervened to rebuke the monarch in the name of the Lord. More simply, he denied the king's claim of final authority and announced instead the supremacy of the will of the Lord, a law that bound the reigning monarch not less than his humblest subject.

This is the background of the work of Amos, whose significance for this line of Israel's thought has already been suggested. . . . His enlarged concept of the nature and authority of God evidently was rooted in a feeling of common human rights, pervasive be-

[1] For another discussion of this passage, see p. 135.

yond the political and religious boundaries of the time. This principle was for him embodied in the person of the God of Israel. But in at least one notable passage he implies the existence of such a force for good existing in and of itself. He says: "Do horses run on the rock, or does one plow the sea, that you should turn justice into gall and the fruit of righteousness into wormwood; you who rejoice in a thing of naught and say, 'Have we not taken to us horns by our own strength?' " (6:12–13). A certain propriety of conduct, he says, is freely recognized in common affairs, but in religious matters his contemporaries outrage the common sense of mankind with their moral and religious aberrations. Ordinary human good sense, he implies, ought to lead one to just conduct and right religious attitudes.

Israel's thought was in general so highly personalized, so fully drawn into the belief in a universal Person who pervaded all and was the moving force in all, that it is important, before we turn to examine the implications of this, to recognize fully the existence of a more humanistic concept of natural law, such as Amos entertained along with his deep faith in divine activity. Even more notable in this regard was the wrestle with the problem of theodicy, which, it is apparent, implies a standard independent of God and in some way beyond Him—a standard to which His conduct is amenable just as that of man. It is scarcely necessary to mention that the Old Testament, particularly in its later expressions, was much concerned with this problem of the justice of God's rule of the world.

Obviously it was paramount in the strange theology of Ecclesiastes. His God was judged by human standards of right and was found wanting. He had guarded his privileges in a most selfish way; further, his major concern seemed to be his own enjoyment, while man, striving and seeking, was circumvented at every turn by this cosmic might, and granted only minor concessions in order to keep him occupied. Man's chief concern in relations with him should be to guard his steps and be cautious of his words, for rash words may get one into untold trouble. Where Ecclesiastes found basis for his theory of ethics in such a philosophy is not stated, although it becomes apparent by careful study. True to the tradition of the wisdom movement, his thought was thoroughly humanistic, rooted in certain convictions as to the nature of the good life and the desirability of specific courses of conduct. He sought to know whether there was any good thing for man; and his conclusion was that the good thing was what would provide abiding satisfaction. So he gave himself to all sorts of conduct without let or hindrance from traditional scruples. Yet it is notable that through this experience, dominated as it seems to have been by a self-interest as crass as that which he ascribed to his God, he paid unconscious tribute to common social ideals of justice and humanity. He was concerned about the rampant injustice of his time, although he put the matter off with the reflection that nothing could be done, for the total of human misery was a constant quantity. He remarked on the selfish hierarchies of officials, each preying on the one below, and, finally, all on the poor peasant. He spoke with apparent censure of the ways of absolute monarchs, before whom speakers could only cringe and watch astutely for opportunity to serve themselves at their expense. By contrast he praised the poor but wise youth, fated to continue to the end in his lowly state, yet better than the powerful monarch whose self-serving would leave at his death not a single person to mourn his going. The wise man who delivered his city by his wisdom when military might had failed: there was something that Ecclesiastes could and did respect. He was a man of deep social feeling, which indeed was a fruitful source of his pessimism by reason of his despair of improving matters. Indeed, at this point he confronts the central problem of a theory of natural law, the existence of conflicting standards of conduct. These selfish rulers acted in accord with universal human impulses. But Ecclesiastes had no thought of commending them on this ground and condoning a return to conditions of the days of the Judges. For over against such norms of life there existed also an instinct for better things, a sense of justice rooted not less deeply in human nature. It would seem, then, that these concepts lie close to the basis of Ecclesiastes' whole system of thought. His norm was the common human feeling for justice, though only vaguely defined. By it God Himself must submit to judgment.

But the treatment of this theme in the Book of Job is notable for its projection of the antithesis of might and right into the conduct

of God Himself. In varying expression this is found throughout the
book. The speeches of Yahweh spend their eloquence in emphasis upon the irresponsible might of God. His power is such and
the complexity of His working so far beyond human understanding
that mere man may not question His ways. The inquiring spirit can
in the end only confess his temerity:

> . . . I have uttered that which I understood not,
>   things too wonderful for me, which I knew not. . . .
> Wherefore I abhor myself,
>   and repent in dust and ashes.

(Job 42:3, 6)

The Elihu speeches are not far from the same position: God "gives
not account of any of His matters" (33:13). Still, these writers
are not unconscious of the problem; they undertake to demonstrate
that God will not do wickedness (34:10 ff.) and are shocked that
Job, presumably, claims his righteousness to be greater than God's
(35:2). In this regard, the Elihu speeches reveal the familiarity
with the Dialogue for which they are well known. For Job's moral
independence outraged the traditional piety of the friends. He refused to bow in contrition before transcendence; on the contrary,
he asked insistently: "Why should God do this?" For him it
would not suffice that absolute might sat enthroned at the center of
the universe; such power must itself answer to common standards
of equity, not less than the lowliest man. On this basis Job sought
a meeting with his great adversary where he might argue the justice of the issue.

Yet at the depth of his black mood he exceeds even Ecclesiastes
in denunciation of an unethical God:

> As for strength: He is mighty;
>   as for justice: who can call Him to account?
> I am upright; I do not regard myself;
>   I despise my own life.
> It is all one! Therefore I say
>   upright and wicked alike He consumes.

(Job 9:19, 21–22)

But the great difference between Job and Ecclesiastes was that the former clung to his faith and worked through to a reasoned position where he could hold that the principles of right which he honored as a man rule correspondingly in the conduct of God.

Yet it will be apparent that, however attractive such views may have proved for the philosophic temper of the wise men, the great mass of Israel's thought, if we may judge by the prominence given it in the literature, went on the conviction that the source of ethics was in the nature and will of God. And the nexus of the two seemingly contradictory view is revealed by the great thinker . . . the author of chapter 8 of the Book of Proverbs. In his concept of wisdom as the vitalizing power in man's restless urge toward better things, which yet was with God before creation and by Him was implanted in the nature of things, there is . . . the clear implication that in such wisdom man gains his truest insight into the essential nature of God. The Hebrew philosopher would have agreed heartily with Socrates in an answer to the latter's famous question. Right was not right because God willed it; He willed it because it was right. For His nature was righteousness.

It is, then, along the line of the growing concept of the universality of the rule of Yahweh and the enlarging of ethical thinking within Israel's religion that we are to trace the advance of a sense of universal standards of right. And the triumph of this concept, apparent in the prophets' condemnation of injustice within Israel, is nowhere better manifested than in the revulsion they felt toward the irresponsibility of the aggressive empires. Isaiah held up to scorn the boast of the Assyrian:

> By the strength of my hands I have done it,
> and by my wisdom, for I have understanding.
> And I have removed the bounds of peoples
> and their treasures I have robbed;
> and as a mighty one I have brought down those enthroned
> My hand has found, like a nest,
> the wealth of the peoples;
> and as one gathers eggs hidden away
> all the earth have I gathered.

> Does an ax boast against the hewer,
>   or a saw make itself greater than its user? . . .
> Therefore will the Lord send
>   upon His fat ones leanness.

(Isaiah 10:13–16)

Not less effective is the brief note of Habakkuk in his account of the violent aggression of the Chaldean foe, the culmination of whose reprehensibility was that "from himself proceed his standards of right and dignity . . . that reprobate, whose own might is his god!" (Habakkuk 1:7, 11).

It is important to realize that in these concepts Israel's thought of natural law attained its characteristic form. The notion of a universal directive force, perhaps impersonal, but in any case independent of the power of the Lord, was but incidental. Emphasis upon it has been necessary in order to insure it adequate attention as a genuine phase of the total of Hebrew thought and to show the measure of its ultimate attainment; for the conviction that Israel regarded the world and all within it as dependent upon the will and activity of God has become axiomatic in our minds to the exclusion of other possibilities. Nor is this a serious error, for the outstanding aspect of Israel's thinking about the world was its personalism; and not least in their thought of a universal law valid and operative in the lives of men did the Hebrew thinkers postulate the personal reality and activity of their God. The supremacy of this faith among the prophets is obvious. But likewise it was the view of the wise men. The "wisdom of God," of which they made so much, was not a detached, impersonal entity; it had emanated from God: more simply, it was God Himself at work among men.

This indeed, is the distinctive contribution of Israel's thinkers to the discussion of natural law. For them it was not an irresponsible force that in some blind way, however benignly, influenced human impulses. It was God in His holiness and righteousness revealing to sinful man His will and their high destiny and only happiness in obedience thereto. From this there resulted all that is characteristic of Hebrew ethics: its white heat of urgency, but also its transcendentalism that set righteousness far beyond human attainment yet held it as a compelling ideal toward which one must strive and aspire. The moral passion of the prophets has become axiomatic; they were concerned with human well-being, it is true, but no such urgency of appeal could have arisen from human considerations. The compelling force that took possession of them "with strength of hand" was the holiness of a personal God who was very near and who sat in judgment upon the unrighteousness of man. And this for Israel was natural law! It was something more than a "supreme unifying, controlling power manifesting itself in the universe at large." It was God Himself in His supremacy and holiness saying, "This is the way; walk you therein."

The role of this concept in shaping positive legislation as well as in criticism of existing laws will be immediately apparent. Nonetheless, it is a noteworthy fact that, until comparatively late times, ethical speculation and sanctions had no recourse to codified law. The ultimate source of right and justice reposed in unwritten codes: more plainly, in the instincts and impulses that stir in the hearts of men. Doubtless the monarchs and other practical folk were ready in citation of the codified legislation of the land, but, for those who gave thought to the matter, the final rule of the hearts of men lay far deeper in a universal norm. The function of this in the legal history of Israel is evident in the work of the prophets. It stirred, too, as an uneasy conscience in the several reforms of the period of the monarchy, even if these were largely cultic. Also, the Book of Deuteronomy is, per se, eloquent testimony to the reality of the movement, for, though it purports to be a "second law," it was in reality a revision of the ancient social legislation that in considerable part Israel had taken over from the Canaanites. So we may safely conclude that an independent attitude of criticism toward the law of the land was widespread among thoughtful men. But, excellent as this is for our present purpose, a further issue forces itself upon the attention. Natural law can exist at all only if it is universal. The crux of the problem is how far Israel's thinkers applied their accepted standards to the laws of foreign nations, or believed that among those peoples there was a stirring such as manifested itself in Israel's own thought.

Investigation of the question is beset with the obvious difficulty that Israel's writers were primarily concerned with Israelite standards and conduct; to the life and thought of foreigners they gave but minor attention. But at least the first eleven chapters of Genesis promise material for our purpose. The heroes and other characters of this narrative may in some measure have been regarded as remote ancestors, but certainly they were not Israelites; and from the stories certain relevant facts stand out. The authors have not the least doubt that God was known among these non-Hebraic peoples, through revelation of a sort similar to or identical with that later given to Israel. His will was their ultimate law, upholding those standards later established in Hebrew society. Cain should not have killed Abel; the rampant "violence" of the time of the flood cried out to high heaven for retribution; the life and conduct of Noah was a standing rebuke to his contemporaries; the builders of the Tower of Babel were guilty of arrogance; etc. Further, the distribution of the peoples of the earth is represented as being in accord with divine purposes; even if not ethically determined, at least it was an expression of that impulse which the writers believed to be the ultimate authority in human life.

Comparable are the results that may be deduced from accounts of Israel's relations with foreign powers. The Egyptians should not have oppressed the Hebrews; the hard labor of the slaves raised a cry to heaven which in turn brought divine retribution in the plagues and the incidents of the Exodus. The lawless oppressions of the Assyrians and Chaldeans were denounced; these peoples outraged all human standards—and made a virtue of it. And for the smaller nations near Palestine, the threats contained in the first and second chapters of the Book of Amos took their rise in a reaction against unhuman conduct; these peoples had practiced barbarities against helpless neighbors, they had forgotten "the brotherly covenant," they had enslaved whole peoples, they had been implacable in their hatreds. On the other hand, the implications of the Servant Songs, and of passages that picture a great movement of Gentile peoples to Jerusalem for worship, as well as the claim in the Book of Malachi that from the rising of the sun to its going-down the Lord's name was great among the Gentiles, all alike indicate recognition of a common human bond among all peoples that rendered foreigners amenable to the same high appeals and impulses as native Hebrews. It will be recognized that we lack formal discussion by Israel's thinkers of the universality of basic

ethical standards; to that extent we are doubtless justified in concluding that the problem was not fully realized. But at least it is
clear that they assumed, even if uncritically, the world-wide rule of
those standards of right which they themselves honored. The words
of Paul . . . may be quoted as expressive of his people's traditional thinking: "For the wrath of God is revealed from heaven
against all unrighteousness of men . . . because that which is
known of God is manifest in them, for God manifested it unto
them."

Yet the problem of natural law looks in still another direction,
for within Palestine, through the centuries of Israel's occupation,
there were notably two groups that provide test cases of Hebrew
consistency; they were the foreign immigrants and the slaves. The
underprivileged condition of both is apparent to every casual reader
of the Old Testament. Of the former, however, it can be affirmed
that progressive thought refused to leave them to the whims of
popular bigotries and suspicions. The concern of the authors of
Deuteronomy for the "sojourner" is a notable feature of the book.
The prophets likewise urged consideration and fellow-feeling toward this noncitizen populace. But it was the priestly document
that took the final step of legislating equal rights and equal responsibilities for the *gerim:* "You shall have one law for the home-born
and for the stranger who sojourns among you" (Exodus 12:49).
The late date commonly ascribed to this legislation and its high
authority in post-Exilic Judaism raise the prescription to a high
significance.

The problem of the slave is not so easily handled: for the thinking of today, the widespread and legalized practice of slavery constitutes a very black stain on the social attainments of ancient
Israel. And, to make the matter worse, no protest was raised
against the institution per se, demanding the equal freedom of all
men. Jeremiah, for example, was indignant because recently
liberated slaves were illegally repossessed, but he says not a word
to the effect that their ever having lost their freedom was a mark
of the iniquity of his contemporaries. . . . Yet the facts are not
so damning as all this may suggest. Slavery in the primitive days
of Israel's history had humane features. The foreign slave, who
was generally a captive in war, owed his life to the institution;

apart from it he would almost certainly have been slaughtered at the time of his people's defeat. The enslavement of Hebrews had an economic basis; one accepted slavery when he could no longer win a livelihood. The condition insured at least subsistence, and to this extent it may be considered, like the institution of blood revenge, a progressive social measure for its time.

The ethics of Old Testament slavery thus depended in large measure upon the character of the slaveowner; and there is abundant evidence to show that, in general, the slave enjoyed a status far above what the term suggests to us. Social distinctions are moderated in the simple, immediate relations of rural life. Master and slave, associated together as they were in tasks and adventures in the field, developed some sense of comradeship. A revealing incident, frequently cited in the study of Hebrew slavery, is that of Saul's consultation with his slave when the two had been for several days searching for lost asses; and it was the slave, not Saul, who had money in his possession to pay a fee to the "man of God." On the other hand, there were, as always, brutal masters who on occasion beat their slaves even to the point of death.

But the important matter is that Israel's conscience did not lie supine under these conditions. Legislation was enacted to protect the slave, and in the great legal revision represented by our Book of Deuteronomy these provisions received notable strengthening. But even more indicative of a Hebrew conscience toward this matter is the ground ascribed for such consideration: "You shall remember that you were a slave in the land of Egypt, and the Lord your God brought you out." "Keep the sabbath day . . . that your male slave and your female slave may rest as well as you." It is to be observed that provision is not specifically for fellow-Hebrews but for any slave.

And its *raison d'être* expresses clearly a sense of common human unity: briefly, a respect for fellow-humans as persons. Beyond this, Hebrew thought on slavery did not go. But it is to be recognized that in this attainment there lay the germ of all future advance. While admitting freely Israel's failure to repudiate slavery, there are then three points to be kept in mind: Hebrew slavery was relatively humane; it was regulated and guarded with increasingly humanitarian legislation; and, third, the slave was recognized as possessing certain inalienable rights on the grounds of his being human. The situation was such that we need not hesitate to include it as an aspect of Israel's thought of natural law.

In course of time that body of literature which we know as the Pentateuch assumed its final shape, and apparently by the fourth century B.C. was "canonized," that is, was accepted as of divine origin and authority. Through the various circumstances that determined its composition there were included certain social codes and much ritual direction, both of which had enjoyed a long history and operation. But now they were endowed with a halo of sanctity. For devout thought, all alike became *ipsissima verba* of the will and revelation of God and, as such, of ultimate authority over human conduct. In this fact, then, we are to see the confluence of the two streams of Israel's law and the termination of the antithesis that marks this line of thinking. Living under foreign rule as they did, subject also to the whims of fallible leaders of their own, the Jews never escaped, in actuality, the problem of positive law; but, for orthodox thought, in the Pentateuch natural law had absorbed and sublimated positive law.

Still, the concept of the unwritten law and its authority continued. It found notable expression in the oral tradition that eventually was codified in the Mishnah. Criticism may smile indulgently at the palpable deception in the claim that this was given to Moses at Sinai along with the Torah, but if we would read the meaning of figurative language, it is apparent that this was but an expression of the sense of a pervasive natural law: the religious impulse and revelation with which the name of Moses was associated was too great to embody itself in written form—not even the Torah was adequate; but it reposed ultimately in the divine impress upon the heart of man. Even in the Old Testament itself, and apparently from a period when the Torah had attained sanctity in Jewish thought, the supremacy of the unwritten law is notably expressed. There are several passages which voice the hope for the future that Israel should then be cleansed of its propensity to sin and transformed into a righteous nation. The following is especially deserving of attention.

> Behold the days come, says the Lord, when I will make a new covenant with the house of Israel, and with the house of Judah, not according to the covenant that I made with their fathers. . . .

but this is the covenant that I will make with the house of Israel after those days, says the Lord: I will put My law in their inward parts and in their hearts I will write it; and I will be their God, and they shall be My people. And they shall teach no more every man his neighbor and his brother saying, Know the Lord; for they shall all know Me from the least unto the greatest of them (Jeremiah 31:31–34).

The law written on the heart, not an external law, should rule men's lives. But it would be a gracious rule: not compulsion, not an infringement of man's freedom but its fulfillment. Men would do the right because they most wished so to do. They would recognize the beauty of goodness, won by its inherent attractiveness. Here is the culmination of Israel's thought about natural law: a glorious day should dawn when man's jungle impulses would atrophy, when right would triumph deep in human nature, and society would pursue its happy course in a state of "anarchy," of "no law," because everyone would do the high and noble thing through his love for it, in obedience to the unwritten law inscribed on his heart!

There remains yet one difficult problem of this line of thinking. When the Torah was canonized and the law of God thus became ostensibly the law of the land, there could be no clash between conscience and authority. Yet it is apparent that such a situation never became an actuality of Israel's life. Even in the period when Jerusalem was under the high priests, the Jews were nonetheless subject to foreign rule; and even if we concede for the sake of argument what notably was not true, that all the officials of the theocracy were high-minded men, still the people were never remote from the problem of what to do in face of a bad law. And even more was this true of earlier ages. A devout answer is immediately at hand. In the words of the apostles faced with some such dilemma, one "ought to obey God rather than man."

Yet the issue is not quite so simple. Paul formulated the crux of it in his seemingly antithetic saying that "the powers that be are ordained of God." Apparently the words of Jesus relative to payment of tribute bear a similar interpretation. "Render unto Caesar the things of Caesar." Both imply recognition that government performs an indispensable function. Without ordered society the bare essentials of civilized life are not possible. Even a bad government provides some measure of security and settled procedure. What then? Are we to weaken the pillars of society by a course of flagrant disobedience of laws that we consider wrong? Or shall we take the opposite course and outrage conscience by supporting a wicked government in the interests of stability? Is there a middle course, and what and where are its bounds?

The revolts instigated by the prophets, notably that of the northern tribes in the time of Rehoboam and of Jehu a century later, were frank acceptance of one horn of the dilemma: direct action for the overthrow of an evil ruler is in harmony with the will of God. But it is notable that subsequent thought repudiated this policy and sought reform within ordered society. The Maccabean revolt, commendable as it seems to us, was likewise given scant honor by the contemporary author of Daniel; it was only "a little help."

This comment may suggest the answer which Hebrew thought finally accepted. For it is apparent that, in repudiating the prowess of Judas and his outlaws, the writer looks rather for divine deliverance. And certainly this is in harmony with the entire apocalyptic movement and with most of the later political thought as it is expressed in the Old Testament. The Lord stirred up the spirit of Cyrus to deliver His people; He showed mercy by inclining the hearts of the kings of Persia to the needs of the Jews in Judea. On the other hand, Daniel and his companions in the Babylonian court "purposed in their heart that they would not defile themselves"; the three who refused to worship the great image were thrown into the furnace. Daniel himself continued his daily devotions in the face of royal prohibition; and in every case deliverance and advancement came to the faithful by supernatural means.

The conclusion is fairly clear. Jewish thought favored an honest acceptance of government, whatever it might be, and loyal conformity to promulgated law, but only within the limits of Jewish conscience. Where law and religion clashed, then the Jew was to honor his religious duty at whatever cost, encouraged, it may be, with the belief that this course would prove in the end wisest even from the practical point of view. Yet such conformity to the rule of government did not mean indifference to public standards of right. But change of government, in that age when it could be brought about humanly only through violence, was regarded as properly in the hands of God. He set up kings and He removed kings in accord with His eternal purposes. One must endure evil days sustained by the conviction that it was the will of God. And, at the worst, oppression was but a transient affair, for soon the kingdom of the saints would be established.

PART III

The Democratic Ideal

Editor's Note

The essence of the democratic ideal, as the term is used in the free societies of the West, is a basic distrust of all government. A distrust of government, to be meaningful, needs to be expressed in constitutional controls on the state and all its agents and servants —in limits on the powers of government, so that the ordinary citizen may be protected against violence, injustice, rapacity, and all forms of oppression and repression. The institutional means used to maximize the democratic ideal will, of course, reflect a people's history and traditions, its culture, and the level of its social and economic development. But through all complexities and variations, expressive of diversified conditions of time and place—if the ideal is there, its vision and force must come through.

Any sensitive reading of the Jewish tradition will show such vision and force. The Torah left room for a king, but in his charge to the Israelites in the Sinai wilderness Moses stressed that the king must be only the first among equals, and that he must be bound by the same law that binds all the citizens. The passage (Deuteronomy 17:18–20) so clearly and beautifully expresses the democratic spirit that it might well serve as a preamble to the constitution of any people who cherish the ideals of freedom and equality under just law:

> And when [the king] sits on the throne of his kingdom, he shall write for himself in a book a copy of this [code of laws], . . . and it shall be with him, and he shall read in it all the days of his life, that he may learn to fear the Lord his God, by keeping all the words of this law and these statutes, and doing them; that his heart may not be lifted up above his brethren, and that he may not

117

turn aside from the commandment, either to the right hand or to the left. . . .

In all literature it would be difficult to find another passage that so succinctly and forcefully expresses what is at the heart of the democratic ideal. But the passage is by no means unique in the Hebrew Bible or Jewish post-Biblical literature. It is characteristic of the political and institutional history of the Jewish people, even as it is expressive of the government and the people of the State of Israel.

Judaism and the Democratic Ideal

MILTON R. KONVITZ

The essence of the democratic ideal is the belief in equality. An explication of this belief in equality leads to cultural and religious pluralism; to constitutional government, with effective checks on the agencies of government; a wide and equitable distribution of property; universal education and emphasis on reason, rather than superstition and force, as instruments of social control and progress; freedom of speech, freedom of the press, and freedom of assembly.

Just as a sharp distinction must be made between the accidental and the essential aspects of democracy, so the same distinction must be made among the various aspects of Judaism. Judaism, too, has had its highest insights, which, though they may have been conditioned by historical events, deserve perpetuation on their own account. On the other hand, like all other social institutions, Judaism has frequently needed to accommodate itself to the accidents of time and place in ways which did not at all times exhibit its own highest ideals. As in the case of democracy, it is the deeper motivation, the profounder insights, rather than the superficial aspects, that have kept alive Judaism as a way of life and as a philosophy of life.

Living in . . . the twentieth century, we, of course, face problems radically different from those faced by the prophets thousands of years ago, or by the great Rabbis responsible for the

Babylonian and Palestinian Talmuds. Freedom of speech must mean something sharply different to a people with a press than it did to a people who prohibited reduction of their learning to writing. This means only that the branches of democracy are different; the root is the same: it is the same wherever and whenever people constitute a society. The problem of human freedom is always the same: though at one time, to achieve more of it, we must fight a civil war to abolish economic and physical slavery; at another time we must fight to abolish racial distinctions in immigration policy; at one time, to achieve more of freedom, we must carry on a fight for woman suffrage; at another time the fight is against the white primary and the poll tax; at one time the fight is for freedom to teach Torah in Javneh; at another time the fight is for freedom to teach the theory of evolution in Tennessee.

The scenes change; the characters and the plot are pretty much the same. This does not mean, necessarily, that the history of mankind can be written in terms of the history of liberty. We are not here concerned with the degree of truth in a Crocean philosophy of history. All we mean to say is that whatever liberty may have meant at different times in the history of mankind, its essential character, as we have stated it, has been always pretty much the same. The struggles have been variations on a theme. The theme has been: human equality and freedom. . . .

When men are judged by any empirical test they are not equal: some are richer than others, some wiser, some swifter, some more beautiful. Yet the essence of democracy is equality. Men reject the empirical tests and assert their equality notwithstanding the evidence adduced by their eyes and ears and other senses. "All men are created equal," said Jefferson in the Declaration of Independence; and he had no footnote references to statistical tables by way of documentation. The belief in equality is a transcendental belief, if you wish; it makes an assertion which may be true only in the world of noumena. But no matter: it is the cornerstone of the democratic faith and the essence of moral idealism. "The basis of democratic development," says Harold Laski, "is therefore the demand that the system of power be erected upon the *similarities* and not the *differences* between men." Here we have the clue to the problem of democracy: differences are not to be eliminated, for it is good that one man paint better than another, that one woman cook better than does her neighbor, that one surgeon operate better than another; yes, and even that one man legislate better than another. But the system of power (political power, economic and social power) must be based on the similarities and not on the differences between men. The demand for equality manifests itself in many relations: there is the demand for equal suffrage; for economic equality; there must be no privilege by birth; there is the demand for educational equality; there must be equality in participation in the results of social developments and improvements; equality before the law (real and not merely formal equality).

At bottom the democratic faith is a moral affirmation: men are not to be used merely as means to an end, as tools; each is an end in himself; his soul is from the source of all life; . . . no matter how lowly his origin, a man is here only by the grace of God—he owes his life to no one but God. He has an equal right to pursue happiness: life, liberty and the pursuit of happiness are his simply by virtue of the fact that he is a live human being. He has his place in the sun, and neither the place nor the sun was made by men.

This faith finds its essence in what Henry Michel called the "eminent dignity of human personality." One of the chief sources of this faith is in the wellsprings of Judaism.

It may be possible to arrive at the philosophy of equality within the framework of secular thought, as e.g., in the systems of John Dewey and Bertrand Russell and in socialist Marxism. Within the framework of a religious system, however, it is probably impossible to arrive at the philosophy of equality in the absence of a belief in ethical monotheism.

For as long as one believes in the existence of a multiplicity of gods, each expressing his own biases and partialities, loving his friends and hating his enemies, and no one supreme god above all others, there is no room provided for accommodation of the beliefs in the fatherhood of God and the brotherhood of man. In ethical monotheism, however, these beliefs are basic. Judaism conceived of God as the creator and ruler of the entire universe: "In the beginning God created the heavens and the earth." He created

Adam and Eve, from whom all mankind have sprung. Humanity lives, therefore, in "one world," one world in every sense of the term; the laws of physical nature are the same everywhere; the laws of human nature are the same everywhere: the heavens and the moral law are the same everywhere.

Not only are the physical laws the same everywhere, but the laws of righteousness too. For God is not only *ehad,* One, but He is God "sanctified in righteousness." He is the judge of all the earth, as Abraham said, and cannot act unjustly. "You are not a God who has pleasure in wickedness; evil shall not sojourn with You; You hate all workers of iniquity." God, as the prophet said, wants to loose the fetters of wickedness, to undo the bands of the yoke, to deal bread to the hungry, to cover the naked, to shelter the homeless—He wants to see all this, and more, accomplished—but through the free agency of man.

Implicit and explicit in the ethical monotheism that is Judaism are, then, the beliefs in the fatherhood of God and the brotherhood of man. Thus Malachi cried out: "Have we not all one Father? Has not One God created us?" Thus is posited the fatherhood principle. But in the same breath the prophet added: "Why do we deal treacherously every man against his brother?" The fatherhood and brotherhood principles go together; they are inseparable: if two men have the same father, are they, then, not brothers?

"God," said the Rabbis, "is on the watch for the nations of the world to repent, so that He may bring them under His wings." When the nations will accept the reign of righteousness, the Kingdom of God will have become established; and God wants this to happen above all else.

The most graphic expression of the fatherhood of God and the brotherhood of man is the statement in the Bible that man was created in the image of God. The Rabbis did not tire of creating homilies on this figurative expression of the oneness of the human family. Thus, R. Joshua b. Levi said: "When a man goes on his road, a troop of angels proceed in front of him and proclaim, 'Make way for the image of the Holy One, blessed be He.' " . . .

. . . It is related that Ben Azzai quoted the verse from Genesis, "This is the book of the generations of Adam," and remarked that this is the greatest principle in the Torah. The same point was made by Rabbi Akiba but in a different statement. He said that the greatest principle in the Torah is "Love your neighbor as yourself." Rabbi Tanhuma put the matter in a third way. He said that one should not say to himself, "Because I am despised, so may my neighbor be cursed with me"; for if one acts in this way he despises a being made in the image of God.

In the Talmud the question is raised why man was created a solitary human being, why were there not created several Adams and several Eves at one time? The answer given is this: "So that it might not be said that some races are better than others."

In the Midrash it is stated that the falling of rain is an event greater than the giving of the Torah, for the Torah is for Israel only, but rain is for the entire world. According to the Mekilta, however, even the Torah is for the entire world: "The Torah was given in the wilderness and in fire and in water. As these three are free to all the inhabitants of the world, so are the words of the Torah free to all the inhabitants of the world."

Are only the righteous among Israel the elect of God? Not at all; for righteousness, like sin, is the great leveler; the sinners among Israel are no better off than the evil ones among the non-Jews; and the righteous Israelites are not preferred to the righteous among the non-Jews. "The just among the Gentiles are the priests of God," says the Midrash. "I call heaven and earth to witness that whether a person be Jew or Gentile, man or woman, manservant or maidservant, according to his acts does the Divine Spirit rest upon him."

The injunctions in the Bible relating to the treatment of a brother were not construed as being directed only to the treatment of Israelites (though all Israelites are brothers) but of all mankind (for all men are brothers). Thus it was said: "The heathen is your neighbor, your brother. To wrong him is a sin." The point is made graphically by the following incident in the Midrash:

> Simon ben Shetah was occupied with preparing flax. His disciples said to him, "Rabbi, desist. We will buy you an ass, and you will not have to work so hard." They went and bought an ass from an Arab, and a pearl was found on it, whereupon they came to him and said, "From now on you need not work any more." "Why?" he asked. They said, "We bought you an ass from an Arab, and

a pearl was found on it." He said to them, "Does its owner know of that?" They answered, "No." He said to them, "Go and give the pearl back to him." "But," they argued, "did not Rabbi Huna, in the name of Rab, say all the world agrees that if you find something which belongs to a heathen, you may keep it?" Their teacher said, "Do you think that Simon ben Shetah is a barbarian? He would prefer to hear the Arab say, 'Blessed be the God of the Jews,' than possess all the riches of the world. . . . It is written, 'You shall not oppress your neighbor.' Now your neighbor is as your brother, and your brother is as your neighbor. Hence you learn that to rob a Gentile is robbery."

In the same spirit it is said in the Talmud that an idolator who studies the Torah is like the High Priest; that a Gentile who lives a godly life is like the High Priest. It is related that Rabbi Judah told the Emperor Antoninus that he would have a share in the world to come even though he was a Gentile; for all men have a share in the world to come as long as they desist from acts of violence. In the spirit of Simon ben Shetah the Talmud states: "In a city where there are both Jews and Gentiles, the collectors of alms collect both from Jews and Gentiles, and feed the poor of both, visit the sick of both, bury both, comfort the mourners whether they be Jews or Gentiles, and restore the lost goods of both."

The Bible begins the story of man not with the birth of Abraham but with the creation of Adam and Eve; and the Rabbis said that Adam was made from dust gathered by God from the four corners of the earth, so that no people should later be able to say that he was made from the dust gathered only in their own corner of the world. And wherever one turns in the writings of the Jews this motif of equality, the fatherhood of God and the brotherhood of man, appears irresistibly. Thus, at the Passover *seder* a drop of wine is to be spilled from the cup at the mention of each of the ten plagues with which the Egyptians were afflicted, the reason being, say the Rabbis, that one's cup of joy cannot be full as long as there is suffering somewhere in the world. . . . Again, at the *seder* the head of the household reads of the drowning of the Egyptian hosts in the Red Sea; and the Rabbis comment on the passage by relating that when the drowning was taking place, angels in heaven commenced to sing the praises of the Lord, but He rebuked them, saying, "My children are drowning, and you would sing!" . . .

. . . According to Isaiah, the Lord says: "Blessed be Egypt My people and Assyria the work of My hands, and Israel Mine inheritance" (19:25). And when Jeremiah speaks of the afflictions that must be visited upon the sinful people of Moab, he says that God weeps: "Therefore will I wail for Moab; yea, I will cry out for all Moab; for the men of Kir-heres shall my heart moan" (48:31). And the Book of Jonah, which occupies so prominent a place in Jewish ritual, relates of God's concern for the salvation of the inhabitants of the city of Nineveh—a city of Gentiles, not of Jews.

. . . Clearly, Judaism, or the ethical monotheism elaborated by the Hebrew Scriptures and the Rabbis, posits as one of its fundamental precepts the equality of all men before God: all men who share righteousness share the grace of God. And righteousness is not considered from the standpoint of ritual observance: works of benevolence, says the Talmud, form the beginning and end of the Torah. . . .

> Wherewith shall I come before the Lord?
> And bow myself before God on high?
> Shall I come before Him with burnt-offerings?
> With calves of a year old?
> Will the Lord be pleased with thousands of rams,
> With ten thousands of rivers of oil?
> Shall I give my first-born for my transgression,
> The fruit of my body for the sin of my soul?
> It has been told you, O man, what is good;
> And what the Lord requires of you;
> Only to do justly and to love mercy
> And to walk humbly with your God
>
> (Micah 6:6–8)

That the ideals of equality and freedom which one finds at the heart of Judaism were not projected merely for "the end of days," but were principles of daily conduct, becomes clear when one

examines some of the institutions . . . characteristic of Judaism.
In their relations with Gentiles the Jews could speak of equality
and freedom only as the ends to be achieved after a long struggle:
both the Jews and the non-Jews will need to realize the nature of
righteousness and strive for it together before they lie down together in equality, no one a lion and no one a lamb, but all
children of the One Father, brothers who have issued from the
same source of life. The ideal was always there; Israel could
preserve itself only by loyalty to its universalistic religion; its mission was never to be treated lightly, let alone forgotten; and every
opportunity was to be taken advantage of to elicit from the non-
Jew a blessing for the One God, and thereby to bring him closer
to righteousness. . . . That is what *Kiddush ha-Shem* means.
. . . Awareness of this mission is illustrated by the dictum in the
Talmud that to cheat a Gentile is even worse than to cheat a Jew,
for besides being a violation of the moral law, such conduct brings
Israel's religion into contempt and causes a *Hillul ha-Shem* (a
desecration of the Name).

In relations among themselves the Jewish people had an opportunity to give the ideal of equality "a local habitation and a name."
The keystone of the Jewish community was the precept that "all
Israel are responsible for one another." The Rabbis relate that
when Moses summoned all Israel before God, he said, "Your
captains, your judges, your elders." But God made him add the
words: "all the people of Israel." This passage receives clarification by the statement of the Rabbis that Moses did not stop with
"all the people of Israel," but went on to add: "your little ones,
your wives, and the stranger that is in your camp"; for, said the
Rabbis, "God's mercies are on male and female alike, on the
wicked equally with the righteous, as it says, 'From the hewer of
your wood to the drawer of your water.' All are equal before God;
hence it says, 'All the people of Israel.'" Rabbi Akiba said that
even the poorest in Israel are looked upon as freemen who have
lost their possessions, "for they are the sons of Abraham, Isaac
and Jacob." In other words, all *men* are equal because all are the
children of Adam and Eve; all *Israelites* are equal because all are
the children of Abraham, Isaac and Jacob—not to mention Adam
and Eve.

The hereditary character of the priesthood in ancient Israel has led to the charge that Judaism recognized a class of privileged persons whose rights were obtained by birth: a hereditary aristocracy. But this is due to a misunderstanding. The priests were not permitted to consider themselves the heads of the community; they were a class whose status was determined by function; they were servants of God in a special sense; but being such servants, they carried obligations rather than privileges. People were not to stand in superstitious fear of them; they had no superior spiritual powers. The Rabbis had freed themselves from almost every trace of sacerdotalism. The priesthood was maintained because the Torah required it; but it was not the priests who blessed Israel; it was God who bestowed the blessing; the priests were not intermediaries, like angels or saints: "It says at the end of the priestly benediction, 'and it is I that will bless them.' One might think that if the priests choose to bless the Israelites, then they are blessed, and if they do not choose, they are not blessed. Therefore it says, 'And it is *I* that will bless them. *I* will bless my people.' "

Nor did the Rabbis themselves constitute a privileged caste. Three crowns were recognized, the crown of the Torah, the crown of the priesthood, and the crown of the kingdom.

> Aaron was worthy of the crown of the priesthood and obtained it, David was worthy of the crown of the kingdom and obtained it. The crown of the Torah remains, so that no man shall have the pretext to say: "If the crown of the priesthood and the crown of the kingdom were yet available, I would have proved myself worthy of them and have obtained them." For the crown of the Torah is available for all. For God says: "Of him who proves himself worthy of *that* crown, I reckon it to him as if all the three were yet available, and he had proved himself worthy of them all. And of everyone who does not prove himself worthy of the crown of the Torah, I reckon it unto him as if all three crowns were yet available, and he had proved himself worthy of none of them."

The crown of the Torah is not inherited; it was worn by men who earned their living by cobbling shoes, weaving flax or making candles. Ben Azzai said: "If any man humiliates himself for the

Torah, eats dry dates and wears dirty clothes, and sits and keeps guard at the doors of the wise, every passer-by thinks him a fool, but at the end you will find that all the Torah is within him"; and if the Torah is within him, he may wear the crown of the Torah. A famous passage in *Pirke Avot* is the following:

> This is the way that is becoming for the study of the Torah: a morsel of bread with salt you must eat, and water by measure you must drink, you must sleep upon the ground, and live a life of trouble, the while you toil in the Torah. If you do thus, "Happy shall you be and it shall be well with you"; happy shall you be in this world, and it shall be well with you in the world to come. Seek not greatness for your self, and crave not honor more than is due to your learning; and desire not the table of kings, for your table is greater than theirs, and your crown greater than theirs; and faithful is He, the master of your work, to pay you the reward of your labor.

As water is priceless, said the Rabbis, so is the Torah priceless; and as water is free for all, so is the Torah free for all. But the Torah was also compared to wine: as wine cannot keep in vessels of gold and silver, but only in cheap earthenware vessels, so the words of the Torah are preserved only in him who makes himself lowly. "The greater the man," says the Midrash, "the humbler he is." Man, especially one who wears the crown of the Torah, must be as humble as is God Himself; wherever you find the greatness of God, there, too, you will find His humbleness. For "God loves nothing better than humility." Said Rabbi Johanan: "The words of the Torah abide only with him who regards himself as nothing." The Torah was not to be used as an ornament with which one might adorn himself; nor was it to be used as a spade with which to dig; knowledge of the Torah was its own reward; it is only to study the Torah that God created man: study of the Torah is his purpose, his end, his happiness and his reward. "Do the words of the Torah for the doing's sake; speak of them for their own sake. Do not say: 'I will learn Torah so that I may be called wise, or sit in the college, or gain long days in the world to come.'" Nor may one charge fees for teaching the Torah; for the words of the Torah are free; God gave the Torah free: "he who takes a fee for the Torah destroys the world."

The humility with which the greatest of the three crowns was to be worn is illustrated by the following incident related in the Talmud:

> One day, at the close of the fig harvest, Rabbi Tarfon was walking in a garden, and he ate some figs which had been left behind. The custodian of the garden came up, caught him, and began to beat him unmercifully. Then Rabbi Tarfon called out and said who he was, whereupon they let him go. Yet all his days did he grieve, saying, "Woe is me, for I have used the crown of the Torah for my own profit." For the teaching ran: "A man must not say, I will study so as to be callled a wise man, or rabbi, or an elder, or to have a seat in the college; but he must study from love. The honor will come of itself."

The Rabbis did not constitute a caste; they generally were not supported by the community but had to carry on a trade or calling from which they might support themselves and their families: "I call heaven and earth to witness," says the Midrash, "that every scholar who eats of his own, and enjoys the fruits of his own labor, and who is not supported by the community, belongs to the class who are called happy; as it is written, 'If you eat the fruit of your hands, happy are you.' " They were teachers, but received no compensation for their teaching; they had to make a living by spending a part of their day in some occupation for which there was a monetary reward: "He who occupies himself with the study of the Torah only is as if he had no God." A man was counseled to spend as little time as possible, however, at his trade or work: only long enough to earn sufficient money to keep body and soul together. It was the duty of everyone to study the Torah at some time during each day: at least two ordinances in the morning and two in the evening; but the more study, the greater the reward (in the world to come). "If a scholar engages in business and is not too successful, it is a good omen for him. God loves his learning and does not want to enrich him." The greatest calumny was to call one an *am ha-aretz*, a boor; to be poor was to be blessed, but to be ignorant was to be cursed. No mitzvah was greater than study: the study of the Torah was superior to all other things— all other things except one: teaching Torah. "He who learns receives but one-fifth of the reward that goes to him who teaches."

It is evident, then, that the crown of the Torah did not carry with it social privileges: the most learned man still needed to continue at his cobbler's bench or carpentry work. On the contrary, it imposed the obligation to teach. The social ideal of Judaism was a community of scholars, where all would be companions. This is what it means to have been created in the image of God: to fulfill the obligation or commandment to study the words of God. This commandment was imposed on *every* Jew equally; it had to be fulfilled by himself, and not by a surrogate.

The schools were commanded not to engage in strife one with the other. Tolerance in scholarly dispute was an obligation. "If a scholar has no *derekh eretz* [good taste, refinement], he is lower than an animal." It is related that Raba would open his discourse with a jest, and let his hearers laugh a little. For years the schools of Hillel and Shammai maintained a dispute over a matter of law, finally a Voice descended in Javneh and cried out: "The words of both are the words of the Living God, but the decision should follow the School of Hillel." It was asked, why, if the words of both are the words of the Living God, was the decision granted to Hillel's school? The reply was: "Because the members of the school of Hillel are amiable of manner and courteous; they teach the opinions of both schools; and furthermore, they always give the opinion of their opponents first." This teaches, said the Rabbis, that whoever abases himself is exalted by God. One was not to assume that the Divine Wisdom rested with him alone and that those who differed from him uttered words of no worth. One was to be a constant fount of tolerance and humility; one must be conscious of the relativity of his own statements even when, or perhaps especially when, the statement related to ultimate truths; for one was always subject to error and sin; all statements of truth were subject to finiteness and contingency. "One says its meaning is this, and another says its meaning is that. One gives such an opinion, his fellow a different one. But they all were given from one shepherd—that is from Moses, who received the teaching from Him who is One and unique in the world." . . .

Judaism is not merely a matter of beliefs and ceremonies, it is a way of life; and the economic aspect of human existence was not a matter of indifference to the prophets and Rabbis. . . . Today we might be tempted to say that one aim was religious while the other was social; but Judaism would reject the distinction. Judaism recognizes no profane virtues; all virtues are sacred; the social function is as religious as the religious function is social. "Rabbi Judah said in the name of Rab: 'A man is forbidden to eat anything until he has fed his beast.' " Was this considered a religious law or a social law? The distinction would not have been comprehensible to either Rabbi Judah or Rab. In Judaism all duties are divine commands. While several duties appear to be arbitrary, nearly all are expressed in laws which our conscience recognizes as obligatory on free will. Economics and ethics are the same; ethics and religion are the same.

. . . The study of the Torah was chiefly the study of social relations, individual and communal problems. The Torah taught that "if two men claim your help, and one is your enemy, help your enemy first"; and the same Torah taught that "he who gives food to a small child, must tell its mother"; and the same Torah taught that one must permit the poor to glean after the reapers, and that one must not take interest on a loan.

Perhaps it was the experience of the Israelites in Egypt that compelled them to project the ideal of social equality and freedom. For in Egypt they saw that when great wealth and political power are in the hands of the same group, the welfare and happiness of the rest of the people are greatly imperiled. Political and economic power must be spread out among all, with little if any disparity in the distribution. If this is not accomplished, and men are unjustly exploited—used as mere means and not as ends; when it is forgotten that every man bears the image of God—physical, spiritual and social pestilence will spread, and insurrection will follow, shaking the community to its very foundations. Masters cannot exploit their workers and God should not see. The excessive wealth of the masters leads to luxury; derived through injustice, wealth breeds further injustice; luxury corrupts what may have been left untouched by the injustice of exploitation. In the end the system collapses; blind injustice leans against the pillar of its palace and is destroyed with it.

Furthermore, as Charles Foster Kent has well pointed out, the experience of Moses showed him that violence does not avail in correcting industrial evils. The only true method is that which he used: "Education and organization of those industrially oppressed; clear presentation of their claims and rights; patient, persistent agitation in order to educate public opinion; and efficient organization to protect their interests."

The Israelites did not win their freedom merely to duplicate among themselves the system they had rejected. They were to build their own community on a basis of moral idealism, ethical religion and social justice. There was to be in the Promised Land no form of political or industrial oppression; for always the Jews were commanded to remember, at every turn, in every crisis, at every temptation to commit an injustice: "Remember that you were a slave in the land of Egypt, and that the Lord your God brought you out from there by a mighty hand and an outstretched arm." Future generations, after the Exodus, . . . were commanded to look upon themselves as though *they,* and not merely their forefathers, had been rescued from the hand of the Egyptian taskmaster. The *freshness* of their freedom was constantly to be before their eyes.

Moreover, they were commanded to remember in humility that it was not by their own strength that they won their freedom, but because God is One who watches over the poor, the fatherless, the afflicted, the helpless, the outcast: He is a just Judge; He loves justice and mercy and righteousness, and requites evil with evil. . . .

In ancient Israel the atmosphere was a thoroughly equalitarian one: all were practically equal and free. Each was represented in the council of the clan or tribe. While slavery was tolerated (it is to be remembered that the United States retained this institution until only three generations ago), the harshness of the master-servant relationship was in many ways mitigated. The Biblical fugitive-slave law, unlike the laws passed by Congress before the Civil War, protected the fugitive; for in Deuteronomy it is provided: "You shall not deliver to his master a bondsman that is escaped from his master unto you. He shall dwell with you in the midst of you, in the place which he shall choose within one of your gates, where he likes it best; you shall not wrong him" (23:16–17). While the institution of private property was recognized and there were laws against theft, clear recognition was given to the fact that property is fundamentally a social object, that property is subject to social control, that society may direct as to how much property a man may possess, how much of his income he may retain for his own use, for how long a period he may divest himself of title to property allotted to him, and so on. Thus it was provided that "when you come into your neighbor's vineyard you may eat grapes until you have enough at your own pleasure . . . when you come into your neighbors's standing corn, you may pluck ears with your hand . . ." (23:25–26).

Among the first laws to protect the rights of laborers are those found in the Bible. The Sabbath was instituted as a social institution, as a day of rest: "in it you shall not do any manner of work, you, nor your son, nor your daughter, nor your man-servant, nor your maid-servant, nor your ox, nor your ass, nor any of your cattle, nor your stranger that is within your gates . . ." (5:14). Wages were to be paid promptly: "You shall not oppress a hired servant that is poor and needy, whether he be of your brethren, or of your strangers that are in your land within your gates. In the same day you shall give him his hire, neither shall the sun go down upon it; for he is poor, and sets his heart upon it; lest he cry against you to the Lord, and it be a sin in you" (24:14–15).

The well-off were forbidden to oppress the impoverished citizen: "No man shall take the mill or the upper millstone to pledge, for he takes a man's life to pledge. . . . When you do lend your neighbor any manner of loan, you shall not go into his house to fetch his pledge. . . . And if he be a poor man, you shall not sleep with his pledge; you shall surely restore to him the pledge when the sun goes down, that he may sleep in his garment, and bless you" (24:6,10,12–13). Bankruptcy laws were instituted, so that a man shall not be borne down by his debts forever, but shall, instead, have an opportunity for a fresh economic start. "At the end of every seven years shall you make a release" (15:1); the creditor shall not exact the debt from his debtor. At the same time, he who has must not close his heart to the importunities of him who has not, and say to himself that "the seventh year, the year of release, is at hand" (15:9), and refuse to lend to the poor; for if this happen, God will hear the cry of the poor man, and the rich man will be guilty of a crime. "You shall surely give him and your heart shall not be grieved when you give unto him" (15:10). The owner of the land was not to think that the land was *really* his, to do with as he pleased; for the land is the Lord's; and the Lord commanded that every seventh year the land must lie fallow; it must not be abused, lest it become a waste place, and all the land a dustbowl. A share of a man's income had to be turned over to the communal authorities for the relief of needy persons. Even when a man builds a house for himself, he must take into consideration the duties he owes his neighbors; he must make a parapet for his roof, so that no one will fall from it.

Time and again the prophets cried out against the economic inequalities that resulted in loss of freedom, injustice and oppression. Men became too rich and too powerful for their own and the community's good. Such rich men were declared enemies of the people and the chief sinners against God. The accumulation of such wealth and the exploitation it entailed were condemned in the strongest terms possible:

> Because they sell the righteous for silver,
> And the needy for a pair of shoes,
> That pant after the dust of the earth on the head of the poor,
> And turn aside the way of the humble . . .
> And they lay themselves down beside every altar,
> Upon clothes taken in pledge,
> And in the house of their God they drink
> The wine of them that have been fined.
>
> (Amos 2:6–8)

Amos foretold such as these what their destiny would be:

> Hear this word,
> Ye kine of Bashan, that are in the mountains of Samaria,
> That oppress the poor, that crush the needy,
> That say to their lords, "Bring, that we may feast."
> The Lord God has sworn by His holiness:
> "Lo, surely the days shall come upon you,

> That you shall be taken away with hooks,
> And your residue with fish-hooks. . . ."
>
> (4:1–3)

Isaiah brought severe charges against the oppressors of the common man:

> Woe unto them that join house to house,
> That lay field to field
> Till there be no room and you be made to dwell
> Alone in the midst of the land!
>
> (5:8)

Just as Judaism posits the ideals of social equality and economic equality, so, too, it posits political freedom and equality. Israel was to be a holy nation, each Israelite was to be a member of "a kingdom of priests, a holy nation." God alone is ruler over Israel. What need is there of a king? No one was permitted to make laws for the nation; for God had given His Torah to His people Israel—to every Israelite; there was no room left for a king. Not even David or Solomon could abrogate the laws of the Sabbath, or of the seventh year, or make oppression of the needy just. Israel was different from all other peoples: its legislation came from God. If a king cannot make laws, of what use can he be? God was the Lawgiver, the Ruler and the Judge. When the Jews asked Samuel to appoint over them a king, he told them of what use a king could be:

> This will be the manner of the king that shall reign over you: he will take your sons and appoint them unto him for his chariots, and to be his horsemen; and they shall run before his chariots. And he shall appoint them unto him for captains of thousands, and captains of fifties; and to plow his ground, and to reap his harvest, and to make his instruments of war, and the instruments of his chariots. And he will take your daughters to be perfumers, and to be cooks, and to be bakers. And he will take your fields and your vineyards, and your oliveyards, even the best of them, and give them to his servants. And he will take the tenth of your seed, and

of your vineyards, and give to his officers, and to his servants.
And he will take your men-servants, and your maid-servants, and
your goodliest young men and your asses, and put them to his work.
He will take the tenth of your flocks; and you shall be his servants
(I Samuel 8:11–17).

The Jews never forgot this lesson of Samuel's; even though they
took upon themselves the yoke of a kingship, they would not
tolerate oppression and despotism. The king was to be a servant
of the people and not their master; he was to rule under God and
not as a substitute for Him. Thus the Jews became a "rebellious"
people; for they would not tolerate a tyrant even if he were of
the seed of David. When Solomon died, the northern tribes rose in
protest against a perpetuation of oppressive measures by Rehoboam, whom Solomon had nominated as his successor. It is related
that Rehoboam and the Israelites met at Shekhem, where he was
asked if he would make lighter their yoke. The king took counsel
with the old men who had served Solomon, and they said to him:
"If you will be a servant unto this people this day, and will serve
them, and answer them, and speak good words to them, then they
will be your servants forever" (I Kings 12:7). The king would
not follow their advice; he "gave no heed to the people." When
the Israelites saw that he disregarded their petition, they said to
him:

> We have no portion in David
> Neither have we inheritance in the son of Jesse;
> Everyman to his tents, O Israel.
>> (II Samuel 20:1)

Even if it meant breaking up the kingdom, Judaism's democratic
ideals had to be asserted and reasserted. Thus it was throughout
Israel's history in Palestine. The people, and sometimes the
prophets speaking for the people, constantly submitted the moral
presuppositions of the ruling caste to scrutiny and re-examination.
The freedom of the private moral judgment was always kept alive.
When Ahab, misguided by Jezebel, his queen, showed his dis-
loyalty to the democratic ideals, a popular uprising ended his

dynasty. Elijah spoke for the conscience of Israel. When Naboth refused to sell his vineyard to the despotic king, and the king, through a perversion of justice, had him murdered, Elijah spoke out against the king, and when the king heard his words, "he rent his clothes and put sackcloth upon his flesh and fasted, and he lay in sackcloth, and went softly" (I Kings 21:27). For the king knew that he could reign only under and within the law; and he was not above the Torah.

And this brings us to our final point, namely, that no people can be free, no democracy can continue to exist, if the rulers selected by the people do not consider themselves bound by the law. There must be limitations on rulers if the individual's rights are to be preserved. The citizen's rights are measured by the restrictions on government. There must, in other words, be a constitution which defines clearly how far the government may go in this matter or that delegated to its authority. Israel had such a constitution in the Torah. No one was above it. Only under the Torah could kings rule and judges judge. As God is righteous, so must the king be; as God defends the weak, so must the king. Only justice is the foundation of a people's happiness and stability. Psalm 72 expresses this thought:

> Give the king Your judgments, O God,
> And Your righteousness unto the king's son;
> That he may judge Your people with righteousness,
> And Your poor with justice . . .
> May he judge the poor of the people,
> And save the children of the needy,
> And crush the oppressor . . .
> He will have pity on the poor and needy,
> And the souls of the needy he will save.
> He will redeem their soul from oppression and violence. . . .

This, in part, is the picture of the ideal king.

Indeed, how could Israel view the status and function of government otherwise; for does not God Himself govern in accordance with law? Judaism is a law-centered religious civilization. All that God does, said Rabbi Akiba, He does by justice; "the procedure

in the heavenly court is governed by law as in an earthly court."
The day has twelve hours, said Rabbi Judah in the name of Rab,
and in the first three God sits and busies Himself with the Torah!
God Himself is bound by the Torah, by His own laws. He made
the world "by law," not arbitrarily. Why, then, should He not
spend His time teaching the Torah to the righteous in heaven?
When Moses went up to heaven, he found God sitting and weaving crowns for the letters, little flourishes on some letters of the
Torah to ornament the Scroll of the Law. The imagination of
the Jewish folk could devise no occupation more worthy of God
than the writing and study of His own Torah; because Israel found
such a delight in the Law: "But his delight is in the law of the
Lord; and in His law does he meditate day and night" (Psalms
1:2).

The ordinances of the Lord are to be desired more than gold;
. . . they are sweeter than the honey and the honeycomb. "I have
rejoiced in the way of Your testimonies. . . . I will delight myself
in Your statutes." The Lord's commandments apply to every significant act in life; as Rabbi Phineas said, one must think of the
commandments when one builds a house, when he makes a door,
when he buys new clothes, when his hair is cut, when his field is
plowed, when his field is sowed, when the harvest is gathered,
"even when you are not occupied with anything, but just taking a
walk. . . ." And the commandments are for *all* the people to
observe: "All are equal before the law. The duty of observance is
for all. For the Torah is the 'inheritance of the congregation of
Jacob.' It does not say 'priests' or 'Levites' or 'Israelites,' but 'the
congregation of Jacob.' "

No one can be above the Law—whether he wear the crown of
Torah, or the priestly crown, or the royal crown—because all men
are equal, all are equally bound by the Law and subject to it,
alike at every point; more than this, the world itself is subject to
the Law; God made the world in accordance with the Law. Is
not then even God Himself bound by the Law? "God created the
world by the Torah: the Torah was His handmaid and His tool
by the aid of which He set bounds to the deep, assigned their
functions to sun and moon, and formed all nature. Without the
Torah the world falls." The same Torah sets bounds to man's

greed, man's injustice; assigns functions to this man and that, and forms civilization.

Without law there is no freedom. Unless a people meditate on the statutes and delight in the Law, they will not be able to walk at ease; unequal strength will lead to unequal justice; and when justice is dead, said Kant, it is better not to be alive. If Judaism projects a *rechtlichbuergerliche Gesellschaft,* it is to be borne in mind that this law-centered society is also an *ethischbuergerliche Gesellschaft,* for the law is within as well as without; and at the center of the ethico-legal system is the injunction of God: "For unto Me are the children of Israel slaves; they are not slaves unto slaves."

Not all democratic institutions were foreseen by the prophets and Rabbis; such agencies are evolved by societies of men as the need for them is felt to be irresistible even by those who would prevent their emergence. But the spirit, the inner values, the energies of democracy are right at the very heart of Judaism.

Foundations of Democracy in the Scriptures and Talmud

LOUIS FINKELSTEIN

The most significant contribution in literature to democratic thought is probably that in the early chapters of Genesis. In the first, we are told that God made man in His image. In the fifth, we are informed that the descendants of Adam were born in his image, and consequently in the image of God. This assertion that all men—all descendants of Adam—are alike the bearers of the image of God, are therefore possessors of supreme dignity, and that all are equal in this dignity, sets the goal toward which all democratic thinking must strive. It is not human equality nor human dignity alone which Scripture stresses. It is the combination of human equality and dignity.

This double basis of democracy is projected from the past into the future in the Pharisaic and rabbinic concept of human immortality. The belief that man's soul is immortal, while not expressly enunciated in the Five Books of Moses, is in fact a corollary of the premise that all men bear God's image. Unless the term "God's image" is taken to refer to a physical appearance—a belief repugnant to ancient Pharisaism and the Talmud—it had to refer to man's spirit. But if man was created with the spirit of God within him, obviously that spirit does not perish with man's body, but survives it. The doctrine of immortality of the soul thus follows inevitably from the principle enunciated in the first chapters of Genesis, when these are interpreted in terms of a God who is entirely spiritual and incorporeal. The doctrine of immortality, in turn, helps to reinforce the belief in human dignity and equality; for it asserts that we are not only equal in the reverence due us because of our divine origin, but also because of our destined immortality. . . .

. . . In Israel two schools of thought developed with regard to the immortality of the soul. The School of Shammai, consisting of the conservative, priestly groups, held that immortality was limited to the righteous in Israel; while their opponents, the School of Hillel, taught that immortality can be obtained even by righteous pagans. . . .

Thus the Book of Daniel (12:2) reads: "And many of them that sleep in the dust of the earth shall awake." It does not say "many of the Hebrews sleeping in the dust of the earth," but "many of them"—of any people, whatsoever. . . .

The theme of human equality recurs again and again in Scripture. . . . In several remarkable passages, the author of Job stresses human equality: "The small and the great are there; and the servant is free from his master" (3:19). "If I did despise the cause of my man-servant or of my maid-servant when they contended with me, What then shall I do when God rises up? And when He remembers what shall I answer Him? Did not He that made me in the womb make him? And did not One fashion us in the womb?" (31:12–15). . . .

Even more important than the proclamation of the theoretical dignity and equality of men, and the weakening and ultimate abolition of institutions symbolizing inequality, was the emergence of a series of institutions destined to make democratic thinking effective. The first of these was that of the lay scholar, as opposed to the hereditary priest. In early times, the interpretation of the Law and the ritual among Jews, as among other oriental peoples, was the prerogative of the hereditary priesthood. The development first of the Scribes and then of the Pharisaic scholars, whose authority derived not from ancestry, but from learning, opened the gates for a democratic interpretation of Scripture and of the Law itself. The manner in which these lay scholars obtained the right to render decisions, and to instruct the priests themselves, is a saga of democratic achievement. Time came when the High Priest, before he entered the sacred shrine to perform the most sacred service of the year (that of the Day of Atonement), had to meet with the lay scholars, to obtain instruction from them, and to promise observation of the ritual as they taught it. Even the right to examine the diseased for the purpose of separating them from the community, given expressly to the priests in Leviticus, was ultimately exercised by lay scholars. The priest acted only as a mouthpiece for the scholar.

It is probably no exaggeration to assert that the whole history of Western religion has been influenced by this emergence of the lay scholar as an authoritative expounder of the Torah. Both in Judaism, and in the religions akin to it, the authority of the hereditary priesthood was replaced by that of men called to the vocation of expounding the faith. Religion interpreted solely by a hereditary priestly caste might have become a force for reaction; but instead became in time the foundation stone of democratic thought and influence throughout the West.

Allied with the emergence of the scholar was that of the House of Prayer, independent of the Temple in Jerusalem. The Temple in Jerusalem represented the authority of the priesthood; the synagogue was from the beginning an institution of democracy. Anyone could lead in the prayers; anyone could read the prescribed sections of the Law; anyone could become the head of the synagogue. The opening of the gates of heaven, as it were, to the masses of the people was a step of the utmost importance in the abolition of special privilege and the conceptions to which special privilege gave birth.

Old institutions, however, die slowly. Even after the Pharisees had established the principle that any scholar could interpret the Law, the Shammaitic group among them sought to limit the instruction in the Law to "those of good family." In reading the controversy between the School of Shammai and the School of Hillel on this point, one is reminded of the modern controversy about opening colleges and universities to all students, solely on the basis of relative ability. Like some modern leaders, the ancient Shammaites held that education should be the prerogative of the elect—the well-to-do who could devote all their time to study. But the House of Hillel insisted—and won its point—that "one should teach anyone," even the sinful, for many sinful in Israel were brought back to righteousness through study of the Torah. . . .

These teachings and institutions were no more important as contributions by the ancient Jewish teachers to democracy than their development of the doctrine of freedom of opinion, and their respect for deviation from the accepted norm of the majority. Precisely because the exposition of the Law became a prerogative of an ever increasing number of scholars, and because the meaning of the Law could be discovered only in free argument, the pre-Pharisaic and Pharisaic teachers arrived at the conclusion that even a rejected view may have sufficient merit to justify its being transmitted to posterity. Hence the Talmud contains on almost every page both the views which became the accepted norm and those which were rejected in its favor. The opposition's conceptions are immortalized together with those of the majority. Thus, though the School of Hillel ultimately prevailed in its arguments with the School of Shammai, hundreds of Shammaitic opinions have been preserved for us. More than that, the Hillelites taught that the School of Shammai was justified in following its own views on the Law and ought not to be urged, much less compelled, to adopt the view of the Hillelites; for the Hillelites maintained, "Both views are the words of the living God."

This extraordinary tolerance of deviation set the pattern for all later Jewish tradition. Many controversies arose regarding the interpretation of the Talmud itself. But Jewish tradition has uniformly held that no one can be asked to forsake the authentic and verified tradition of his fathers in the interpretation of Jewish law.

Perhaps the most powerful expression of this tolerance for opposition is that given by Rabban Gamaliel I, the grandson of Hillel, and preserved not in the Talmudic writings, but in the Book of Acts. When Peter and the other Apostles were brought before the Sanhedrin to stand trial on the charge of teaching an anti-Jewish doctrine, the Book of Acts records that Gamaliel "a doctor of the law, had in reputation among all the people," stood up and spoke on their behalf. The climax of his address, which cited precedents in favor of tolerance of deviation, is the verse: "And now I say unto you, refrain from these men, and let them alone; for if this counsel or this work be of men, it will come to nought; but if it be of God, you cannot overthrow it, lest haply you be found even to fight against God" (Acts 5:38–39).

The question of whether these were the precise words of Rabban Gamaliel on this occasion is not relevant; the important fact is that the Book of Acts, not otherwise friendly to the Pharisees, records that this great Pharisaic leader set down the principle that deviation from accepted or majority opinion is not a punishable offense. No matter how certain he and his colleagues might be that the teaching of the Apostles was erroneous, penalties could not be inflicted on them. On the contrary, it was assumed that if the teaching was entirely in error it would fail; and if it had a place in the divine plan, to seek to crush it would be wrong.

With this background it is not at all surprising to find that the Jewish communities of Europe in the tenth and the eleventh centuries, surrounded by a feudal system which left little room for democratic thought and practice, remained islands of freedom and equality. The famous "ordinances of the communities," established by the Jewish settlements in the Rhineland, and later in France and in Germany generally, were models of legislation by will of the people. Under the leadership of the great scholar, Rabbenu Gershom, called "the Light of the Dispersion," these various communities even came together in the first part of the eleventh century and established a constitution limiting the authority of the community itself against its individual members. Among the rights reserved to the individual who believed himself wronged, yet could not obtain redress in the regularly constituted courts, was that of interrupting the service in the synagogue, until arrangements were made to hear him. This right of preventing the congregation from proceeding with worship until they were willing to see justice done, was one of the most formidable means of protecting the weak against the strong.

In this way the democratic tradition of Judaism, beginning with the very origins of the faith, continued right through the Middle Ages.

Democratic Aspirations in
Talmudic Judaism

BEN ZION BOKSER

The Talmudic conception of mankind is that of a unity, deriving its character from a common origin and a common destiny. The basic elements of this doctrine are already enunciated in the Bible, which traces the origins of the human race to a single person who was formed by God in His own image. It is in the Talmud, however, that this doctrine reaches it fullest maturity. . . .

Human behavior may be infinitely varied, but human nature, which underlies it, is essentially the same. Man is a creature of earth and at the same time a child of God, infused with the divine spirit. Appraised in moral categories, all people are endowed with the tendency to see in their own persons the ultimate ends of their being and the tendency to seek transcendent ends toward which their own persons are but contributing instruments. Out of these two tendencies flow good and evil, which thus reside, in varying measure, to be sure, in every individual as part of his indigenous equipment for life. If you but probe sufficiently, one Talmudic maxim advises, you will discover that "even the greatest of sinners" abounds in good deeds as a pomegranate abounds in seeds (*Eruvin* 19a). On the other hand, the greatest of saints have their share of moral imperfection (*Sanhedrin* 101a). All human beings are, so to say, cut from the same cloth and there are no absolute distinctions between them. . . .

The Talmud speaks repeatedly of the dignity of free labor.

Creative labor, no matter how humble, is always honorable and is a form of divine worship, for it contributes to the maintenance and development of civilization. "Flay dead cattle on a highway," runs a Talmudic proverb, "and say not 'I am a priest, I am a great man and it is beneath my dignity'" (*Pesahim* 113a, *Bava Batra* 110a). One of the responsibilities which every parent owes his son is to teach him a trade (*Kiddushin* 29a). The Talmudists themselves, because their academic work was a labor of love which offered no remuneration, pursued various handicrafts as well as farming and commerce to earn a livelihood. . . .

Even he who had endangered social security in the commission of crime has not forfeited his inherent worth as a person. The Talmud ordained with great emphasis that every person charged with the violation of some law be given a fair trial and before the law all were to be scrupulously equal, whether a king or a pauper. One of two litigants was not to appear in court in expensive robes when the other came in tatters, lest there be a swaying of the juror-judges (*Shevuot* 31a).

Particularly in criminal cases did the Talmud seek to protect the accused against a miscarriage of justice. Circumstantial evidence, however convincing, was not acceptable (*Tosephta Sanhedrin* 8:3). . . . The juror-judges could reverse a vote from guilty to not guilty, but not vice versa. The younger members of the court were first to announce their vote, so as not to be influenced by the actions of their seniors. Whereas in civil cases a majority of one was sufficient to establish guilt, in criminal cases a majority of two was required.

Even when he was found guilty, a man had not lost his link to the human brotherhood. The larger ends of safeguarding the community might require his extermination, but whatever punishment was inflicted upon him had to be humanized by a persistent love and not brutalized by vengeance (*Sanhedrin* 43a, 45a). Certain Talmudists advocated the abolition of capital punishment, and it was agreed that any court that inflicts capital punishment once every seven years had exhibited brutality (*Mishnah Makkot* 1:10). The execution even of the most violent criminal is a cosmic tragedy. For he, too, was formed in the divine image and had been endowed with infinite possibilities for good.

In the hierarchy of Jewish values the knowledge and practice of the Torah represented the apex, but the master of the Torah was not to hold himself aloof from or superior to other men. He was to be "modest, humble . . . to make himself beloved of men, to be gracious in his relations even with subordinates . . . to judge man according to his deeds" (*Derekh Eretz Zuta* I). "To show pride in one's learning is to become like the carcass of a dead beast from which all men turn away in disgust" (*Avot de Rabbi Nathan* Ch. 11). The true master of Torah will be inspired by a greater learning and piety not to aggrandize himself over others or to detach himself from the common people and cultivate his virtues in the privacy of his own home, but to teach and lead the common people to a nobler way of life. He who has insights that can broaden the horizons of his neighbor's life and does not communicate them is robbing his neighbor of his due. The gifts of the spirit, like the gifts of substances, are a trust to be shared with others (*Sanhedrin* 91b).

Throughout Talmudic times, the Jews lived under the domination of foreign imperialisms: in Palestine under the Romans and in Babylonia under the Parthians and neo-Persians. Whether a free Jewish commonwealth would have developed a democratic representative government, we do not know. But within the framework of the limited autonomy which the Jews enjoyed, they did develop certain democratic institutions. The most important instrument of Jewish autonomy was Jewish civil and religious law, and the Talmud developed the theory that the ultimate sanction of all law is the consent of the people who are to be governed by it. For the Talmud, of course, all authority, including the authority behind the makers and interpreters of law, flowed from the divine source which manifests itself in every form of human leadership. But man is endowed with free will, and his unrestrained conscience must give its assent to every legal institution that is to have moral claims over him. Judges and legislators must not enact decrees unless a majority of the people find it possible to conform to them. Any decree which is resisted by a popular majority has, *ipso facto,* lost its validity and been rendered obsolete. Indeed, the Talmud even traced the authority of the Bible itself not so much to its divine source as to the consent of the people who fully agreed to live by it.

Social stability frequently calls for disciplined behavior. In the

field of social and religious conduct the Talmud called upon
individuals to conform to the majority decisions of the duly constituted authorities who interpreted Jewish law. In the field of
opinion, however, the individual remained essentially free to believe and speak in accordance with the dictates of his own conscience. Indeed, there has never been formulated an official creed
in Israel as a criterion of loyalty to the mandates of Jewish life.
And even in law, the minority could continue defending its position in the hope that the majority might eventually be moved to
reconsider its judgment (*Mishnah Eduyot* 1:5).

The Talmudists developed a system of democratically constituted town councils which were charged with the administration
of local municipalities. All those residing in a community for a
year or over enjoyed the right to participate in the election of
the seven town councillors. The functions of these town councils
were far-reaching, including the supervision of economic, religious,
educational and philanthropic activities of the people. On important issues town meetings were held in which the will of the people could be ascertained more directly (*Megillah* 27a). Certain
local officials were, of course, appointed by the head of the Jewish
community, the patriarch in Palestine and the exilarch in Babylonia. But the most important requirement in all such appoint-
ments was that they meet with the public approval. In the words
of the Talmud, "We must not appoint a leader over the community without first consulting them, as it is said, 'See, the Lord
has called by name Bezalel, the son of Uri' (Exodus 35:30).
The Holy One, Blessed be He, asked Moses, 'Is Bezalel acceptable
to you?' He replied, 'Sovereign of the universe, if he is acceptable
to You, how much more so to me!' God said to him, 'Nevertheless
go and consult the people . . .' " (*Berakhot* 55a).

The social process frequently brings individuals into a position
where they exercise power over the lives of others. In the social
theory of Talmudic Judaism, it then becomes the task of the
community to develop such instruments of social control as will
rationalize that power with moderation and justice. The Talmudists
declared individual property rights as subject to their consistency
with the public welfare. When it is to serve the public interest,
these rights may be modified or suspended altogether (*Yevamot*
89b). Acting on this principle, Talmudic legislation regulated

wages and hours of labor, commodity prices and rates of profit (*Bava Batra* 8b). It was similarly the task of the community to provide other facilities for promoting the public welfare, such as public baths, competent medical services and adequate educational facilities for all, at least on an elementary level.

The poor had a claim upon the community for support in proportion to their accustomed standard of living. The more affluent individuals were to share their possessions with them, as members of a family circle were obligated to share with their own kin. To place the administration of poor relief on a more efficient and respectable basis, it was eventually institutionalized. Begging from door to door was discouraged. Indigent townsmen were given a weekly allowance for food and clothing. Transients received their allowance daily. Ready food was also kept available to cope with immediate needs. For the poor traveler and the homeless, public inns were frequently built on the highroads. All these facilities were maintained from the proceeds of a general tax to which all residents of a community contributed. Perhaps the most interesting form of poor relief, from a modern standpoint, is a public works project for the assistance of the unemployed. The details of the project have been preserved by Josephus, but it was instituted in Talmudic times: "So when the people saw that the workmen were unemployed who were above 18,000 and that they, receiving no wages, were in want . . . they persuaded him [King Agrippa] to rebuild the eastern cloisters . . . he denied the petitioners their request in the matter, but he did not obstruct them when they desired the city might be paved with white stone. . . ."[1]

The same concern for the values of humanitarianism and democracy appears in the Talmudic legislation bearing on the various aspects of family life. The Talmud does not regard the individual man as a self-sufficient personality. He is completed through matrimony. "The unmarried person lives without joy, without blessing and without good. He is not a man in the full sense of the term; as it is said (Genesis 5:2), 'male and female created He them, and blessed them and called their name man'" (*Yevamot* 62b, 63a).

Happiness in married life involves many compromises, but these

[1] *Antiquities* XX, 9:7.

must be assumed in freedom. They should not be imposed through constraint from any external source. In the words of the Babylonian teacher Rab, "A man is forbidden to give his minor daughter in marriage without her consent. He must wait until she grows up and says, 'I wish to marry so and so' " (*Kiddushin* 41a). If he did give her in marriage as a minor, she could protest the marriage on reaching maturity and have it annulled without divorce. The man's choice, too, should be voluntary and an expression of considered choice. "A man should not marry a woman without knowing her, lest he subsequently discover blemishes in her and come to hate her" (*ibid.*).

As the more dominant partner in the family circle, the husband was exhorted to treat his wife with tenderness and sympathetic understanding. "Whoever loves his wife as himself and honors her more than himself . . . to him may be applied the verse (Job 5:24), 'You shall know that your tent is in peace' " (*Yevamot* 62b). Before the children, father and mother were equals. They were both to be accorded the very same devotion and respect (*Kiddushin* 30b).

The Talmud regards divorce as the greatest of all domestic tragedies. "Whoever divorces the wife of his youth, even the altar sheds tears on her behalf, as it is written (*Malachi* 3:13, 14) 'And this again you do; you cover the altar of the Lord with tears . . . because the Lord has been witness between you and the wife of your youth, against whom you have dealt treacherously' " (*Gittin* 90b). There are occasions, however, when husband and wife cannot harmonize their natures and irreconcilable differences develop between them. The Talmud then sanctions divorce, as preferable to a life of continuing bitterness and distress. . . .

For the Talmudists, children are the noblest fulfillment of married life. For it is man's elemental duty to the continuity of life to bring children into the world and to raise them properly. Nevertheless, where conception was likely to prove dangerous to the mother, birth control was recommended. In the words of the Talmud, "Three types of women should employ an absorbent to prevent conception: a minor, a pregnant woman and a nursing mother; a minor lest pregnancy prove fatal, a pregnant woman lest she have an abortion, and a nursing mother because of the danger to her young infant" (*Tosephta Niddah* 2:6, *Yevamot* 12b). . . .

Perhaps the most significant triumph for democracy in Talmudic Judaism was the development of a system of free, universal education. The Jewish school system began with higher rather than elementary education. The most important institution of higher education was the Sanhedrin itself and the hierarchy of various lower courts, which functioned under its supervision. Their deliberations were made accessible to advanced students who were preparing themselves for ordination and they were even permitted to participate in the discussions. Witnessing the conflicts of personalities, the play of minds and the manipulation of dialectic by which the Torah supplementation was evolved represented a vivid and unforgettable educational experience. In addition, the leaders of Pharisaic and rabbinic Judaism conducted formal instruction in their own schools. Some of these schools were particularly famous. The Schools of Shammai and Hillel were continued even after their founders were gone. Akiba's school, which was finally conducted at B'nai Brak, is said to have had an enrollment of 12,000 students, like a modern metropolitan university.

In early times these schools charged tuition fees which were payable upon admission to each lecture. And many made great sacrifices to attend, frequently working their way through school. . . . This admission fee was abolished after the destruction of the Temple and higher education became wholly free. In addition, lectures were offered in the evening, which facilitated attendance for those who had to work for a livelihood during the day (*Pesaḥim* 72b).

Elementary education was originally left to the home, but in time this, too, was institutionalized. As the Talmud relates it: "Were it not for Joshua ben Gemala [High Priest who was in office in the latter part of the first century], the Torah would have been forgotten in Israel. In antiquity every father taught his own child. Those who were without fathers to teach them were thus left without education. Later on, schools were established in Jerusalem to which the children were to be sent from all over the country. But these, too, were inadequate. Thereupon, they estab-

lished regional schools to which youths of 16 or 17 were admitted. But it was soon apparent that adolescents could not first
begin to subject themselves to school discipline. Finally, therefore, local schools were instituted in each city and town and
children were enrolled at the age of six or seven." Classes were
generally conducted in the synagogue buildings, though they were
frequently transferred to the outdoors. There were, according to
the Talmud, 394 schools in Jerusalem before its destruction by
the Romans in 70 C.E. (*Ketuvot* 105a). The curriculum concentrated on Biblical literature, Midrash and, later on, the Mishnah
also.

The Pharisees and Rabbis were equally devoted to educating the
general public. Their formal lectures in the schools were generally
open to lay auditors. In addition, they utilized the synagogue
service, which brought out large numbers, as an opportunity for
educational work. The liturgy itself, which was eventually recited
thrice daily by every Jew, was an affirmation of the fundamental
beliefs of Judaism. Readings from the Torah, with appropriate
elucidations in the Aramaic vernacular, had been made an integral part of the synagogue ritual ever since the days of the
Sopherim. Four times weekly, Saturday morning and afternoon,
Monday and Thursday, as well as on all feasts and holidays, and
on the new moon, the Jewish laity thus listened to Scripture les-
sons.

Under the inspiration of the synagogue, smaller groups of people formed into individual study circles, meeting at convenient
hours on week days or the Sabbath for the study of Scriptures or
some other branch of Jewish tradition. This was later enhanced
with the introduction of the popular sermon on Friday evening
and Saturday morning; and there were special sermons before
each holiday.

Some of the Rabbis were not particularly gifted with eloquence
and it, therefore, became customary for an additional functionary,
the orator-commentator, to attach himself to the rabbi. In academy
and synagogue alike this rabbi would first communicate his message to the commentator, who then made that the theme of his
oration before the public. The synagogues in every community,
in addition to providing for religious worship, also functioned as

popular universities, diffusing the knowledge of the Torah among the common people.

The sanctity of human life implied for the Talmudists a similar concern for the national community. For each society, too, makes its unique contribution to the fulfillments of history. The Talmudists speak of Israel as being particularly creative in the field of religion, whereas other peoples achieved comparable distinction in other fields, in the arts and sciences. There were some who spoke with admiration of Roman law, of the Roman system of public markets, bridges and baths. The collective welfare of all humanity is contingent upon the welfare of every individual people, and the sacrificial cult of the Second Temple in Jerusalem included, during the Feast of Tabernacles, 70 offerings invoking God's aid for each of the 70 nations of the world (*Sukkah* 55b).

The aberration of human sin will occasionally drive groups to seek dominion over others. Thus in Talmudic times, the Jews suffered heavily from the oppression of Roman imperialism. The Talmudists decried this oppression and encouraged their people's resistance to it. They denounced the Jewish tax farmer as a reprobate and robber, because he collaborated with the Roman system of extortion and oppression. Deceiving the Roman tax-collector they put on a par with deceiving a pirate, for Rome had no moral right to the country which she had occupied by force (*Mishnah Nedarim* 3:4). The Pharisaic ostracism of the publican, which was but another name for the Jewish tax-collector, was not, as has frequently been interpreted, an expression of self-righteousness. It was the reaction of liberty-loving men against those who, for a consideration, were willing to make themselves the partners of an alien imperialism in the plunder and oppression of their own people.

At the same time, the Talmudists guarded against transmuting the temporary historical struggles of their people against various imperialist oppressor-states into enduring hatreds against other nations. . . .

Even in the face of the tragedy inflicted upon their people by the Romans, the Talmudists sought to avoid hatred. Individual teachers spoke sharply in denunciation of Roman tyranny. But their collective reactions, as summarized, for instance, in the liturgy of that day, is dedicated not to the denunciation of Rome, but to Jewish self-criticism. "It is because of our sins that we have been banished from our land," is the principal motif in the liturgical reaction to the national disaster. And the way of redemption toward which they were taught to strive was moral regeneration in their inner personal and social lives and the interpenetration of the same ideals of a loftier morality among all mankind. In time, the strife of nations, like the strife of individuals, will come to an end in the discovery of their universal interdependence (*Mishpatim Tanḥuma* 12). Israel's cry of justice will be vindicated in a universal fulfillment when the "kingdom of wickedness" shall pass away and all mankind join to form "one fellowship to do the divine will with a perfect heart." [2]

But the Talmudic conception of man implied a reciprocal responsibility from individual men and nations to the collective human community. For the fulfillment of the larger organism is dependent upon the integrated functioning of its constituent parts. The unique gifts of energy, substance or spirit with which an individual is endowed must all be directed to larger human service. As one Talmudist interprets it, the second commandment ordains not alone repose on the seventh day of the week, but also creative labor on the six days. "For is it not written, 'Six days shall you do your work and on the seventh day shall you rest.' " [3] The Talmud denounced asceticism, even when religiously motivated, as sinful, for it withdrew essential creative energies from the tasks of civilization (*Taanit* 11a). . . .

The responsibilities of service rest similarly on every society. The Talmud called upon the Jews to share with the rest of mankind their achievements in the field where they believed they had distinguished themselves, the field of religion and morality. . . .

Implementing the ideal of its mission, the Judaism of the early Talmudic period proselytized extensively throughout the pagan world. Judaism became, in the words of Professor George Foot Moore, "the first great missionary religion of the Mediterranean world." [4] Because it conceded salvation even to those who were

2 From the liturgy of the New Year, composed by Abba Areka.
3 *Avot de Rabbi Nathan* II ch. 21.
4 *Judaism in the First Centuries of the Christian Era* (Cambridge, 1927), I, 324.

outside its fellowship, Jewish missionaries did not seek only formal conversions. With equal diligence, they sought to make what were known to the Romans as *metuentes* or "God fearing men," sympathizers of Judaism who, while not conforming to the Jewish ceremonial discipline, would yet order their lives by Jewish ideals of personal and social morality. Through this dissemination of the unique values in Jewish tradition, the Jewish people were to meet their responsibilities to the larger human community of which they recognized themselves to be a part.

PART IV

Freedom of Conscience

Editor's Note

"There is another man within me that's angry with me," wrote Sir Thomas Browne in his *Religio Medici* three centuries ago. Every human being has this experience of transcendence: the movement within himself from one self to another self, or the movement from one level or layer of self to another, or the movement from what feels like his phenomenal or superficial self to his deeper—or higher—self.

And often the self to which one has moved sits in judgment and condemns the self from which he has moved; and when this happens we think of the former as constituting one's real self, and the voice with which the real self speaks as the voice of conscience.

That voice, when it makes itself heard, compels one to act out of the fundamental necessities and forces of one's life, as a response to one's deepest, most sacred emotions. In such moments one feels that he is working with God, or with the basic needs of human nature, and that God is working with and through him to assert and vindicate an ineluctable truth.

Conscience is thus a name for one's deepest convictions, for which a person would be willing, if necessary, to sacrifice all that is dearest to him, including his very life. It is that which he identifies with his soul, with his real or highest self: his religion, his moral and spiritual imperatives.

History has recorded the life stories of men who have come to represent this ideal force in human life—men like Socrates and Thomas More. For Jews, conscience has been the central fact of their history as a people. For them it has been the voice of the Lord God walking in the garden in the cool of the day, calling

159

to Everyman, "Where are you?"—i.e., "Where are *you?*" For them it has been the voice of God as He spoke through a thick cloud at Sinai, or through a whirlwind; the voice heard through a mother's weeping in Ramah; or a still small voice after a wind, an earthquake, and a fire. The Jews left Egypt not merely to be free from Egyptian slavery, but to be free to live their own lives in accordance with their own deepest convictions regarding the true, the good, and the holy—"the secret things [that] belong unto the Lord our God" (Deuteronomy 29:29)—and which are, therefore, beyond the reach of kings.

It is in this conception of conscience that we can find the roots of our basic liberties: freedom of religion, and the separation of church and state; freedom of speech and press, freedom of assembly and association; and the right of privacy. For a man to enjoy the right to be himself, to be true to his deepest self, he needs the freedom to seek the truth. There must therefore be what Justice Holmes called "free trade in ideas"—an intellectual and spiritual market place where monopolistic practices are not tolerated.

Conscience and Civil Disobedience in the Jewish Tradition

MILTON R. KONVITZ

In the first chapter of Exodus it is related that the new ruler of Egypt, alarmed by the increase in the number of Israelites, spoke to the Hebrew midwives and directed them to kill all male infants born to Hebrew women. "But the midwives feared God," the Bible goes on to relate, "and did not as the king of Egypt commanded them, but saved the men-children alive" (1:15–17). Thereupon the king issued a new decree, directed not to the midwives but to the people generally, who were ordered to kill all newborn Hebrew males by throwing them into the river Nile (1:22).

These events, which may have happened some thirty-four hundred years ago, relate to what may well be the first recorded instance in history of what is today called non-violent civil disobedience. From the Biblical text it is not clear that the midwives were themselves Hebrews; for they acted as they did not because they were Hebrews but because they "feared God." The text twice mentions the fact that they "feared God"—or, as we say today, that they listened to the voice of conscience rather than to the law of the state or the voice of the king.

In the First Book of Samuel there is another clear and dramatic instance of non-violent civil disobedience. It is related that when

161

King Saul learned that a certain priest had given David food and other assistance, he ordered the priest to appear before him and decreed his death and the death of all his kin. The crucial words of the Biblical text are as follows: "And the king said to the guard who stood about him, 'Turn and kill the priests of the Lord; because their hand also is with David, and they knew that he fled, and did not disclose it to me.' But the servants of the king would not put forth their hand to fall upon the priests of the Lord" (1 Samuel 22:17). This may be the first recorded instance of non-violent civil disobedience by military men in refusing to obey superior orders. It is not clear why the men of the guard refused to lay hands on the priests and their families—because the victims belonged to the priestly class, or because they were civilians; whatever the reason, their action was a clear case of civil disobedience.

In the Book of Daniel we find the first instance of what became a pattern in Jewish life and history: the worship of God without regard to the fact that such worship had been prohibited at the price of one's life. The book relates (chapter 6) that Darius the king had appointed Daniel chief of his officers. The officers then conspired to bring about the fall of Daniel, and to this end they contrived an ingenious trap. They induced Darius to issue a decree that for thirty days no man was to offer petition to any man or god except to the king, on pain of death in the lion's den. Daniel, however, went on to pray to God three times daily, with the window of his chamber open toward Jerusalem. His enemies came upon Daniel when he was thus petitioning God rather than Darius, and then naturally went with their report to the king. After trying to find a way out, the king felt compelled to order his law to be enforced, and Daniel was put into the den of lions. The following morning, however, the king found Daniel unharmed, saved by an angel.

The case of Daniel, it should be noted, differs from our two previous instances. In the cases of the Egyptian midwives and Saul's guards, there was simply a refusal to commit an act which was deeply felt to be inconceivable by the persons ordered to perform it. In the case of Daniel, however, there was a positive act: he did not merely *refuse* to perform an act; he *performed* an act in violation of a law. Furthermore, while the first two cases involved the moral conscience—orders to commit murder—the case of Daniel was an act in the realm of religious worship. While these differences are significant, the concept of non-violent civil disobedience is broad enough to accommodate these as well as additional types of conduct.

The four Books of Maccabees in the Apocrypha offer numerous instances of civil disobedience during the period of the Hellenization of Judea, when the Second Temple was defiled and was dedicated to Zeus Olympius. Some Jews assisted in the work of Hellenization and even in the persecution of fellow Jews who tried to obstruct the process. The Syrian overlords forbade the Jews to offer sacrifices and to observe the Sabbath and festivals. They were compelled to make and to worship idols, to sacrifice swine, and to leave their sons uncircumcised. Disobedience meant death. But I Maccabees records (chapter 1) that "many in Israel were firmly resolved in their hearts not to eat unclean food. They preferred to die rather than be defiled by food and break the holy covenant, and they did die." When the king's officers came to Modin to enforce the decrees against religious observances, Mattathias answered them with these resounding words: "Yet will I, my sons and brothers, walk in the covenant of our fathers. . . . We will not listen to the decrees of the king by going astray from our worship, either to the right or to the left." And then he issued his call: "Let everyone who is zealous for the Law, and would maintain the covenant, follow me" (I Maccabees 2).

The second Book of Maccabees records many dramatic instances of martyrdom when Jews resorted to civil disobedience: women hurled from the city wall with their infants held to their breasts because they had violated the law prohibiting circumcision; men who had secretly observed the Sabbath in caves burned alive. Special mention may be made of Eliezar, one of the foremost scribes, whom the authorities tried to compel to eat swine's flesh which apparently had been used in a forbidden sacrifice. The officers tried to induce him to bring his own meat but pretend that he was eating meat of the sacrifice as ordered by the king. But he refused, saying that if he were to comply, the young would say that old Eliezar had been converted to heathenism and would thus be led astray by his example. He died on the rack (cf. IV Maccabees 5).

The second and fourth Books of Maccabees relate the story of the martyrdom of a mother and seven brothers who refused to eat forbidden food associated with idolatrous sacrifices. The position of non-violent civil disobedience is stated without ambiguity by them as they cry out to the king's officers: "It is certain that we are ready to die rather than transgress the laws of our fathers" (II Maccabees 7:2). The seven brothers, called Maccabees by the Church, became models for Christian martyrs; and though the Rabbis rejected the Books of the Apocrypha from the canon of Sacred Scriptures, they too made a great deal of their story.

What may be the first recorded instance of *mass* non-violent civil disobedience is found in Josephus' *Antiquities of the Jews* (Book 18, chapter 8).[1] The incident he relates took place in the reign of Emperor Caligula (37–41) and revolved around the latter's decision to place his statue in the Temple in Jerusalem. Petronius, the emperor's agent, was given a large army but was instructed to try, in the first instance, to persuade the Jews to permit the installation of the statue peacefully. If, however, they refused, then Petronius was to install the statue by force. Petronius got ready an army of Romans and auxiliaries to carry out this mission and in due course arrived at Acre (referred to as Ptolemais). What happened after that is graphically reported by Josephus:

> But there came ten thousands of the Jews to Petronius at Ptolemais to offer their petitions to him that he would not compel them to violate the law of their forefathers. "But if," they said, "you are wholly resolved to bring the statue and install it, then you must first kill us, and then do what you have resolved on. For while we are alive we cannot permit such things as are forbidden by our law and by the determination of our forefathers that such prohibitions are examples of virtue."
>
> Petronius, however, was angry at them, and said: ". . . Caesar has sent me. I am compelled to observe his decrees. . . ." Then the Jews replied: "Since, therefore, you are so disposed, O Petronius, that you will not disobey Caesar's orders, neither will we transgress the commands of our law. . . ."
>
> When Petronius saw by their words that their determination was hard to be removed, and that . . . he would not be able to be

[1] But see Haim Cohn, *The Trial and Death of Jesus* (New York, 1971), p. 341, note 23.

obedient to Caligula in the dedication of his statue, and that there must be a great deal of bloodshed, he took his friends and servants and hastened to Tiberias, to see how the Jews there felt about the affair; but many ten thousands of Jews met Petronius again when he came to Tiberias. . . .

Then Petronius came to them (at Tiberias): "Will you then make war with Caesar, regardless of his great preparations for war and your own weakness?" They replied: "We will not by any means make war with Caesar, but we will die before we see our laws transgressed." Then they threw themselves down on their faces and stretched out their throats and said that they were ready to be slain. And this they did for forty days, neglecting to till their soil, though this was the season which called for sowing. Thus they continued firm in their resolution and proposed to themselves to die willingly rather than see the statue dedicated.

When matters were in this state . . . Petronius determined to listen to the petitioners in this matter. He called the Jews together in Tiberias, who came many ten thousands in number. . . . Said Petronius: "I do not think it just to have such a regard to my own safety and honor as to refuse to sacrifice them for your preservation, who are so many in number and who endeavor to preserve the regard that is due to your law. . . . I will, therefore, send to Caligula and let him know your resolutions, and I will assist your cause as far as I am able, so that you may not suffer on account of your honest designs, and may God assist you . . . But if Caligula should be angry and turn the violence of his rage on me, I would rather undergo that danger and affliction on my body or soul than see so many of you perish. . . ."

When Petronius had said this and had dismissed the assembly of Jews, he asked the principal men among them to look after their fields, to speak kindly to the people and to encourage them to have hope. . . . He then wrote to Caligula . . . to entreat him not to drive so many ten thousands of these men to distraction; that if he were to slay these men, he would be publicly cursed for all future ages.

Recording the same incidents, Philo reports the Jewish plea to Petronius in essentially the same words as Josephus. The core of the plea, according to Philo, was as follows:

We are evacuating our cities, withdrawing from our houses and lands; . . . We should think ourselves gainers thereby, not givers.

One thing only we ask in return for all, that no violent changes should be made in this temple. . . . But if we cannot persuade you, we give up ourselves for destruction that we may not live to see a calamity worse than death. We hear that forces of cavalry and infantry have been prepared against us if we oppose the installation [of the image of Caesar]. No one is so mad as to oppose a master when he is a slave. We [therefore] gladly put our throats at your disposal.[2]

With the instances before us—from the Hebrew Scriptures, the Apocrypha, and Josephus—it is now possible to state the essential elements for a case of civil disobedience:

1. There was a law or an official decree.

2. Those whose obedience was commanded considered the law to be unconscionable.

3. They refused to obey.[3]

4. They resorted to non-violent resistance.

5. They stood ready to put their lives on the line; they showed a readiness to suffer for their conscience.

6. The incident in Josephus discloses an additional element— i.e., civil disobedience, in which the above five elements are manifested, seeks to convert the opponent, to achieve reconciliation by the assertion of the force of truth and love in the place of fear, hate, and falsehood.

The texts cited above do not formulate a principle of civil disobedience in abstract terms. The ancient Hebraic mind did not tend to conceptualize but moved instead in an existential way, within a specific configuration of facts and forces. It did not become engaged in philosophic analysis beyond the small range disclosed by the Wisdom Literature. But with our hindsight it is not difficult to see the modern philosophy of civil disobedience prefigured in the cited incidents. Neither Thoreau nor Gandhi

[2] Philo, *De Legatione ad Gaium*, vol. 10 of *Philosophical Works*, Loeb Classical Library (Cambridge, Mass.: Harvard University Press, 1929–62), pp. 232 ff.

[3] It may be noted that while the Egyptian midwives refused to assist in the proposed genocide of the Israelites, they did not openly avow their intent knowingly to violate the king's decree. They resorted to a subterfuge by claiming that the Hebrew women did not really require the services of midwives (Exodus 1:19).

nor Martin Luther King detracted from or added to the elements of civil disobedience as formulated above. Each of them, because of his own situation, tended, however, to emphasize one element or another. Thoreau stressed the duty of conscience to assert itself against the evil law or state action. Gandhi emphasized the need of resistance to be non-violent and to seek by that means and the practice of humility to penetrate to the heart of the enemy, to transform him into friend. Dr. King put first the need to be non-violent and the readiness to submit to penalty for willful breach of the law. What element is singled out for stress at any one time is decided not abstractly but by the circumstances of time, place, and people.

In the light of some of the events in the late 1960's—demonstrations by black students, by opponents of the Vietnam war on college campuses, by welfare recipients and others making demands of government officials—perhaps the element in non-violent civil disobedience that most needs emphasizing, apart from the stress on non-violence, is the willingness to submit oneself to the penalty of the law that has been broken. Such submission is important for several reasons.

First, it clearly marks off the civil disobedient from the ordinary criminal who tries to suppress evidence of his action and escape punishment. It also marks him off from the person who seeks to *evade* a law which he considers unconscionable by flight to another jurisdiction—e.g., the thousands of American draftees who have gone to Sweden or Canada because of their opposition to the Vietnam war, but who feared that they could not prove their conscientious objection to the satisfaction of the Selective Service authorities or the courts. This is not the place to consider the moral arguments for or against *evasion* of a law considered unconscionable; all that is meant is that there are significant differences between civil disobedience and evasion.

We should also note that readiness to submit to legal punishment does not preclude a willingness to appeal one's conviction through a hierarchy of courts. This was the practice of Martin Luther King, and at times he succeeded in persuading the Supreme Court that the law under which he or demonstrators associated with him were convicted was in fact unconstitutional. A willing submission to the penalty implies a valid judgment of conviction under a law sustained by the Constitution.

Second, the posture of readiness to suffer the punishment prescribed by the law demonstrates the seriousness with which the defendant considers the law that he has knowingly violated and the response of his conscience to its demands; for in effect the defendant says he would rather lose his liberty, or even his life, than obey the law which is against his conscience. In the words of the second Book of Maccabees, he says: "It is certain that I am ready to die rather than transgress the law of my conscience." To break the law and to fail or refuse to submit to its sanction may lead to the inference that the defendant wants to have the best of both worlds: to break the law for the sake of his conscience, but at the same time to treat the law as if it were a mere scrap of paper and not a test of his conscience.

By willingly submitting to the law's penalty the defendant shows himself—as well as the community—that he has faced his conscience squarely. A member of society accepts or tolerates the burden of countless laws which he does not approve or like. He makes no claim that he has the power to veto or nullify laws which he, for one reason or another, dislikes. By resorting to civil disobedience and submitting to the sanction of the breached law, the defendant shows that he has deliberated; that he has weighed and measured; that he is not acting on a mere impulse or whim; that he has made a decision that is of supreme importance to himself.

Third, by showing his willingness to accept the punishment, the defendant declares or affirms his membership in the community and his respect for the rule of the law. This will mark him off from the radical revolutionary and the anarchist, who may wish to subvert the whole social order. This was the position taken by Gandhi and King, both of whom could have looked to Socrates as the classical model of this argument. When Socrates was in prison awaiting execution, his friends urged him to make the escape which they had arranged. But Socrates spurned the suggestion. He himself, he argued, would *do* no wrong; but it was not against his conscience *to suffer* a wrong. It was his duty, he said, willingly to accept the punishment even if the verdict of guilty was an injustice. For he was not, Socrates in effect said, an anarchist. He profoundly respected the legal order. It had its imperfections—witness the unjust judgment against him; but it is a citizen's duty to respect the legal order as such, for without it life as a human being would be impossible. Who, he asked in the *Crito,* would care for a city without laws? Goodness and integrity, institutions and laws, he said, are the most precious possessions of mankind.

This must, indeed, be the position if civil disobedience is to be differentiated from the acts of the anarchist and social revolutionary, who wish to subvert the entire legal and social order. He who resorts to civil disobedience "obeys the laws of the state to which he belongs, not out of the fear of the sanctions, but because he considers them to be good for the welfare of society," wrote Gandhi. "But there come occasions, generally rare, when he considers certain laws to be so unjust as to render obedience to them a dishonor. He then openly and civilly breaks them and quietly suffers the penalty for their breach." [4]

In the same spirit of submission to the rule of law Martin Luther King wrote from his Birmingham cell: "I submit that an individual who breaks a law that conscience tells him is unjust, and willingly accepts the penalty by staying in jail . . . is in reality expressing the very highest respect for law."

Finally, breaking the immoral law openly and standing ready to pay the price demanded by the very law that was broken will, it is hoped, have the effect of opening the eyes of others to the way the law in question offends the conscience. This happened, according to Josephus, when the Roman general saw the anguish and suffering of the Jews, and their fixed determination to face torture and death rather than permit the perversion of their religion. This is the appeal that non-violent civil disobedience is supposed to make to the instincts of truth, justice, and peace as it pushes out ignorance, prejudice, and hate.

Leaving out for the moment the incident from the Book of Daniel, the Biblical instances of civil disobedience already cited—the Egyptian midwives and the case of Saul and his guards—in-

[4] Mohandas K. Gandhi, *Non-Violent Resistance,* ed. Bharatan Kumarappa (New York: Schocken Books, 1961), p. 7.

volved orders to commit murder. The cases cited from the Books of the Maccabees and from Josephus involved orders to commit the sin of idolatry. Now a man of conscience may readily agree that he would prefer martyrdom rather than commit murder or practice idolatry. But what of laws or decrees that call for acts not so heinous as murder or idolatry but that are nonetheless against the conscience? In the course of the war that Hadrian waged to destroy Judaism and the Jewish nation, countless Jews stood ready for martyrdom. But the Rabbis saw that indiscriminate martyrdom might itself be a peril to Jewish survival. With this consideration before them, they decreed that the duty to prefer martyrdom be restricted to three transgressions: murder, idolatry, and incest (or adultery or gross unchastity). The Rabbis attached this legal principle to Leviticus 18:5: "And you shall guard My statutes and My ordinances, by doing which a man shall live." They concluded from this passage that the Torah was given to enhance life rather than to induce death. The emphasis of the Torah is on holy living and not on holy dying. The Rabbis also pointed to the fact that the passage stated that the statutes and ordinances are such that by observing them "a man" shall live—not an Israelite, but a man. With these two highly significant interpretations in mind, the Rabbis felt that martyrdom had to be limited to instances that involved laws transgressing the most basic principles of what came later to be called natural law or the laws of nature. (There can hardly be any question about murder and incest falling into this category.[5] Idolatry was so closely associated with grossly immoral practices that it could rank with the transgressions of the basic precepts of natural law, and that association was made and stressed by the prophets of the Bible and the Rabbis of the Talmud.)

The *locus classicus* of the legal formulation of the principle concerning martyrdom is in the Babylonian Talmud:

> For every law of the Torah the rule is that a man may transgress the commandment rather than suffer death—excepting idolatry, incest and murder. . . . Murder may not be committed (even)

---

[5] Compare the Oedipus cycle in Greek drama for a similar feeling of revulsion against an incestuous act.

to save one's life. . . . For example, someone came to Raba and told him: "The general of my town has ordered me to go and kill a named person, and if not, the general will kill me." Raba said to him: "Let the general kill you rather than that you should commit murder. Who knows that your blood is redder? Maybe his blood is redder!" (*Sanhedrin* 74a).

In the face, then, of laws or orders that command idolatry, incest, or murder, the above-stated halakhic (legal, jurisprudential) principle calls for the duty of civil disobedience, even at the cost of one's life.[6]

What of the incident from the Book of Daniel? As the story is related, Daniel was not called on to perform any act at all. If he had not petitioned (prayed) at all for thirty days, he would have complied with the king's decree. Why, then, did he resort to civil disobedience? Was his conduct consistent with the halakhic principle later formulated by the Rabbis?

It seems that the incident may be interpreted consistently with the above principle. The Persians believed that their king was a god; accordingly, they set a trap for Daniel, for they suspected that he would refuse to pray to the king as one prays to God. Had Daniel failed to offer prayers to anyone for thirty days, his enemies could have used this as evidence of a rejection by him of a belief in the king as a divinity. From this point of view, the story in its essentials is not significantly different from the story in Josephus of Caligula's desire to have his statue installed in the Temple on Mount Moriah. By praying to God while looking out the window that faced toward Jerusalem, Daniel acted out his

[6] In post-Talmudic Judaism, authorities did not all agree that Halakhah imposed an absolute duty freely to choose martyrdom under the circumstances in view of the great degree of duress. They also stressed the question whether the cardinal sin was required to be committed publicly or secretly. The post-Talmudic discussions are not considered in this essay. See Samuel Belkin, *In His Image* (New York: Abelard-Schuman, 1960), 210–211; David Daube, *Collaboration With Tyranny in Rabbinic Law* (New York: Oxford University Press, 1965), especially pp. 26–27, 31, 35–36, 40, 83; Henri Clavier, *The Duty and the Right of Resistance* (Strasbourg and Oxford, 1956); and Samuel G. Broude, "Civil Disobedience and the Jewish Tradition," in *Judaism and Ethics,* ed. Daniel J. Silver (New York: Ktav, 1970).

rejection of Persian idolatry. Accordingly, the story of Daniel is not only an instance of civil disobedience, but is also an instance of the later legal formulation of the duty of civil disobedience to avoid the commission of idolatry, incest, or murder.

Going beyond the three-fold principle of the duty of civil disobedience, Halakhah formulated a duty of civil disobedience that is operative even when the act that is commanded falls short of constituting idolatry. This second principle applies only in times of persecution, when the government seems determined to destroy Judaism. In such circumstances, when one is ordered to violate a commandment in public (i.e., in the presence of ten adult Jews), he must refuse to comply with the order, even at the cost of his life. This is the principle of *Kiddush ha-Shem* (sanctification of the Name). To violate a commandment under these circumstances would be a desecration of the Name (*Ḥillul ha-Shem*). The principle applies, under these circumstances, even if the religious commandment is a relatively minor one—even if it involves merely the deviation from an established custom in Jewry. In such a case, the principle that applies is the same as that when idolatry is commanded: "Let yourself be killed but do not transgress the law of the Torah."

While the threefold principle involving the duty of civil disobedience applies to any man, for it is based on the demands of natural law, the second principle, limited to the persecution of Judaism, applies only to Jews. While the cases of Eliezar and of the mother and the seven brothers, as related in Maccabees, could be interpreted as involving the ban on idolatry, they could also be interpreted, more simply perhaps, as falling under the second principle. For the Jews were ordered to violate a dietary ban in a time of religious persecution, and under circumstances which would have given their compliance publicity within the Jewish community. Their death was therefore a martyrdom, a *Kiddush ha-Shem*.

The second principle may at times appear to run counter to the thinking of the Rabbis when they decided to limit the duty of civil disobedience to idolatry, incest, and murder. For was not the time of Emperor Hadrian a time of religious persecution? If in such a time the second principle is also operative, may not its operation itself be a threat to Jewish existence and survival? The contradiction was probably resolved by Jewish community leaders *ad hoc* in the light of the facts and circumstances as they were known and interpreted at the time. It may thus be that the nature of the Hadrianic persecution, and the character and temper of the people, made the threefold principle necessary, and that it was sufficient to meet the danger. Other persecutions, like that described in II Maccabees, called for the additional principle of *Kiddush ha-Shem*.

The relations between law and conscience—conscience in which civil disobedience is rooted—in classical Jewish thought are extremely subtle and complex.[7] In the present discussion we shall limit our exploration to three aspects:

1. Conscience, as a specific concept of value, does not appear in the Hebrew Scriptures. It is, however, clearly implied. The story of Cain and Abel would have no point unless conscience were assumed; for there had been no supernatural revelation of a law against murder before one brother killed the other, nor was there at that time an enacted criminal code. The same may be said of the judgment on Sodom and the other cities of the plain; and so, too, of Noah and the judgment on his generation; and so, too, of the judgments on Egypt and on the people of Canaan. Much of the Bible, including many passages of the prophets, assumes that there are laws written on the tablets of the heart (Proverbs 7:3), that there is a law in the heart (Deuteronomy 30:14).[8]

The words of Jeremiah (31:32), "I will put my law in their inward parts, and in their hearts will I write it," were not only a promise but also a statement of basic belief as to the nature of man. Without this belief in a law written by God on the tablets of the heart of every man, God could not be the judge of all the universe, of all peoples and nations. Without this belief, God would be only the tribal God of Israel, and He could not have been their judge before the revelation of the Ten Commandments at Sinai; without this belief, the commandments not to kill, not to commit adultery, or not to commit theft would have binding force only on

[7] See Milton R. Konvitz, "Law and Morals: In the Hebrew Scriptures, Plato, and Aristotle," in L. Finkelstein, ed., *Social Responsibility in an Age of Revolution* (New York: Jewish Theological Seminary, 1971).

[8] Cf. Romans 2:14–15.

Israel. Indeed, it may be argued that the conception of man made in the image of God means primarily that man is made with a moral conscience—and with the freedom to act against it. It is this that the Bible means when it states that the Egyptian midwives "feared God"; that Amalek, when he acted cruelly, showed that "he feared not God" (Deuteronomy 25:18); that Abraham pretended to be the brother of Sarah because when they came to Gerar he thought, "Surely the fear of God is not in this place; and they will slay me for my wife's sake" (Genesis 20:11).

Indeed, in Biblical contemplation, there may be said to be a special category of sin which is an act committed "against the Lord," that is, a sin which implies the denial of the existence of God, or atheism. This applies to a wrong done to another person secretly, under circumstances where there are no witnesses—no witnesses but God. In Leviticus this type of sin is referred to as follows: "If any one sin, and commit a trespass against the Lord, and deal falsely with his neighbor in a matter of deposit, or of pledge, or of robbery, or have oppressed his neighbor; or have found that which was lost, and deal falsely therein, and swear to a lie; in any of all these that a man does, sinning therein . . ." (Leviticus 5:21, 22). Rabbi Akiba attached great significance to the phrase "against the Lord," for, he believed, it points up the fact that the guilty man denies that God was a witness to the deposit or the other acts, and thus impliedly he denies God's existence or presence. This, in my view, gives the phrase in Leviticus the same meaning as the phrase "feared God," and is a meaning based on what we generally speak of as conscience.

It was with such views in mind, and especially the story of Noah and the flood, that the Rabbis of the Talmud formulated what they called "the seven commandments given to the descendants of Noah" (*Sanhedrin* 56a). These commandments prohibit idolatry, murder, theft, incest, blasphemy, and the eating of flesh taken from living animals, and require the establishment of courts of justice.[9] How were these seven commandments "given" and to whom? They were "given" on the "tablets of the heart," and to every man everywhere, since Noah was a kind of second Adam.

9 Cf. Jubilees 7:22; Acts 15:20, 29.

These commandments spell out, therefore, a natural law, a law binding on the conscience of every man, and from which no man, nation, or generation can claim exemption.

2. This principle of a law of nature, elaborated into the seven commandments given to the descendants of Noah, is obviously the source from which Jewish tradition selected the threefold principle of civil disobedience: that a man must choose to die, if necessary, rather than obey a law or decree that he commit murder, incest, or idolatry.

One significant aspect is that the duty of civil disobedience is not extended to all of the seven commandments but only to those three. Thus, if the order is to commit theft, for example, on the pain of death, the person should commit the theft.[10]

Suppose that the sanction for a refusal to commit theft, however, is imprisonment, not death. May a person, then, resort to civil disobedience and choose to go to prison rather than commit the wrong? The principle is silent as to such cases. The principle only states explicitly that one must choose to suffer a wrong rather than commit it when the wrong to be committed is idolatry, incest, or murder. And the principle implies only that when the wrong to be suffered is death as a penalty, one must commit the wrong ordered—except idolatry, incest, or murder—and avoid death. A great deal is, therefore, left open—when the wrongs commanded are other than the three cardinal ones, or when the penalty threatened for disobedience is something other than death.

3. Finally, our discussion should have demonstrated the distinctly halakhic approach to the problem of conscience versus law that is an expression of the genius of classical, normative Judaism. The legal order provides a constitutional or higher law by which a man is commanded to disobey certain orders, even when they are made by the king or other high officers of the state. Halakhic normative Judaism thus speaks not of a right but of a *duty*, a *legal* duty, of civil disobedience. Thus, while it recognizes conscience, or "the fear of God," or the laws written on the tablets of the heart, it converts morality into law by demanding that, given

10 See Maimonides, *Hilkhot Yesodei Ha-Torah*, 5, 4. Cf. Belkin, *op. cit.*, pp. 102, 132.

proper circumstances, the higher law become the living law—a living law that contradicts, and even nullifies, the enacted law—or what wrongly pretends to be the law.

The dialectic of the conceptual relations between the demands of conscience (or of the inner or natural law) and those of enacted law or orders of the state is probably impossible to express with any precision, or in terms of logical consistency. The ancient Jewish authorities were wise not to make the attempt but instead resorted to existential terms by conjuring up the case of the governor of the town ordering X to go and kill Y. What did Raba say to X? "Let the governor slay you rather than that you should commit murder. Who knows that your blood is redder? Perhaps Y's blood is redder than yours." Thus, as is often the case in Hebraic-rabbinic thought, an example symbolizes a principle,[11] the commentary becomes the text—as if there were a fear of making the word into a thing, of accepting the notion that in the beginning was the Logos, the word. For the ultimate sanctity is life, God's creation, and not what is said about it in some abstract formula. Yet life, sacred as it is, is given and sustained for certain ends. If these ends are threatened—by coerced idolatry, immorality, or "the shedding of blood"—life becomes worthless and must well be given up. Yet the ends are such only because they enhance life. It is "holy living" and not "holy dying" that is sought and hoped for and cherished.

But the values for which life itself must, if the tragic need arises, be sacrificed, are very few. This perhaps explains the silence of the Talmud regarding the 960 men, women, and children who defended Masada, the fortress on the Dead Sea, in the course of the Judean revolt against Rome. Especially repulsive to the Rabbis must have been the agreement among the members of the garrison's council, as their final act of defiance, to kill the members of their own families and to put one another to death. As against the nationalist Zealots, the Rabbis stressed the need to save the lives of Jews from fruitless martyrdom; the value of non-violent, non-military action; and, of supreme importance to them, the winning

---

[11] Cf. Daube, *op. cit.,* 99–100.

of the right to continue to study and to teach Torah without distraction or fear.[12]

In the light of the Talmudic principles of non-violent civil disobedience, the attitude of the Rabbis to Masada and its defenders, led by Eliezar ben Yair, is entirely understandable. To them, what was indispensable for life was not political independence but the independence of their religious life and the values it contained and sustained (which included, of course, as a minimum, life in conformity with the natural law as formulated in the seven commandments to the descendants of Noah—a natural law which, it could have been reasonably assumed, the Roman overlords would respect and observe).

The unsympathetic critic may say that we have constructed a rather heavy and imposing superstructure on a meager foundation of small incidents, like that of the Egyptian midwives and Saul's bodyguards. Until our own tumultuous days, one would not have thought of such incidents as implying and foreshadowing a principle so momentous for the human spirit as that of civil disobedience. But often it takes many centuries and a great deal of history to disclose the existence of an ideal, theory, or principle. In the Preface to his *Poems* (edition of 1853), Matthew Arnold glibly wrote: "An action like the action of the *Antigone* of Sophocles, which turns upon the conflict between the heroine's duty to her brother's corpse and that to the laws of her country, is no longer one in which it is possible that we should feel a deep interest." One may be sure that when read in 1853 this judgment seemed to be eminently to the point. But would Arnold have made this statement in 1953 after the Nürnberg Tribunal judgments, after the other many war-crime trials, after the Eichmann Trial? Would he have made this statement in the light of Gandhi's non-violent struggle to end untouchability in India? Would he have made this judgment in the 1960's in the light of the lunch-counter sit-ins led by Martin Luther King?

Great actions, whether those of a bereaved young girl, midwives,

[12] Cf. Bernard Heller, "Masada and the Talmud," *Tradition,* vol. 31 (Winter 1968).

or young soldiers engaged to protect their king, have a way of surviving the ravages of time, and demonstrate, when the moment is appropriate, their relevance and significance for that which is "permanent in the human soul." That demonstration can be made by Antigone or Socrates, by Thomas More or Bronson Alcott or Thoreau, by Gandhi or Martin Luther King, or by thousands of nameless Jews who were not afraid of a Roman general, nor of the Roman emperor who sent him, nor of death, but who did have the "fear of God"—a "fear" that gives boundless courage to a spirit that suddenly discovers itself as boundless. These men and women found it easy to act but impossible or difficult to give a rational account of their actions. But this is natural, for conscience demands that the act be justified before God and not necessarily before men; God knows the heart and its inner thoughts and secrets.

And God does not demand great sacrifice when the occasion is not one of transcendent importance; God makes demands only when man is called upon to perpetrate murder or commit immorality or idolatry. Only then does the law of God demand violation of the law of man at the cost of one's life. Civil disobedience is not offered as an everyday method for meeting unwelcome situations, for the amelioration of which society and individuals must find other methods and agencies.

Beyond this, however, Jewish tradition and Halakhah place the highest value on martyrdom that is the price paid for defiance of a tyrant whose policy it is to destroy the Jewish religion. In the solemn service of Yom Kippur, a prominent place is given to a recital of the heroism and martyrdom of the ten great scholars who, during the Hadrianic persecutions, steadfastly refused to accept the prohibitions on observances and the ban on study of Torah. At the risk of their lives they acted in defiance of imperial edicts and gladly suffered torture and death in order to sanctify the Name of their God (*Kiddush ha-Shem*). Within the Jewish tradition of non-violent civil disobedience, these ten martyrs have played a role in the education of the Jewish conscience that is at least comparable to that of Socrates in Western society: as witnesses to the force of the moral and religious conscience and its imperious claims to obedience—claims more pressing than those of any state or emperor.

Freedom of Religion—
Absolute and Inalienable

MOSES MENDELSSOHN *

The task of the church is to convince people, with all the emphasis
at its command, of the truth of the principles and views it proclaims. The church must show them that duties toward men are
also duties toward God and that to reject them is to live in deepest misery. It must show them that by serving the state we truly
serve God; that law and justice are the commands of God; that
charity is His sacred will; and that the true acknowledgment of
the Creator cannot leave even a residue of hatred for our fellow-
men in any human soul. To teach this is the charge, duty, and
vocation of religion; to preach this is the charge, duty, and vocation of its ministers. It is inconceivable to me how men could ever
have permitted religion to teach, and its ministers to preach, exactly the opposite.

If, however, the character of a nation—its cultural development,
its growing prosperity, increasing population, excessive luxury, and
other conditions and circumstances—makes it impossible to govern
the people on the basis of their attitudes alone, the state will have
to resort to public measures such as the enforcement of the law
by coercion, the punishment of crime, and the rewarding of merit.
If a citizen is unwilling to defend his country because he lacks a
sense of duty, he will have to be tempted by rewards or compelled
by force (to fulfill his obligation). If men have lost their feeling

* Translation by Alfred Jospe.

for the intrinsic worth of justice or if they no longer realize that honesty in word and deed is true happiness, it becomes necessary for the state to correct injustice and punish fraud.

In this way, however, the state attains society's true goal only halfway. External inducements cannot make an individual happy, even though they may affect him to some extent. The man who avoids deception because he loves righteousness is happier than the man who avoids it merely because he is afraid of the arbitrary punishments the state metes out for fraud. To his fellow-man, by way of contrast, it does not matter why the wrong is not committed, or by what means his rights and property are protected. The country will be defended regardless of whether a citizen fights for it out of patriotism or out of fear of punishment—even though the defenders themselves will be happy in the former and unhappy in the latter case. If it is impossible for society to achieve inner happiness, at least it will be possible to bring about external tranquility and security.

The state will thus be content with mere deeds—with conduct without conviction, with conformity of action without concurrence in thought. Even though a person may have no regard for laws, he must obey them as soon as they have been enacted. The state may grant the individual citizen the right to criticize laws, but not to act in accordance with his criticism. This right a citizen has to renounce as a member of society, for no society can exist without this renunciation.

Not so with religion. It knows no act not founded on conviction, no work without spirit, no need without inner concurrence, no consensus concerning action without agreement upon its meaning. Religious deeds without religious motivation are empty mechanical motions (literally, "puppetry"), not service of God. Religious deeds must spring from conviction; they can neither be purchased by the promise of a reward nor enforced by the threat of punishment.

Nor is religion concerned with those civil acts that have been motivated by force rather than by conviction. As long as the state exerts its influence only through reward and punishment, it cannot expect any assistance from religion. For as long as this condition exists, man's duties toward God are disregarded, and the relationship between man and his Creator has become inoperative. The only assistance that religion can render the state is through teaching and comforting. It can use its divine teachings to instill ideas in the citizen that are of benefit to the community; and it can bring spiritual comfort to the unfortunate creature who has been condemned to death as a sacrifice to the common good.

Here we have a first essential difference between state and religion. The state commands and coerces, religion teaches and persuades. The state issues laws, religion issues commandments. The state possesses physical power and uses it when necessary; the power of religion is love and charity. The one abandons the lawbreaker and expels him from society; the other draws him close and seeks to instruct or at least to comfort him, not always without profit, even during the last moments of his earthly life. In one word: civil society, viewed as a moral person, has the right of coercion; in fact, it has secured this right through the social contract. Religious society neither demands the right of coercion nor can it possibly obtain it by any contract. . . .

Principles are free. Convictions, by their very nature, cannot be influenced by coercion or bribe. They belong in the realm of man's cognitive power. Their only criterion is whether they are true or untrue. Good and evil, on the other hand, are related to man's capacity for approval or disapproval. Fear and hope guide his impulses. Reward and punishment direct his will; they spur his initiative, encourage, tempt, or deter him.

If principles are to make us happy, they must never be the result of outside pressures or wheedling. The sole criterion by which their validity is to be judged is their rationality. To use any other criterion, to mix it up, for instance, with notions of good and evil, is to invite an unauthorized judge to make the decision.

Thus, neither church nor state has the right to impose any restraint upon man's principles and convictions or to make his status, rights or claims contingent upon these principles and convictions. Nor may they use any other foreign criterion that might interfere with his cognitive power and weaken his understanding of the truth.

Not even a social contract can grant this right to the state or church. A contract involving things which by their very nature are inalienable is self-contradictory and *ipso facto* void.

No oath can possibly change this fact. Oaths do not engender new responsibilities; they are simply solemn affirmations of those obligations which we are duty-bound by nature or contract to fulfill in any case. An oath which does not involve any responsibility is a useless and perhaps even blasphemous invocation of God's name. It certainly cannot be binding in any way.

Moreover, men can swear only to what can be supported and verified by the evidence of their senses—to what they have seen, heard, touched. Thoughts, intellectual perceptions, however, can never be verified by oath.

To abjure or adjure any principles and doctrines is therefore inadmissible. But even if we have done either, we are still not obligated to anything save regret for the unforgiveable lack of prudence with which we have acted. If I were to swear to a certain opinion this very moment, I would be afraid to disavow it a moment later. Furthermore, I have merely sworn a meaningless oath even if I retain my opinion; but I have not committed perjury even if I change it later.

We must not forget that, according to my principles, the state is not authorized to make a person's income, position, or status contingent upon his affirmation of specific doctrines. Teachers, for instance, should be appointed solely in accordance with their ability to teach wisdom and virtue and to disseminate the basic verities upon which the well-being of society is founded. In all other matters, however, teachers should be free to act in accordance with their knowledge and conscience. Otherwise, endless confusion and conflict would ensue, until finally even a man of virtue might find himself in a position in which he is tempted to yield to hypocrisy or to betray his conscience. The rules of reason cannot be broken with impunity. . . .

As far as basic convictions and principles are concerned, religion and state are in agreement that both must avoid any semblance of coercion or bribe and that they must confine themselves to instruction, admonishment, persuasion, guidance. However, they differ with regard to actions. The relationship between man and man involves acts as such; the relationship between God and man involves acts only insofar as they are conducive to stimulating the growth of conviction. An act designed to promote the common welfare is no less beneficial for having been enforced; but a religious act is religious only to the degree to which it is performed voluntarily and with proper intent.

Consequently, the state may compel its citizens to act in ways that will promote the common good. It can reward and punish, grant offices and bestow honors. It can admonish or shame people into actions of whose intrinsic value they would otherwise not be aware. For this reason it is possible, and, in fact, necessary to grant the state the right as well as the power to use compulsion. Hence, the state must, by social contract, be defined as a moral person, capable of exercising rights and holding property with which it can do as it pleases.

Divinely inspired religion is something utterly different. It does not separate act from conviction in the same way in which the state does. For religion, an act is the expression of conviction. Religion is a moral person, too, but its rights cannot be enforced by coercion. It does not prod men on with an iron rod; it guides them with the gentle hand of love. It draws no avenging sword, dispenses no worldly goods, arrogates unto itself no right to earthly possessions, and makes no claim to legal power over any person's mind. Its sole weapons are reason and persuasion; its strength is the divine power of truth. The punishments it threatens as well as the reward it promises are but manifestations of love—salutary and beneficial to the person who recognizes them. It is by these signs that I recognize you, daughter of God, religion, who alone, in truth, are all-saving on earth as well as in heaven! . . .

As far as their civil rights are concerned, the adherents of all religions are equal, with the sole exception of those whose beliefs run counter to the fundamental rules governing human and civil conduct. Such beliefs can obviously not claim any right in the state, and those who are unfortunate enough to hold these beliefs can expect toleration only as long as they do not disturb the social order by unjust or harmful acts. If they do, they must be punished, not for their beliefs but for their actions. . . .

Judaism a Free, Pluralistic Faith

Among the precepts and ordinances of the Mosaic Law, there is none saying, "You shall believe" or "You shall not believe." All say, "You shall do" or "You shall not do." You are not commanded to believe, for faith accepts no commands; it accepts only what comes to it by reasoned conviction.

All commandments of the divine law are addressed to man's will, to his capacity to act. In fact, the original Hebrew term (*emunah*) that is usually translated as "faith" means, in most cases, merely "trust," confidence or firm reliance on pledge and promise: "Abraham trusted in the Lord, and He counted it to him for righteousness" (Genesis 15:6); "And Israel saw . . . and trusted the Lord and Moses, His servant" (Exodus 14:31). Whenever the text refers to eternal verities, it does not use the term "believe" but "understand" and "know": "Know that the Lord is God, and there is none beside Him" (Deuteronomy 4:35); "Therefore know this day and take it to heart that the Lord alone is God, in the heavens above and on the earth below, and there is none else" (*ibid.,* 4:39); "Hear, O Israel, the Lord our God, the Lord is One" (*ibid.,* 6:4). Nowhere does a passage say, "Believe, O Israel, and you will be blessed; do not doubt, O Israel, lest you will be punished." Commandment and prohibition, reward and punishment apply only to acts of commission and omission. These acts are governed by our ideas of good and evil and hence are affected by our hopes and fears. Beliefs and doubts, however, intellectual assent or dissent are governed neither by our wishes or desires nor by our fears and hopes but by what we perceive to be true or false.

For this reason, Judaism has no symbolic books, no articles of faith. No one has to swear to creedal symbols or subscribe, by solemn oath, to certain articles of faith. We do not require the affirmation of specific doctrines by oath. In fact, we consider this practice incompatible with the true spirit of Judaism. Maimonides was the first thinker to whom it occurred by chance to try to condense the religion of his fathers into a certain number of principles. According to his explanation, he wanted religion, like all other sciences, to have axioms from which everything else could be deduced. This accidental effort produced the Thirteen Articles of Faith, to which we owe the hymn *Yigdal,* as well as some valuable writings by Ḥasdai, Albo, and Abravanel. But these are the only results which Maimonides' effort to formulate specific articles of faith has produced. Thank God, they have not been forged into shackles for our beliefs. Ḥasdai opposes them and proposes certain changes. Albo limits their number and wants to recognize only three basic principles, which correspond more or less to those which Herbert of Cherbury later proposed as basis for a catechism. Still others, especially Luria and his disciples, the neo-Kabbalists, refuse to recognize any fixed number of fundamental tenets and maintain that everything in our teachings is axiomatic. Yet all these controversies were conducted, as all controversies of this kind should be, with earnestness and zeal but without animosity and bitterness. And although Maimonides' Thirteen Articles of Faith have been accepted by the majority of our people, no one, to the best of my knowledge, has ever accused Albo of being a heretic because he attempted to reduce their number and to base them on more universal rational principles. In matters of this kind, we still heed the important dictum of our sages, "Although this one permits and the other prohibits, both teach the words of the living God." . . .

Diversity Is the Plan of Providence
—a Union of Faiths Is Not Tolerance

A union of faiths, if it were ever to come about, could have only the most disastrous consequences for reason and freedom of conscience. Suppose people were able to reach agreement concerning the doctrinal formulations they want to introduce as basic creed; suppose one could also manage to find symbols to which none of the religious groups now dominant in Europe could object—what would be gained by this? Would it mean that all of you had arrived at the same views about religious truths?

No one who has the slightest insight into human nature can possibly come to this conclusion. This would merely be agreement on words, on a formula. The unifiers of faith would simply be collaborating in pinching off a bit from some concepts here and there, in enlarging the texture of words elsewhere, until they become so vague and loose that any ideas, regardless of their inner differences, can, if necessary, be squeezed in. Everybody would merely be attaching to the same words a different meaning, peculiarly his own. Therefore, do you still want to boast that you have united mankind in faith, that you have brought the flock under the care of its one shepherd? Alas, if the goal of this universal delusion were to be realized, I am afraid man's barely liberated mind would once again be confined behind bars. The shy animal would soon have let itself be captured and put in harness again. Be as undemanding and conciliatory as you may wish, as soon as you link faith to symbol, tie conviction to words, lay down unalterably your articles of faith, the unfortunate wretch who arrives a day later and dares to find fault even with these inoffensive, purified words will be in terrible trouble. He is a disturber of the peace! Off to the stake with him!

Brothers, if you care for true godliness, let us not pretend that conformity exists where diversity is obviously the plan and goal of Providence. Not one among us thinks and feels exactly like his fellow-man. Why, then, should we deceive each other with lies? It is sad enough that we are doing this in our daily relations, in conversations that are of no particular importance. But why also in matters which concern our temporal and eternal welfare, our very destiny? Why should we use masks to make ourselves unrecognizable to each other in the most important concerns of life, when God has given each of us his own distinctive face for some good reason? Would this not mean that we oppose Providence as far as we can; that we try, in fact, to frustrate the very purpose of creation; and that we deliberately act contrary to our own vocation and destiny in this life and the life to come?

Rulers of the earth! If an unimportant coinhabitant may be permitted to lift his voice and to address you: Do not trust your counselors who, in smooth phrases, seek to mislead you into such a harmful course of action. They are either deluded themselves and cannot see the enemy of mankind lurking in the background, or they deliberately try to deceive you. Our most precious possession—the freedom to think—will be lost if you listen to their counsel. For the sake of your happiness as well as ours, remember that "a union of faiths is not tolerance." It is the very opposite. For the sake of your happiness and ours, do not use your powerful prestige to give the force of law to some eternal truth that is immaterial to civic well-being; do not transform some religious doctrine to which the state should be indifferent into a statute of the land! Concentrate on what men should or should not do; judge them wisely by their actions; and let us retain the freedom of thought and speech with which the Father of all mankind has endowed us as our inalienable heritage and immutable right.

Should, however, the link between privilege and personal conviction have become so solidified over the years that the time has not yet come to abolish it completely without serious damage, try at least to diminish its pernicious influence as much as you can and set wise limits to an obsolete prejudice.

At least prepare the way for your more fortunate descendants to (reach) that height of culture, that universal human tolerance for which reason is still sighing in vain. Reward and punish no doctrine; hold out no allurement or bribe to anyone for the adoption of a particular faith. Let every man who does not disturb the public welfare, who obeys the law, acts righteously toward you and his fellow-men be allowed to speak as he thinks, to pray to God after his own fashion or after the fashion of his fathers, and to seek eternal salvation where he thinks he may find it. Permit no one in your country to search someone else's heart or to judge someone else's thoughts. Let no one usurp a right which the Omniscient has reserved to Himself. If we render unto Caesar what is Caesar's, then let us also render unto God what is God's. Love truth! Love peace! . . .

Judaism Seeks No Converts

According to the principles of my religion, I am not expected to try to convert anyone not born in my faith. Even though many people think that the zeal for proselytizing originated in Judaism, it is, in fact, completely alien to it. Our rabbis hold unanimously that the written as well as the oral laws that constitute our revealed religion are binding only for our own people. *"Moses* had given *us* the law; it is the inheritance of the House of *Jacob"* (Deuteronomy 33:4). All other nations were enjoined by God to observe the law of nature and the religion of the patriarchs. All who live in accordance with this religion of nature and of reason are called "the righteous among other nations"; they too are entitled to eternal bliss. Far from being obsessed by any desire to proselytize, our rabbis require us to discourage as forcefully as we can anyone who asks to be converted. We are to ask him to consider the heavy burden he would have to shoulder needlessly by taking this step. We are to point out that, in his present state, he is obligated to fulfill only the Noahide laws in order to be saved but that upon his conversion he will have to observe strictly all the laws of his new faith or expect the punishment which God metes out to the lawbreaker. Finally, we are to paint a faithful picture of the misery and destitution of our people and of the contempt in which they are held, in order to keep him from a hasty decision he may later regret.

As you see, the religion of my fathers does not ask to be propagated. We are not to send missionaries to the two Indies or to Greenland in order to preach our faith to distant nations. . . . Anyone not born into our community need not observe its laws. The fact that we consider their observance incumbent upon us alone cannot possibly offend our neighbors. Do they think our views are absurd? No need to quarrel about it. We act in accordance with our convictions and do not mind if others question the validity of our laws, which, as we ourselves emphasize, are not binding on them. Whether they are acting fairly, peaceably, and charitably when they mock our laws and traditions is, of course, something else that must be left to their own consciences. As long as we do not want to convince or convert others, we have no quarrel with them.

If a Confucius or a Solon were to live among our contemporaries, I could, according to my religion, love and admire the great man without succumbing to the ridiculous desire to convert him. Convert a Confucius or Solon? What for? Since he is not a member of the household of Jacob, our religious laws do not apply to him. And as far as the general principles of religion are concerned, we should have little trouble agreeing on them. Do I think he can be saved? It seems to me that anyone who leads men to virtue in this life cannot be damned in the next. . . .

It is my good fortune to count among my friends many an excellent man who is not of my faith. We love each other sincerely, although both of us suspect or assume that we differ in matters of faith. I enjoy the pleasure of his company and feel enriched by it.

But at no time has my heart whispered to me, "What a pity that this beautiful soul should be lost. . . ." Only that man will be troubled by such regrets who believes that there is no salvation outside his church.

The Right of Dissent and
Intellectual Liberty

ROBERT GORDIS

In post-Biblical Judaism there developed a common body of
generally shared beliefs and doctrines, but, within exceedingly
broad limits, one was free to interpret them as one chose and to
battle for one's view in the market place of ideas. *The nexus binding the Jewish community together lay not in an authoritative creed,
but in a shared experience,* as embodied in a common history in the
past, a common way of life in the present, and the conviction of a
common destiny in the future.

Undoubtedly, the natural human tendency to suppress unpalatable and unpopular views operated in Israel, sometimes with great
vigor. Always, however, it encountered the formidable opposition
of a tradition which had underscored the right to dissent. Since
practice rather than creed was the instrument of unity in Israel,
the effort to achieve conformity in the group tended to be more
successful in the field of law rather than in the area of theology.

The point need not be labored that the heart of the democratic
world view lies in the right to dissent. The tragic experience of our
own age has revealed how elections, ballot boxes, and all the trap-
pings of parliamentarianism may become the instrument of totali-
tarian tyranny. The right to dissent had very ancient roots in Judaism: in fact, it was older than Judaism itself. Its origins are to be
sought in the primitive democratic institution of the *Edah* or *Ka-*

190

hal, . . .[1] which went back to the nomadic period preceding the settlement in Palestine. . . . All the members of the *Edah* were equal, free to protest any injustice and to demand the righting of any alleged wrong. Even the lowliest member of the group could demand and would receive a hearing.

With the rise of the Hebrew monarchy and the breakdown of the tribal structure, the demand for conformity and obedience grew in power. But the right to dissent and to express unpopular ideas remained the jealously guarded privilege of the prophets. Most prophets undoubtedly shared the opinions and the prejudices of their contemporaries and never ran afoul of duly constituted authority, whose mouthpiece they were. The prophetic literature that has survived in the Bible is not their work. It is almost entirely the work of the dissident minority, the unpopular and unprofessional seers of their day, who insisted that they spoke the word of God. These prophets scornfully denied any connection between themselves and the respectable majority whom they stigmatized as "false prophets." An instructive instance is afforded by the diametrically opposite messages proclaimed by two prophets of the eighth century B.C.E., before the kings of Israel and Judah, Ahab and Jehoshaphat, as they were embarking upon a campaign against Aram (Syria). The one prophet, Zedekiah ben Kenaanah, prophesied the desired victory in war. But the prophet Micaiah ben Imlah announced defeat and declared that his opponent was possessed by a spirit of deception and falsehood (see I Kings 22:1–28). A hundred years later, his namesake, the prophet Micah the Morashtite, went further and declared that the popular prophets of his time were not mistaken but corrupted: "When they can bite with their teeth, they announce peace, but whoso does not feed their maws, against him they declare war" (Micah 3:5). A similar confrontation occurs in Jeremiah's time, when his message is challenged by the "false prophet" Hananiah (see Jeremiah 28). By and large, the Bible chronicles the activity of the "true prophets," whether they were court prophets like Nathan, who did not hesitate to confront his royal master

---

[1] *Edah,* a religious congregation of ten or more adult Jews; a term first used by Exilic writers of the Hebrew Scriptures. *Kahal* meant, in pre-Exilic writings, a predominantly secular assembly. Both words came, however, to be used of religious gatherings of Jews.

David and to declare, "You are the man," or independent figures like Samuel, Ahijah, Elijah and Elisha, who spoke out as they saw fit from their homes or in the public arena.

Undoubtedly, superior power succeeded often enough in silencing the unpalatable message of the great prophets. Amos was driven from sanctuary in Bethel and told to go back to his native Judah whence he came.[2] Jeremiah, who counseled submission to Babylonia in order to preserve the nation, was naturally hated and despised as disloyal, since his activity coincided with the attack by the enemy upon the very gates of Jerusalem. His contemporary, the prophet Uriah, who lacked Jeremiah's powerful friends, fled to Egypt but to no avail. The king sent a squad of men to bring him back and had him killed (see Jeremiah 26:20 ff.). Undoubtedly, other, similar incidents have not survived in our sources. However, royal tyranny and mob passion remained incapable of extirpating the tradition of freedom of expression cherished by the prophets.

The persistency of this principle of free speech is highlighted by the account of the trial of the prophet Jeremiah for treason, which took place in the reign of King Jehoiakim (circa 608–597 B.C.E.). With the threat of the Babylonian conqueror close at hand, Jeremiah, who had announced the impending destruction of the Temple, was charged with subversion by "the priests, the prophets and the people." He was tried before "the lords and the people" in the New Gate of the Temple. He maintained his position, however, and the elders cited in his defense the century-old precedent of the prophet Micah the Morashite, who had similarly prophesied the destruction of Jerusalem and yet had not been killed by King Hezekiah. Jeremiah was accordingly freed on the ground that "he does not deserve to die, for in the name of the Lord, our God, has he spoken unto us."

It is pertinent to inquire whether the same freedom of expression extended to others outside the prophetic circle. The prophets, being under the divine afflatus, might be granted a measure of immunity on the ground that it was the Lord speaking through them. While direct evidence is lacking, it can be taken for granted that

[2] Cf. Amos 7:10–17, especially 7:12. There are, however, no grounds for the widely held assumption that his expulsion from the Northern Kingdom meant the end of his prophetic activity. . . .

unpopular ideas expressed by those who claimed no prophetic role met stronger opposition. Yet two observations are in order. The conviction of a prophetic call was undoubtedly far more widespread among the ancients than our modern, sophisticated standpoint would normally assume. Whoever had a message to proclaim, particularly if it ran counter to accepted prejudice and opinion, would naturally find his sanction and strength in the conviction that "thus says the Lord." In the second instance, the variety of content, outlook, and mood in the Bible . . . offers objective testimony to the latitude of opinion which prevailed in the life of the Hebrew people and which is reflected in the tripartite division of the Hebrew Bible. Not only did the priests, prophets, and wisdom teachers differ from one another, but there were important differences and even conflicts within each group. Yet they all were permitted to function and indeed preserve considerable sections of their literary activity for posterity, as the pages of the Bible bear witness.

The deeply rooted democratic emphasis in the tradition, which we have described, made freedom of expression a fundamental of the Hebrew way of life. Such freedom necessarily depended on access to knowledge by all the people. Our sources, unfortunately, reveal little information about the system of education in Biblical days. We are compelled to fall back upon minor incidents and accidental phrases which reveal the wide diffusion of literacy even in this early period. In a period as primitive as that of the Judges, Gideon captures at random a youth who is able to write down the names of the leaders of the settlement of Sukkot (see Judges 8:15). The prophet Isaiah describes the remnant of destruction as so slight that "a child can write them" (Isaiah 10:7). The prophet Habakkuk refers with equal casualness to the ability to read (Habakkuk 2:2).

The Torah was given to the entire people, and the famous call to love God "with all your heart" is concretized immediately thereafter by the injunction to "teach these words diligently to one's children and write them on the doorposts of one's house and gate" (Deuteronomy 6:4, 6). We know little of the schools which undoubtedly existed in Biblical times. The priesthood probably restricted its instruction in the Torah to the scions of the hereditary clan, though it is noteworthy that Moses himself is not described as a priest. On the other hand, the prophets came from every sector of society, and we may be sure that the prophetic guilds were open to all who knocked, irrespective of class or background. Elsewhere, we have sought to demonstrate that the wisdom academies served primarily the youth of the upper classes, the merchant princes, the landed gentry, and the government officials, but here there was no overt exclusion, only the operation of impersonal economic factors. In sum, the tradition of learning for all, so pervasive in later Judaism, found its roots in the Biblical era.

The Babylonian Exile (587–538 B.C.E.) is often regarded, particularly by critical scholars, as marking the transformation of the Hebrew nation into the Jewish church, from an ethnic group to a religious community. It is true that the national independence of the First Temple period now gave way to limited autonomy under foreign rulers, whether Persian, Seleucid, or Roman, except for the brief flash of Maccabean freedom which lasted only eighty years (142–63 B.C.E.). The Exile and the Return therefore constitute a convenient dividing line between Biblical and Rabbinic Judaism. What took place was a shift in emphasis, but the transition was both more gradual in tempo and less far-reaching in character than is usually assumed. With the loss of national independence, the bond of group unity was no longer allegiance to the state or even to the land, but to the Torah, which was both the faith and the culture of Israel.

Nonetheless, Biblical and Rabbinic Judaism overlap. Important sections in the Bible were composed or compiled during the Exile and after the Return and, conversely, the beginnings of the Oral Law are to be sought in the pre-Exilic period. Essentially, however, the Second Commonwealth period marks the birth and development of Rabbinic Judaism. It was with Ezra the Scribe that the Torah of Moses won acceptance as the basic law governing the life of the people. There now began a vast and complicated process of interpretation, amplification, and extension of the Biblical text in order to meet new insights and conditions. The creation of this vast Oral Law absorbed the spiritual energies of Jewry for nearly a millennium, from the days of Ezra (the middle of the fifth century B.C.E.) to the sixth century of the Christian Era. The Oral Law was officially put into writing in two stages, that of the Mishnah in the third century and that of the Gemara, its elaborate commentary and expansion, three centuries later.

The Oral Law was the result of widespread intellectual activity by the masses of the people. Unlike the priests, who continued to conduct the Temple ritual as a hereditary and aristocratic caste, the teachers and students of the Torah, in the Pharisaic "houses of study," were recruited from all levels of society. The study of the Torah became the most significant form of worship, the entire liturgy of prayer growing up around the public reading and exposition of Scriptures. The cultivation of Torah, far from being regarded as the province of a special group, was the duty and privilege of every male Jew. To be sure, many did not fulfill the obligation, but the Mishnah emphasizes, in spite of much experience to the contrary, that "the ignorant person can not truly fear sin, nor the uneducated be pious." The most popular and familiar tractate of the Mishnah, *Avot,* generally referred to as the *Ethics of the Fathers,* in which this line appears (2:5), is basically a panegyric on the study of Torah and a guide to its pursuit and is intended for no special class but for all the people.

The Biblical injunction for the father himself to instruct his son necessarily became unworkable as the body of learning increased. Talmudic sources attribute the establishment of schools in each town to the Pharisaic teacher, Simon ben Shetah, or to the High Priest, Joshua ben Gemala. At all events, a system of education, probably compulsory in character, existed before the first century of the Christian Era. Among enumerated duties of a father toward his son was the teaching of the Torah, of a gainful occupation, and how to swim, besides marrying him off properly.

So important did the study of the Torah by the people become that the entire history of the Jewish people is associated with the building of schools and with the effort to diffuse learning among all the people. The rabbinic conviction that knowledge was the only firm foundation of piety remained unshaken until the present day.

The Mishnah is the literary and religious monument of Pharisaic Judaism. Actually, the Pharisees were not a sect; they represented the vast majority of the people who belonged to the lower and middle classes. The strictures levelled against the Pharisees in the

New Testament are recognized by competent scholars as being the result of polemic zeal rather than of objective evaluation, and constitute an oblique recognition of the debt of early Christianity to Pharisaic Judaism. Basically, Pharisaism represented the liberal interpretation of Scripture as against a conservative adherence to the letter of the Law advocated by the upper-class Sadducees. So pervasive was Pharisaic influence that it gave birth to a variety of splinter sects which took on one or another Pharisaic doctrine and carried it to extremes or to its logical conclusion—it all depends upon the point of view! Such were the Essenes, with their emphasis upon ritual and ethical purity; the various Apocalyptic sects, with their profound conviction that the Kingdom of God was at hand, from whom the early Judeo-Christian Church emerged; and the Zealots, who insisted upon fighting the Roman tyranny instead of passively awaiting the advent of the Messiah. The recently discovered Dead Sea Scrolls extend and complicate our knowledge of the number of sectarian trends in Palestine during the fateful centuries at the beginning of the Christian Era.

It is noteworthy that in this welter of controversy, no effort was made to compel conformity of outlook or expression. The Pharisees were strongly opposed to the Sadducean denial of the validity of the Oral Law and of such important religious doctrines as bodily resurrection, and the Talmud records many arguments between the two groups. Yet no heresy trial or excommunication of the Sadducees is recorded in the thousands of pages of rabbinical literature. Within the rabbinical schools, too, there were far-reaching differences of opinion, the Talmud as a whole being a massive monument of controversy. The basic principle for deciding the law was derived from Exodus, chapter 23:2, the last clause of which was taken to mean "the majority is to be followed." The Mishnah, however, was careful to record the minority opinions on each issue. Some of the divergences represented entire schools of thought, like the Schools of Hillel and of Shammai. When the decision was finally made in favor of the Hillelites, the judgment was added that one was nevertheless free to follow the Shammaite position as long as one did it consistently. The phrasing here is significant: "He who *acts* according to the School of Shammai is free to do so." The emphasis was upon conformity in practice, not upon unanimity in belief.

In general, there was little conscious speculation on metaphysical issues in rabbinic Judaism. It was only as the Jewish tradition came into contact with Greek thought that the exemplars of Judaism were led to examine the traditional body of belief and seek to buttress it against the corrosive acids of philosophy. Greek influence, which came to the fore principally in ancient Alexandria and in medieval Europe, was not limited to philosophy. A wide familiarity prevailed in Palestinian Jewish circles with the Greek language and many aspects of Hellenistic religion, folklore, and popular literature, while the influence of Roman law upon Talmudic jurisprudence is not inconsiderable.

With the destruction of the Temple by the Romans in 70, the last vestiges of Jewish autonomy all but disappeared, and the scattered Jewish communities throughout the world had no visible spiritual center. Weakened from within, normative Judaism now faced a threefold attack. The Sadducean opposition to the authority of the Oral Law and to the resurrection of the body was now dwarfed by the challenge of the nascent faith of Christianity, which declared that the old dispensation had been nullified by the advent of the Savior. Greek thought, both in its philosophic and gnostic forms, continued to exert a powerful fascination as well.

The closest approach to a creedal formulation occurs in a passage in the *Mishnah Sanhedrin*. It is couched in negative terms because it is directed against these challenges: "He who says that the Torah is not from Heaven, he who denies the resurrection, and the Epicurean [3] have no share in the world to come." Rabbi Akiba adds his minority view and says, "Also he who reads Apocryphal books [4] and pronounces magical incantations over wounds." Within these broad limits, however, which included the freedom to interpret the doctrines of divine revelation and resurrection literally or figuratively, the right to differ was jealously guarded. This in spite of the growing need to create some basis of unity to replace the destruction of the center in Jerusalem. The Sanhedrin in Jerusalem was

[3] The term is generally used of an adherent of Greek philosophy of any school and hence a skeptic with regard to Judaism.
[4] Because they were largely products of the dissident sects and frequently sustained interpolations in line with the teaching of the Christian Church.

no longer in existence, and so, by a bold assumption of authority, the ancient scholar Joḥanan ben Zakkai and a group of scholars who assembled at the seacoast town of Jamnia, after the destruction of the Temple, constituted themselves an Academy. This institution, they declared, represented the continuation of the religious authority of the Sanhedrin. The Academy at Jamnia was not the only one; others, headed by independent scholars, continued to command the loyalty of disciples. However, the felt need for a single center and the prestige of the Patriarch, who was the president of the school at Jamnia besides being the official head of the Jewish community legally recognized by the Roman authority, finally gave the Academy of Jamnia, which later moved to Usha, and to other sites in Palestine, universally recognized hegemony.

Since the authority of the Academy was entirely unofficial, it was felt that some instrument of enforcement was needed. Thus the institution of the *ḥerem,* "ban" or "excommunication," came into being. Rabbinic sources distinguish three types of ban: the *nezifah,* "rebuke," usually imposed for a week; the *niddui,* "separation," which was a suspension for a thirty-day period; and, finally, the *ḥerem,* or the *shamta,* "excommunication" or "ban," which was final and subject to recall only by the submission and penance of the offender.

The origin of the ban is shrouded in obscurity. The Hebrew term *ḥerem* occurs in the oldest sections of the Bible. In pre-Exilic times, *ḥerem,* which, according to its etymology, means "sacred," "dedicated to the deity," referred to living persons, animals, or possessions forbidden to human use and hence consigned to destruction. In the post-Exilic Book of Ezra, the term is still used in its older sense, but with an addendum reflecting the later rabbinic usage: "Whoever will not come within three days to the council of the princes and the elders shall have all his property placed under the ban and he himself shall be separated from the community of the exile" (Ezra 10:8). As has been noted already, the ban was not invoked against the Sadducees or any of the dissident sects of the Second Temple period. It is not until after the destruction of the central authority of the Temple and the Sanhedrin in the year 70 that it begins to appear in our sources. Its function has been well described as "an instrument for the promotion of public conduct as well as the enforcement of public morality." The emphasis in Judaism upon practice rather than upon doctrine is clear in the poignant career of the second-century sage, Elisha ben Abuyah, who was the teacher of the famous Rabbi Meir, one of the architects of the Mishnah. According to a rabbinic tradition, Elisha ben Abuyah was one of four scholars who entered the enticing garden of theosophical speculation and thus sought to penetrate the mysteries of creation. While his three colleagues emerged with their faith basically unshaken, Elisha ben Abuyah came out "transformed," a heretic. The sources differ with regard to the nature of his heterodoxy, whether it consisted of his opposition to the ceremonial law, of his denial of divine justice in this world or the next, or of an effort to wean the youth away from the study of the Torah. It is noteworthy, however, that no formal excommunication is recorded in our sources. His faithful pupil, Rabbi Meir, continued to associate with him and learn from him. The Talmud defends his conduct by citing a proverb, a widespread saying that might well serve as a guidepost for our age: "Rabbi Meir found a half-ripe date; its fruit he ate, its husk he cast away."

The *niddui* was employed in the case of other scholars like Akabiah ben Mahalalel and Eliezer ben Hyrcanus. Both of these scholars were independent stalwarts of conservative views, sympathetic to the Shammaite position, who persisted in maintaining their point of view on several legal issues after the Hillelite majority had ruled against them. Both of them continued to be held in high veneration, but if the authority of the Academy was to be maintained the ban had to be invoked against them. . . .

Basically, however, the offenses for which excommunication might be used fall into three principal categories:

1. *The weakening of the authority of the Jewish court.*

The ban might be invoked for insulting the scholars or the messenger of the court, for refusing to appear before the Jewish court, or declining to abide by its decision, and for having recourse to a non-Jewish agency, thus avoiding the jurisdiction of the Jewish authorities altogether.

2. *The violation of religious or ethical standards.*

The ban could be used against one who dealt lightly with a Biblical or a rabbinical precept, or ignored the additional day of the Festivals, customary in the Diaspora. It was permitted against a Jew who profaned the name of God by unseemly behavior or who sold ritually prohibited meat as kosher, or who, after divorcing his wife, continued to have business dealings with her where there was a temptation for intimate relations forbidden by the Jewish tradition.

3. Malfeasance in office.

The ban was permitted against a priest who failed to give priestly gifts, a slaughterer not sufficiently scrupulous in observing the law, a rabbi whose conduct made him subject to public scandal, or a leader who had invoked the excommunication unjustly upon an accused.

It is obvious that in this catalogue of offenses punishable by the ban, the influence of medieval conditions is marked. With the extinction of the Palestinian and Babylonian centers about the tenth century, the last vestiges of central religious authority in Jewry disappeared. In the first half of the Middle Ages, Spain, France, Germany, and Italy became the major centers of Jewish population. Each community, local and regional, was now governed by its own authorities and judged by the courts which it created. Lacking the scope and prestige of earlier institutions, the rabbinical leadership strove to strengthen its authority. This was especially necessary, since Jews were now living as distinct, alien communities, dependent on the goodwill of their hosts for their rights to residence. At times, the right to corporal punishment was granted by the state to the Jewish community, the Jews of Spain even possessing the power to execute grave offenders. Generally, however, the authority of the Jewish court was greatly restricted, and the basic sanction for adherence to Jewish law was the voluntary adherence of the vast majority of Jews to the decisions of their religious and judicial leadership. Where such adherence was not forthcoming, the ban became virtually the only available weapon, for it meant social and economic isolation in this world, and divine displeasure in the next.

Undoubtedly, to be excommunicated was a powerful sanction, but the isolation which it imposed was not so unmitigated as is sometimes pictured. Maimonides specifies, to be sure, that "he is not hired for labor nor does one hire oneself to him, one does not engage in business with him," but he adds: *"except that one may engage in business with him slightly to the degree needed for his support."* Karo adds that one who eats and drinks with the person under the ban is not himself excommunicated, though the court has the discretion to do so, if the offense is particularly grave. In practice, the ban was often more severely applied than religious authorities approved.

Since the ban was the principal instrument for enforcing authority in the Middle Ages, it was added to whatever regulations individual scholars or synods adopted for their communities. Such were the early anonymous synods in Europe, as well as their famous successors in the eleventh and twelfth centuries associated with Rabbi Gershom, "The Light of the Exile" (born in 960), with Rashi, the French Jewish commentator and scholar (1040–1105), and with his grandson, Rabbi Jacob Tam. The contrast between the decisions of these rabbinical synods and the deliberations of the various church councils of the period highlights the far-reaching difference in emphasis between the two traditions. The Jewish synods are concerned primarily with matters of morals, rather than with faith; the contrary is the case in the Christian leadership. To validate the authority of these courts, the sources speak of a *herem bet din,* "the vow of the court," an obligation assumed to have been taken by the various European communities to recognize the decisions of their rabbis. By the year 1000 its use was widespread. There are grounds for assuming that, like the social contract of Rousseau, it had no foundation in historical fact, but was a symbolic idea necessary to establish continuity with the old communities of Palestine and Babylonia. Another use of the ban was the *herem hayishuv,* "the ban on settlement," by which a community could determine what new resident might be accepted within its confines. Here economic and housing considerations were the prime factor.

Harking back in spirit to the primitive democracy of the *Edah* was the custom of interrupting public prayers in order to call public attention to private wrongs. It served to arouse public opinion against arbitrary power and thus helped secure a hearing for the weaker elements in society. Beginning in Germany, the practice continued to flourish in Eastern Europe until virtually our day.

The ban of Rabbi Gershom and his synod was invoked, for

example, in the area of family law. His ordinance forbade polygamy among Jews in Christian Europe, a practice virtually extinct long before, and declared a divorce issued against the will of the wife null and void, an important step in the enfranchisement of women. Other ordinances protected tenants against unjust evictions and forbade the opening of letters addressed to someone else, an important provision when private travelers carried all correspondence.

The ordinances of Rashi and Jacob Tam reflect the same general areas of interest. Many sought to safeguard and extend the rights of women, to strengthen the authority of the courts to protect the community against informers, and to minimize physical brawls. An ordinance which sheds light on the diffusion of education is the ordinance of Rabbenu Tam forbidding the cutting off of the margin of a book, even it it is one's own property. Margins were, of course, frequently used for comments and critiques of the text in the manuscript. Similarly, a Rhineland ordinance adopted before 1220 forbade the community to seize books left in trust for unpaid taxes.

Particularly in the later Middle Ages, many Jewish communities felt constrained to adopt sumptuary legislation to limit the finery that might be worn by the womenfolk. While ascetic tendencies played some part, the principal motives were to avoid arousing the envy of Gentile neighbors, to prevent the impoverishing of socially ambitious families, and to minimize social differences between rich and poor.

The power of the ban could easily lead to abuses, and medieval ordinances are replete with provisions against its arbitrary and unjust use by individual rabbis and scholars. These efforts did not succeed, and ultimately the abuses weakened the effectiveness of the ban and it became meaningless in ghetto life. It should not be overlooked that the state frequently compelled the use of the ban in order to collect taxes or to establish its authority in other areas. Such bans were declared null and void by the rabbinical authorities.

The Crusades, which played so significant a role in liberating the spirit of Christian Europe, had a drastically opposite effect on Jewish life. The Dark Ages for Jewry coincide, not with the first half of the Middle Ages, but with the second, when Europe was discovering broader horizons. The Crusaders, in marching across Europe, attacked and all but destroyed the long-established Rhineland communities. In spite of the effort of such leaders as St. Bernard of Clairvaux to prevent excesses, the friendly relationships between Jews and Christians became rarer, often interdicted by law. In the wake of the rise of unitary monarchies in Western Europe came the expulsion of the Jews from England in 1290, their expulsion from France in 1306, until the final act of the tragedy in 1394, and their expulsion from Spain in 1492. The Black Death in 1348–49, which wrought havoc with the European population, let loose deep prejudices against the Jews. Jewish life became increasingly precarious, and the segregated community of the ghetto became more and more the rule after that catastrophe.

The crusade of extermination waged by the Church against the heretical sects of the Waldensians and the Albigensians (1229) underscored the pressure toward conformity in Catholic Europe. The Inquisition became a fearsome reminder of the determination of the Church to stamp out heresy.

As Jewish contacts with the world at large became restricted and Jews were driven into Central and Eastern Europe, a narrowing of outlook resulted. In medieval Germany and Eastern Europe there was little of the vital intellectual life characteristic of Mohammedan Spain or Christian Provence and Italy, to which Jews had richly contributed and from which they had freely drawn. The natural sciences, philosophy, philology, and poetry, which had been part of the intellectual equipment of an educated man, whether Jewish, Christian, or Mohammedan, virtually did not exist. The level of culture of the East European Jewish communities did not sink to the illiteracy of the environment because of the rich, religious culture which the Jews brought with them. But owing to the lack of any stimulation from without, Jewish intellectual interests were limited to the confines of the Talmud, the Codes, and the commentaries. Even the study of the Bible as an independent discipline fell into desuetude. When it was revived in the nineteenth century, it was under the impact of the Enlightenment and was resented in traditional circles as an attack upon the citadel of tradition.

In the narrowing of horizons in the later Middle Ages, the intellectual factor was reinforced by more practical considerations.

As the Jewish communities felt their right of domicile becoming more precarious, there was a growing feeling that unfamiliar or heterodox ideas might arouse the hostility of the Church or the state and further weaken the Jewish position. To forestall such unpleasant consequences as the burning of books by the Inquisition, a practice in which it was freely indulging, the rabbinical synod of Ferrara in 1554 forebade the publication of a book without the sanction of three rabbis and of the head of the community in which it was printed. In 1603, the Frankfort synod adopted a similar ordinance. The tangible dangers involved in publishing a book which the Inquisition might not approve are graphically depicted in the fears expressed by the Italian rabbi, Leon da Modena, in 1637. Similarly, the Spanish Jewish community in London expressly motivates its enactment of censorship, "because it thus conduces to our preservation." Another, lesser factor was the desire to avoid poorly printed, error-ridden editions.

Long before the invention of printing, the problem of freedom of expression versus group security had arisen. The rationalist philosopher Maimonides, the great Talmudic authority of his day and author of a monumental Code of Jewish law, as well as of the great philosophic work *Guide to the Perplexed,* during his lifetime, remained unassailable. But after his death his enemies became active. Some objected to his Code, in which he set forth the law without citing his sources, often expressing an independent viewpoint. Others objected to his philosophic speculations in general. As the traditionalists began the campaign, the liberals rallied to his defence. The war was long and bitter, extending from Baghdad to Provence and Spain. The Northern French scholars, unfamiliar with philosophy, pronounced a ban against the study of Maimonides' philosophical writings. Solomon of Montpellier, the leader of the anti-Maimonidists, denounced the *Guide* to the Dominican order, and a public bonfire was made of the book in the public square in Paris in 1233. This led to a revulsion of feeling and the liberals were now reinforced by the moderates, but the struggle continued. Finally, the great rabbinical authority Rabbi Solomon ibn Adret of Barcelona (1235–1310) issued a ban intended as a compromise that satisfied no one. He proscribed the study of philosophy and the sciences (except medicine) by anyone under the age of twenty-five, and then only if he had thoroughly studied the Talmud and rabbinical literature. The liberals responded with a counter-ban. One fundamental fact became clear: *The ban was effective in the field of communal policy and private morality, because it had the sanction of the people. It proved increasingly ineffective in the area of belief and opinion, where conformity had never been sought and was less and less evident.*

Curiously, Maimonides, because of his love of systematic and logical thought, was himself the unconscious cause of a threat to freedom of thought. Uncompromisingly rationalistic, he declared that to ascribe any physical form to the deity was tantamount to heresy and deprived one of a share in the world to come. Nowhere is the genius of Judaism better revealed than in the printed page of Maimonides' Code, where this statement is countered by the comment of his unsparing critic, Rabbi Abraham ben David of Posquières, who wrote: "Better and greater men than Maimonides have ascribed a physical form to God, basing themselves on their understanding of Scriptural passages and even more so on some legends and utterances, which give wrong ideas." The critic's standpoint is clear. He too denies physical form to God, but he affirms the right to maintain backward ideas in Judaism.

Maimonides sought also to systematize the articles of belief in Judaism and formulated his "Thirteen Principles" in his *Commentary on the Mishnah*. Their all-embracing character, the clarity of their formulation, and the authority of their author gave them wide popularity, and they are printed in the traditional prayerbook as an appendix. Lesser men, however, did not hesitate to quarrel with both the content and the number of articles of belief in the Creed of Maimonides. It never became an official confession of faith.

The spirit of medieval Jewish life may be observed from another angle. The invention of printing found no more enthusiastic devotees than the Jewish community. About twenty-five years after the invention of the art, Hebrew books were being printed, in 1475, in three different places in Italy. By the middle of the sixteenth century, the Bible, with all its rabbinic commentaries, the Babylonian Talmud, the Palestinian Talmud, and the other classic works, were already in print, to be republished time without number.

While . . . it became customary to solicit favorable statements by scholars for books, the primary purpose was to commend them to purchasers. No such institution as an official imprimatur ever came into being, and works of every conceivable standpoint continued to flow from the presses.

There was also no *Index* of forbidden books in Judaism. The authoritative Code, the *Shulḥan Arukh,* declares in one passage that it is forbidden on the Sabbath to read "secular poetry, fables, books dealing with wars and love poetry." The authoritative commentary of Moses Isserles declares that the objection does not apply to books on these subjects in Hebrew, and adds that the practice was to be lenient on the subject.

The one author specifically mentioned in this mild interdict was Immanuel of Rome (1268–1330), a physician, Bible commentator, poet, and wit who was an intimate friend of Dante. He wrote a Hebrew imitation of Dante's *Divine Comedy.* In the spirit of the Renaissance, he did not hesitate to use the language of Holy Writ, not merely for secular poetry, for which there was a respectable tradition in Judaism, but for work marked by dazzling combinations of phrases that can only be described as erotic and suggestive. Yet even his work was not completely forbidden. Of purely local importance was the action of nine Italian cities, in 1574, forbidding the reading of the critical historical work *Me'or Enayim* by Azariah dei Rossi.

Two other great issues rocked late medieval Jewry: the Messianic movement headed by the pseudo-Messiah Shabetai Z'vi (1626–76); and the controversy between Rabbi Jacob Emden (1697–1776) and Rabbi Jonathan Eybeschütz (1670–1764). In both instances, bans and counterbans were freely employed, but they no longer carried any genuine power to enforce obedience.

Seventeenth-century Holland witnessed the two most famous acts of excommunication in Jewish history. The Jewish community in Holland consisted largely of refugees from Spain and Portugal and of their descendants. Many of them had previously lived as nominal Christians or Marranos in the Iberian peninsula, secretly cherishing their ancestral faith and planning for the day when they might escape to a land where they could profess Judaism openly. Holland offered such a refuge, and here a deeply loyal, highly cultured Jewish community came into being in the sixteenth century. The process of return, however, was fraught with more than a little psychological anguish and spiritual peril.

One such instance is afforded by the tragic case of Uriel Acosta (1585–1640). Acosta was born in Portugal, the son of a Marrano family of means and distinction. Reared as a strict Catholic, he had been treasurer of an endowed church in Oporto. Between 1600 and 1615, he and his four brothers emigrated to Holland and formally accepted Judaism. His conception of his ancestral faith had been fashioned in Portugal, on the basis of his reading of the Old Testament. What he found in Amsterdam was, of course, not Biblical religion but normative Judaism, with a system of laws and observances for which he was not prepared and against which he carried over the negative attitude derived from Paulinian antinomianism. Acosta began by inveighing against Pharisaism, but his questing spirit did not stop there. He wrote a book denying the immortality of the soul and retribution, and was called to account by the rabbinical court. He was denounced to the city government and imprisoned, whereupon in 1663 he recanted, becoming, in his own phrase, "an ape among apes." His ideas continued to develop along heterodox lines and he became a deist, denying the divine character of the Bible and the binding character of ritual law. Finally, the major ban was invoked against him. Lacking the fortitude to persist in his position and isolated from his people, Acosta once again recanted and was subjected to public penance and ignominy. Deeply humiliated, he wrote a bitter apologia for his life, called *Exemplar Humanae Vitae,* and shot himself in 1640.

Of sterner mettle and of far greater consistency of outlook was Baruch (Benedict) Spinoza. Spinoza was born of Marrano ancestry in Amsterdam in 1632 and received an excellent traditional training in the Academy of his native city. In addition to a thorough grounding in Bible and Talmud, he was familiar with the rationalistic commentary of Abraham ibn Ezra, and with the works of Maimonides and of other Jewish philosophers. He went, however, further afield, and came under the influence of Descartes. His ideas on God and the nature of man went far beyond the confines of traditional religion, however liberally interpreted. His teacher, Rabbi Saul Morteira, is reported to have offered him a thousand florins if he would refrain from expressing his heretical views publicly. As late as 1654, Spinoza was called to the Torah at a synagogue service. Two years later, however, on July 27, 1656, he was publicly excommunicated. Actually, he had already taken up residence outside of the Jewish community before that date.

The basic motivation for the ban is revealed here, too, by the fact that the act was at once communicated to the Amsterdam magistracy. It was obvious that the Jewish community, living on sufferance even in free Holland, was fearful lest its status be jeopardized by harboring and tolerating a heretic whose views were regarded as subversive of all religion. That these fears were not groundless is clear from the fact that Spinoza's *Tractatus Theologico-Politicus* was published in 1670 anonymously, and was promptly proscribed by the synods of Doort and the States-General of Holland, Zealand, and West Friesland.

These dramatic instances of the use of the ban should not obscure the fact that they were highly exceptional. In the everyday business of conducting Jewish community life, the effective use of the ban by rabbinical courts was principally as a sanction for enforcing obedience to constituted authority, the discharge of communal obligations, and the maintenance of personal and group morality.

One other effort was made to invoke the ban in the area of faith, this time in the eighteenth century. A folk movement, pietistic in character, called Ḥasidism, had arisen in Eastern Europe, spreading through Poland, Rumania, and Russia. The Ḥasidic movement arose as the protest of the lower, uneducated groups against the scholars and leaders of Rabbinic Judaism, whose energies were concentrated on the abstruse and casuistic study of the Talmud, the Codes, and the commentaries. Ḥasidism emphasized the role of emotion and fervor in religion rather than intellectuality and learning, and declared that the joy of the commandments, rather than the duty of their performance, was the touchstone of the religious life. As the tide of Ḥasidism threatened to inundate all of East European Jewry, the great luminary Elijah, the Gaon of Vilna (1720–97), was prevailed upon to lend his august authority to a ban against the sect, which was issued in 1777 and repeated in

1781. As he himself anticipated, this *ḥerem* did not avail. Ultimately, the sect abated its hostility against Rabbinic Judaism,
and today the Ḥasidim and their "opponents," together with a me-
diating group, are within the household of Orthodox Judaism. . . .

When the Reform movement first began to appear in Central
Europe, some Orthodox rabbis in Central and Eastern Europe, ig-
noring the far-reaching changes which had taken place in their
traditional authority, sought to stem the tide by employing the time-
honored instrument of the ban against the innovators. It had proved
largely ineffective in the field of ideas even in the Middle Ages;
now, however, it was completely worthless. It served only to drive
deeper the wedge between the traditionalists and the non-tradi-
tionalists.

In Eastern Europe, the impact of modernism made itself felt
particularly in the area of education. The revival of Hebrew as a
modern language, to be read for secular purposes, and the study of
its grammar and of the Bible, became the hallmarks of the revolt
against the curriculum of the traditional *ḥeder* (elementary school)
and yeshivah (academy). These institutions limited all study to
the Pentateuch, the Talmud, and rabbinic literature. Essentially,
the new trends marked a return to the wider horizons of the Golden
Age in Spain, and what they lacked in depth they compensated for
by greater breadth. But the traditionalists and modernists were at
one in insisting that access to knowledge was the duty, not merely
the right, of every Jew. Ultimately, as is so often the case in intellectual history, it became clear that the differences between the
antagonists were not so irreconcilable as had first appeared. Except
for an extremist fringe, traditional circles made room for the modern types of study in their schools in Europe, Israel, and America. . . .

The long stream of Jewish historical experience through time
has many windings, with untold currents and cross-currents within
it. Yet the basic drift is unmistakable. By and large, the Jewish people has preferred to build its unity upon a common historical experience in the past and a sense of a common destiny in the future.
Its most creative periods, those of the Bible and the Talmud, were
precisely the eras of greatest variety of standpoint, marked by con-

troversy. Even in the medieval period, the age of the greatest homogeneity of outlook, the Jewish tradition refused to accept a creed as a test of loyalty and founded its unity upon a common way of life, which did not lack significant differences in the pattern of practice. Basic to this way of life was the study of Torah on every level, from the most elementary to the most advanced, an activity pursued by every segment of society. The centrality of Torah in the Jewish world view served to buttress both aspects of freedom of the spirit, the right of dissent and of free access to knowledge. The unique success of Judaism in preserving not only its identity but its vitality indicates that there are more potent factors making for group security than an artificially imposed conformity from without.

Moreover, in making action rather than belief the touchstone of loyalty, the Jewish tradition helped to preserve freedom, which is the necessary condition for creativity and growth for any society, and without which it cannot endure long in a dynamic world. Finally, Judaism demonstrated its attachment to justice, for only actions may be judged fairly by human agencies; beliefs and convictions are too subtle for any bar of judgment except that of God.

Judaism did not always adhere to the dictates of its innermost nature, particularly under the bitter lash of perils. But the sixteenth-century Rabbi Judah Loew of Prague spoke for the tradition when he declared: "Even if the words spoken are directed against one's faith and religion, do not tell a man not to speak and to suppress his words. Otherwise there will be no clarification in religious matters. On the contrary, one should tell a person to express whatever he wants . . . and he should not claim that he would have said more, had he been given the opportunity. . . . Thus my opinion is contrary to what some people think. They think that when it is forbidden to speak against religion, religion is strengthened. . . . But it is not so. The elimination of the opinions of those who are opposed to religion undermines religion and weakens it."

Thus for thirty centuries Jewish tradition and experience have exhibited the basic democratic faith that freedom of the human spirit, in all its manifestations, justifies man's audacious faith that "he is little less than God." The oldest living tradition of the Western world would counsel modern democracy that this freedom is to be guarded jealously and is to be limited only temporarily, when there is the gravest duress of a clear and present danger. It was this faith in freedom, characteristic of the Hebrew tradition, that John Milton expressed in his *Areopagitica:* "Let truth and falsehood grapple. Who has ever known truth to be worsted in a fair and full encounter?"

PART V

Life, Liberty, and the Pursuit of Happiness

Editor's Note

Religions, almost by definition, tend to teach that men will attain moral perfection and a high spiritual state by abstention from the normal pleasures of life and ordinary material satisfactions. A religious existence and an ascetic life are almost synonymous terms.

But Judaism, on the contrary, has never propagated self-mortification and extreme self-denial as religious ideals. In numerous ways Judaism has affirmed the belief, expressed simply and forcefully in Psalm 115, that

> The heavens are the heavens of the Lord,
> *But the earth He has given to man.*

Much of Judaism can be said to be a commentary on this text. It explains, for example, the strong prophetic element in Judaism and in Jewish experience; for if one believes that the earth is the stage on which man must play his role, he will be greatly concerned with what he finds on that stage and will feel compelled to re-arrange things—to be a *re-former*—so that they may more closely approximate his heart's desire.

When Thomas Jefferson wrote, in the Declaration of Independence, that men have "certain unalienable rights," and that among these are "life, liberty, and the pursuit of happiness," he was affirming and confirming a belief that has its roots deep in the Jewish tradition and Jewish consciousness.

The Good Life

MILTON R. KONVITZ

For thousands of years most religions and philosophies have idealized suffering and poverty. Self-denial, poverty, indifference to nature and the social environment have been guiding ideals. Society was to be organized into classes, and millions of people, especially women, were born into slavery, untouchability, and degradation, from which only death could free them. Life was short, brutish, painful and ugly; why, then, should it not be a great virtue to deny life? Since finite things present to the senses brought only pain and humiliation, was it not wisdom to deny their reality, to think of them as illusory, and to look elsewhere—to the infinite or the hereafter—for the true and the real? Only when man withdraws from a life of action, only when he ceases to be concerned with what is relative and longs for the Absolute does he establish some relation with Brahma or with the Absolute Reality or with God: the ideal was the solitary soul, without wife or children, without property, without personal attachments or private ambitions.

This ideal of renunciation of the world has been held not only by peoples of the Far East. Christianity, too, emphasized that happiness could be found only within the soul or in heaven. The good man was not to take thought of pleasure or food or drink or clothing: "Take no heed for the morrow, for the morrow shall take thought for the things of itself. . . . It is easier for the camel to go through the eye of the needle than for a rich man to enter into the kingdom of God. . . . Lay not up for yourselves treasures upon earth . . . but lay up for yourselves treasures in heaven. . . .

216

Blessed are they that mourn. . . . Blessed are the meek. . . ."
The Christian ideal was austerity and monasticism. Contempt for
the world, renunciation of the world was the rule to be followed
by the wise, pious Christian. The flesh was to be mortified. "Do not
love the world or the things in the world," wrote John in his first
Epistle. "If anyone loves the world, love for the Father is not in
him. For all that is in the world, the lust of the flesh, and the lust
of the eyes and the pride of life, is not of the Father but is of the
world."

Writing in the eleventh century, Peter Damiani said: "Therefore,
dearest brothers, seize the arms of all the virtues . . . and fight
not on behalf of fields or cities, nor for children or wives, but for
your souls which rise above every emotion of relationship." Especially, he said, should one fast, and learn to be content with but
few garments, and these should be mean ones; for why care for
and nourish the body? "Is it not a mass of putrefaction, is it not
worms, dust, and ashes?" A. L. Goodhart relates that some years
ago when he called on a distinguished Oxford philosopher, he
heard him say in a worried voice to one of his pupils: "I am not
at all happy about pleasure." Christianity and most other religions
of the world have never been happy about pleasure. What pleasure
can a man take in the body or in the world or in life when he is
taught that the body and the world and life are nothing but corruption and gateways to hell?

Traditionally the Christian view of life emphasized the duality
and enmity of matter and spirit, body and soul, the here and the
hereafter, and identified life and virtue only with spirit or soul. As
long as this ideology ruled the minds and lives of people, there was
no room for the emancipation of slaves and women, no chance for
the ideals of equality and freedom, no opportunity for universal
education. People did not see that they were in fact living not a
spiritual but a materialistic life, for they were subject to matter—
to plagues and epidemics, to hunger, to discomfort, to pain and
suffering, to cold and ignorance, to the brute and brutal facts of a
brutish existence.

It was only two hundred years ago that men, in revolt against the
ideal of other-worldliness, began to question the premises on which
the miserable state of this world was based. They began to speak

of happiness, and of its possibility and its virtue. Voltaire, Pope, Helvetius, Samuel Johnson, Montesquieu, and Swift—to name a few of the leaders—revolted against the religion of their day and said that it was a man's duty and right to plant his feet firmly on the solid ground, and that man should not aim at the blissful state of angels and ghosts. Let us, they said, look at the near rather than the distant, at the useful rather than the useless, the tangible rather than the speculative, the relative rather than the absolute, this life rather than the next, the earth rather than heaven. "Let us cultivate our garden," said Voltaire. These men and their followers—among them Thomas Paine and Thomas Jefferson—started a revolution in the minds of men. People began to assert the right to the pursuit of happiness. "I want to be happy!" was the first article of faith that they wrote into their religious, moral, and constitutional codes. When Jeremy Bentham proposed that a society should aim to achieve the greatest happiness of the greatest number, he shocked his contemporaries.

An order of society that supplies a man only what is absolutely necessary for his existence is a system fit for beasts, not men. "The superfluous," said Voltaire, "is very necessary."

The ideas of the eighteenth-century rationalists and humanists had in them an explosive quality, and they were let loose in full force in 1776 and in 1789. Things have not been the same since.

These ideas prepared people for a friendly reception of science and technology. Labor-saving devices were welcomed as blessings to mankind. Utilitarianism, democracy, and humanitarianism found in the new machines means for actualizing their ideals. The new gospel of happiness was spread, not by societies for the propagation of a religious faith, but by the steam engine and similar contraptions. The Industrial Revolution was hitched to the American and French revolutions to wipe out poverty, ignorance, slavery, class consciousness, and misery.

Today in one way or another all people everywhere seek to make the gospel of happiness their own. The leaders of people everywhere clamor for "know-how" and technical assistance. They are beginning to see that it is spiritual, and not materialistic, to transcend the matter-of-factness of matter, to conquer nature, to make matter the servant, rather than to let it be the master, of man's interests. They see that by conquering, assimilating, matter, man transcends himself as well as matter.

Not escape from life but involvement in and betterment of life has been the Jewish ideal. Insofar as the peoples of the world now accept this view, they accept at least part of the teaching that has come out of Zion. For Judaism has never preached that the body is evil, that the earth is profane, that poverty is a blessing, that scarcity is better than plenty. Judaism has always affirmed life; it has not attempted to meet life's problems by renunciation. Judaism has never put an abyss between good and evil, the saved and the damned, the selfish virtues and the social virtues, body and soul, earth and heaven, the city of God and the city of man, revelation and intelligence, time and eternity, man and woman, religion and culture.

Let us take, first of all, the plain fact of the length of life. In the whole of the Hebrew Scriptures we find a persistent emphasis on the desirability of a long span of years. Abraham "died in a good old age, an old man, and full of years"; David "died in a good old age." I cannot recall a single Biblical hero who died young. It is not until one turns to the New Testament that one reads of an important person dying young, for Jesus was only in his early thirties when he died; and he was the first Jew whose death was given great significance. In the Hebrew Scriptures the emphasis is always on life, not death. The essence of this Biblical affirmation of life is stated in Psalm 115: "May the Lord increase you, you and your children. . . . The heavens are the heavens of the Lord; but the earth has He given to the children of men. The dead praise not the Lord, neither any that go down into silence; but we [the living] will bless the Lord from this time forth and for evermore."

"And you shall love the Lord your God with all your heart, and with all your soul, and with all your might." The Rabbis say that "with all your heart" means "with all your desires, including the *yetzer hara*" (the "evil inclination"). The Jew must make even his passions and ambitions means which contribute to the service of God. The "evil inclination" is not to be rooted out; it is to be made the servant rather than the master of the whole person. Martin Buber has commented on this attitude of Judaism in the following beautiful passage:

> One should, and one must, truly live with all, but one should live with all in holiness, one should hallow all that one does in one's natural life. No renunciation is commanded. One eats in holiness, tastes the food in holiness, and the table becomes an altar. One works in holiness, and he raises up the sparks which hide themselves in all tools. One walks in holiness across the fields, and the soft songs of all herbs, which they voice to God, enter into the song of our soul. One drinks in holiness to each other and with one's companions, and it is as if they read together in the Torah. One dances the roundelay in holiness, and a brightness shines over the gathering. A husband is united with his wife in holiness, and the *Shekhinah* rests over them.[1]

Speaking of the I-Thou relationship, and obviously echoing Buber, Paul Tillich, in his *Biblical Religion and the Search for Ultimate Reality*, has written: "Through stars and stones, trees and animals, growth and catastrophe; through tools and houses, sculpture and melody, poems and prose, laws and customs; through parts of the body and functions of the mind, family relations and voluntary communities, historical leaders and national elevation; through time and space, being and non-being, ideals and virtues, the holy can encounter us."

Cherbonnier's reinterpretation of the doctrine of sin in the light of Biblical teaching leads him to affirm the goodness of creation, and the radical freedom of man, and to call the doctrine of original sin and belief in predestination Christian misconceptions. In reach-

---

[1] Rabbi Naḥman b. Samuel said: "But is the *yetzer hara,* the evil inclination, 'very good' (Genesis 1:31)? Yes, for if it were not for the evil inclination, man would not build a house, or take a wife, or beget a child, or engage in business, as it says, 'All labor and skillful work comes of a man's rivalry with his neighbor'" (*Genesis Rabba* 9:7). The Mishnah states that: Man is bound to bless [God] for the evil even as he blesses [God] for the good, for it is written, *And you shall love the Lord your God with all your heart and with all your soul and with all your might.* With all your heart—with both your impulses, your good impulse and your evil impulse (*Berakhot* 9:5).

ing this conclusion he finds it necessary to challenge Augustine, Aquinas, Luther, and Calvin, in the name of and for the sake of Biblical religion. Insofar as Christianity manifests, he says, "a negative view of the world in general and a repressive attitude toward the flesh in particular," it has been infiltrated by "pagan value judgments." When Thomas Aquinas placed matter on the lower half of his scale of realities, says Cherbonnier, he bifurcated human nature into mind and matter, and thereby sacrificed the Bible to Aristotle. The God of the Bible wants, he says, "not the annihilation of unruly passions, but their conversion, for the greatest power of evil may also be transformed into even greater forces for good." The Bible does not demand *"disuse* but redemption"; and he speaks of the "joyous affirmation of the goodness of the present life" as an essential Biblical outlook.

Cherbonnier, Paul Tillich, and Reinhold Niebuhr, as they try to rediscover Biblical religion, come much closer to what Jews recognize as authentic Judaism than to what Christians recognize as authentic Christianity.

Throughout the Hebrew Scriptures "freedom from want" is held up as a divine ideal for man. This is the picture of the Promised Land that the Lord presented to the vision of the Israelites: "a good land, a land of brooks of water, of fountains and depths, springing forth in valleys and hills; a land of wheat and barley, and vines and fig-trees and pomegranates; a land of olive trees and honey; a land wherein you shall eat bread without scarceness, you shall not lack anything in it. . . . And you shall eat and be satisfied" (Deuteronomy 8:7–10). Job, we must remember, the man of Uz who "was blameless and upright, one who feared God, and turned away from evil," had a wife and ten children, seven thousand sheep, three thousand camels, five hundred yoke of oxen, five hundred she-asses, and very many servants. He was a rich man, yet there is no intimation that Job could enter heaven any more than could one of his three thousand camels go through the eye of a needle.

The genius of Judaism has been, not to reduce the sacred to the profane or secular, but to raise the secular to the sacred, the material to the spiritual. Just as Judaism raised the seventh day to the Sabbath, so it seeks to raise every weekday to the Sabbath; so that in the end there would be, not the distinction between the sacred and the secular, but between the sacred and the sacred—*bein kodesh le-kodesh.*

Certainly the Bible does not fail to remind us that man does not live by bread alone. There is always the danger that "when you have eaten and are satisfied, and have built goodly houses, and dwelt therein; and when your herds and your flocks multiply, and your silver and your gold is multiplied, and all that you have is multiplied; then your heart is lifted up, and you forget the Lord your God . . ." (Deuteronomy 8:11–14). But this risk does not entail a degradation of the values that inhere in the pursuit of happiness. "Materialism" is not necessarily atheistic or pagan, no more than "spiritualism" is necessarily godly. A healthy man may waste his life in futile objectives, but his health is not, therefore, at fault or an evil, and we do not blame a man's legs because he uses them to take him to places that are unworthy of him.

The ideal of Judaism is a kingdom of heaven on this earth in which every man will live under his own vine and his own fig tree, enjoying God's bounty free from want and fear, in a social order based on justice, freedom, and righteousness: an order of society which combines God's bounty with God's law—man walking in the way which the Lord commanded him, and God prolonging man's days, and blessing the fruit of his body and the fruit of his land, the nation constituting a kingdom of priests, a holy people.

"The ant is knowing and wise, but he doesn't know enough to take a vacation," Clarence Day once said. "The worshipper of energy is too physically energetic to see that he cannot explore certain higher fields until he is still." But Judaism, with its institution of the Sabbath day and the Sabbatical and Jubilee years, and with the emphasis that it places on study as a form of worship, has taught the Jew to avoid imitating the ant. The Jew has been taught to stand still. But a vacation is important only if one customarily works, and to stand still is important only if one ordinarily is in motion. Judaism tries to be true to a healthy rhythm of life—work and rest, affirmation and denial; the whole human being must be outer-oriented and inner-oriented, committed and suspended, involved and withdrawn. Judaism teaches self-denial for the sake of greater affirmation. Asceticism is, thus, not stagnation but the Sabbatical pause, the Sabbatical rest, the Sabbatical withdrawal.

This asceticism in Judaism reflects that awareness that life is reproduced and perpetuated only with pain ("in pain you shall bring forth children"); that sustenance from the earth can be won only by toil; that the days are "swifter than a runner" and go by "like skiffs of reed, like an eagle swooping on the prey," and that man is, after a day and a night, turned back to dust. Much of the Bible, and of Jewish literature generally, reads like an ode on melancholy that exposes and sighs over the vanities of life, the endless heartache, and the feeling that the man of wisdom will ever be "half in love with easeful Death."

Maimonides conveys the sense of the classic Jewish approach that sees the need for balance:

> Perhaps a man may say: "Since passion and glory and similar things are evil qualities to cultivate and lead to man's departure from this world, I will separate myself from them in greater measure," and [he] will seek their contrary extreme to such an extent that he will not eat meat, nor drink wine, not marry, nor dwell in a decent home, nor wear comely apparel, but will clothe himself in sackcloth and coarse wool like idolator's priests. This, too, is the wrong way, not to be followed. Whoever persists in such a course is termed a sinner (*Hilkhot De'ot* 3, 1).

And Judah Halevi in *The Kuzari* reflected the same harmonious combination of the sacred and the everyday, which is Judaism's definition of human happiness:

> The divine law imposes no asceticism on us. It rather desires that we should keep the equipoise, and grant every mental and physical faculty its due, as much as it can bear, without overburdening one faculty at the expense of another. Prolonged fasting is no act of piety for a weak person—who . . . is not greedy. . . . Neither is diminution of wealth an act of piety, if it [wealth] is gained in a lawful way, and if its acquisition does not interfere with study and good works, especially for him who has a household and children. He may spend part of it in alms-giving, which would not be displeasing to God; . . . Our law, as a whole, is divided between

fear, love, and joy, by each of which one can approach God. Your contribution on a fast day does nothing the nearer to God than your joy on the Sabbath and holy days, if it is the outcome of a devout heart. . . . You thank Him in mind and words and if your joy lead you so far as to sing and dance, it becomes worship and a bond of union between you and the Divine Influence.[2]

[2] Judah Halevi, *The Kuzari* (New York: Schocken Books, 1964).

The Right of Privacy

NORMAN LAMM

At the very beginning of the Biblical account of man, we are informed of the association of the feeling of shame, the reaction to the violation of privacy, with man's moral nature. Adam and Eve ate of the fruit of the tree of knowledge of good and evil, after which "the eyes of them both were opened, and they knew that they were naked; and they sewed fig leaves together, and made themselves girdles" (Genesis 3:7). The need to decide between good and evil gave man self-consciousness and a sense of privacy which was affronted by his exposure. The respect for physical privacy is again alluded to in the story of Noah and Ham.[1] The abhorrence of exposure of what should remain concealed is evidenced in the Biblical idiom for illicit sexual relations: *giluy arayot,* literally, "the uncovering of nakedness." Rabbinic tradition discovers the virtue of privacy in the blessing uttered over Israel by the Gentile prophet Balaam, "And Balaam lifted up his eyes and he saw Israel dwelling tribe by tribe" (Numbers 24:2). What is it that he saw that so inspired him? The tradition answers: he saw that the entrances to their tents were not directly opposite each other, so that one family did not visually intrude upon the privacy of the other.[2]

Even more to the point is a specific commandment in the Bible

---

[1] Genesis 9:20–27. See Milton R. Konvitz, "Privacy and the Law: A Philosophical Prelude," *Law and Contemporary Problems,* vol. 31, no. 272 (1966).

[2] *Bava Batra* 60a. Thus, the end of the verse, "and the spirit of God came up on *him*" (Numbers 24:2) refers to Israel, not Balaam.

which declares a man's home a sanctuary which may not be violated by his creditors: "When you do lend your neighbor any manner of loan, you shall not go into his house to fetch his pledge. You shall stand without, and the man to whom you did lend shall bring forth the pledge without to you." [3] "You shall stand without" is the Biblical way of saying, "do not violate the privacy of his home." [4]

The Halakhah differentiates between two forms of invasion of privacy: intrusion and disclosure. [5]

The first case of intrusion concerns the Biblical law just mentioned, that of the creditor desiring to seize collateral from the home of the debtor. The Talmud records two opinions as to whether this prohibition applies only to ordinary citizens acting on their own or also to the representative of the court; it decides that even the court officer may not invade the premises of the borrower to seize collateral. [6] The courts are thus not permitted any invasion of privacy denied to private citizens; the only difference between them is that only by court order may the borrower's possessions be seized forcibly outside his home. [7]

---

[3] Deuteronomy 24:10–11. However, this holds true only for civil cases. In criminal cases there is no sanctuary; thus Exodus 21:14.

[4] "For by entering [by force] and viewing the interior of his home, he will feel humbled and shamed" (R. Joseph Bekhor Shor, commentary to this verse).

[5] These are two of the four categories within the concept of privacy as analyzed by Dean Prosser, "Privacy," *California Law Review,* vol. 48, no. 383 (1960).

[6] *Bava Metz'ia* 113a, b; Maimonides, "Laws of Creditor and Debtor," 3:4, in *The Book of Civil Laws* (Book 13 of *The Code of Maimonides*), trans. Jacob Rabinowitz (New Haven: Yale University Press, 1949). This prohibition applies to the case of a lender who failed to secure collateral at the time of the loan but seeks it as security later, before the time of the loan has expired. When, however, the money owed is not a loan but wages or rent, entry is permitted (Baraita in *Bava Metz'ia* 115a, as against *Sifre;* Maimonides, *op. cit.,* 3:7). The latter category includes the return of stolen articles (commentaries to *Shulḥan Arukh, Hoshen Mishpat* 97:14). The difference is this: a loan was meant to be spent by the borrower, and hence forced entry to secure collateral is an illegitimate invasion of the privacy of his home. But articles that are stolen or wages that are withheld do not belong even temporarily to the one now in possession, and entry and seizure in such a case, therefore, outweigh the concern and respect for privacy.

[7] Maimonides, *op. cit.,* 3:4.

The most important contribution of the Halakhah to privacy law, however, is not the problem of physical trespass but that of a more subtle form of intrusion: visual penetration of a neighbor's domain. This is termed *hezek re'iyah,* "visual damage," incurred by viewing or prying.

That such non-physical invasion of privacy is proscribed we learn from the Mishnah, which prohibits installing windows facing the courtyard of a neighbor.[8] The question, however, is whether this prohibition is more than a moral exhortation and is legally actionable. Two contradictory opinions are recorded in the Talmud. One maintains that *hezek re'iyah* is not considered a substantial damage. The other opinion is that visual surveillance is considered a substantial damage. It is this second opinion, that holds visual penetration of privacy as tortious as actual trespass, that is accepted by the Halakhah as authoritative.[9] Basically, this means that even in advance of actual privacy invasion, action may be brought to prevent such invasion from occurring. Thus, if two partners jointly acquired or inherited a tract of land, and decide to divide it and thus dissolve their partnership, each has the right to demand that the other share the expense of erecting a fence at least four cubits high, i.e., high enough to prevent each from spying on the other and thus violating his privacy.

Interestingly, the Halakhah does not simply permit one of the erstwhile partners to build a fence for his own protection, and then require his neighbor to share the expense because he, too, is a beneficiary, but demands the construction of the wall, so that each prevents *himself* from spying on his neighbor. Thus, Rabbi Naḥman said in the name of Samuel that if a man's roof adjoins his neighbor's courtyard—i.e., the two properties are on an incline, so that the roof of one is approximately on a level with the yard of the other—the owner of the roof must construct a parapet four cubits high (*Bava Batra,* 6b). Hence, without the obstruction between them, the owner of the roof could see all that occurs in his neigh-

---

[8] *Bava Batra* 3:7. The Mishnah speaks only of the courtyard of partners, but its intention is to prohibit opening windows into *even* a partner's courtyard, and certainly into that of a stranger; so in the Gemara, *Bava Batra* 59b.

[9] *Bava Batra* 2b, 3a, *et passim.* Maimonides, "Laws of Neighbors," 2:14, in *The Book of Civil Laws, op. cit.*

bor's courtyard and thus deprive him of his privacy. This viewing is regarded as substantial a damage as if he had physically invaded his premises. Therefore, it is incumbent upon the owner of the roof to construct the wall and bear all the expenses, and so avoid damaging his neighbor by denying him his privacy. It is thus not the potentially aggrieved party who would benefit from the wall, who has to pay for it, but the one who threatens to perform the intrusion.

Thus, the Halakhah insists upon the responsibility of each individual not to put himself into a position where he can pry into his neighbor's personal domain, and this responsibility can be enforced by the courts.[10]

It should be added that while the discussion in the Talmud concerns visual access to a neighbor's domain, the principle may be expanded to cover eavesdropping as well. Thus, one prominent medieval commentator, Rabbi Menahem Meiri,[11] decides that while we must guard against *hezek re'iyah,* visual surveillance, we need not worry about *hezek shemiyah,* aural surveillance. Hence, the wall the partners can demand of each other must be solid enough to prevent over*looking* each other's affairs, but need not be so strong that it prevents over*hearing* each other's conversations. But the reason Meiri gives is not that eavesdropping is any less heinous than spying as an invasion of privacy, but that people normally speak softly when they think they will be overheard. Where this reason does not apply, such as in wiretapping or electronic "bugging," then obviously *hezek shemiyah* is as serious a violation and a damage as *hezek re'iyah.* All forms of surveillance—natural, mechanical, and electronic, visual or aural—are included in the Halakhah's strictures on *hezek re'iyah.*

The gravity of non-physical intrusion is only partially evident from the fact that the Halakhah regards it as tortious, in that prevention of such intrusion is legally enforceable. More important is the fact that such surveillance is considered not only as a violation of civil law, but, what is more serious in the context of Judaism, it is considered as *issur,* a religious transgression. Visual or

[10] On the moral background of this law as an outgrowth of the rabbinic concept of the sanctity of the individual, see Samuel Belkin, *In His Image, op. cit.,* pp. 126–128.

[11] *Bet Ha-behira* to *Bava Batra,* ed. Sofer, p. 6.

aural invasion of privacy is primarily a moral offense, and the civil law and its requirements of monetary compensation are derivative from it.

The Halakhah considers intrusion and disclosure as two separate instances of the violation of privacy. Interestingly, the Biblical commandment concerning forced entry by the creditor into the debtor's home to secure a pledge—a case of intrusion—is immediately preceded by the commandment to remember the plague that afflicted Miriam who was punished for speaking ill of Moses to their brother, Aaron—a case of disclosure.

The law against disclosure is usually divided into three separate parts: slander (i.e., false and defamatory information), talebearing, and gossip. The last term refers to the circulation of reports which are true; the "evil tongue" is nevertheless forbidden because it is socially disruptive, since it puts the victim in an unfavorable light. However, in its broadest and deepest sense disclosure is not so much an act of instigating social disharmony as the invasion of personal privacy. Thus, the Mishnah teaches that, after a trial presided over by more than one judge, each of them is forbidden to reveal which of the judges voted for acquittal and which for conviction (*Sanhedrin* 3:7). The Talmud relates that the famed teacher, R. Ami, expelled a scholar from the academy because he revealed a report he had heard confidentially twenty-two years earlier. Information received confidentally may not be disclosed even if it is not damaging or derogatory as long as the original source has not expressly released it (*Yoma* 4b). Even if the original source subsequently revealed this information publicly, the first listener is still bound by the confidence until released—a remarkable example of the ethics of information. Unauthorized disclosure, whether the original information was received by complete consent or by illegal intrusion, whether ethically or unethically, remains prohibited by the Halakhah.

We have discussed so far two kinds of intrusion, visual and aural. But the "Peeping Tom" and the eavesdropper are not the only kinds of practitioners of this "dirty business," as Justice Oliver Wendell Holmes called it, with which the Halakhah is concerned. Another form of invasion of privacy is reading another's mail. Letters sent through the mail are protected by the Fourth Amendment, according to a Supreme Court ruling in 1877. In Halakhah, a law protecting the privacy of mail was enacted a thousand years earlier, by Rabbi Gershom, "The Light of the Exile"; the decree might well be older than that. . . .

But the Halakhah comprises more than civil law; it includes a moral code. And its legal limit on voyeurism is matched by its ethical curb on the citizen's potential exhibitionism. It regards privacy not only as a *legal right* but also as a *moral duty*. We are bidden to protect our own privacy from the eyes and ears of our neighbors. The Talmud (*Yoma* 86b) quotes Rav as pointing out a contradiction between two verses. David says, "Happy is he whose transgression is concealed, whose sin is covered," [12] whereas Solomon states "He that covers his transgressions shall not prosper" (Proverbs 28:13). One of the two solutions offered by the Talmud is that David discourages the revealing of sins not publicly known; here the atonement should be pursued privately only between man and God. Solomon, however, encourages the public acknowledgment of sins that are already widely known. What is not known to others I may not reveal about myself. A man has the moral duty to protect his own privacy, to safeguard his own intimacies from the inquisitiveness of his neighbors (*Yoma* 86b). The Talmud records an opinion that once a man has confessed his sins to God on the Day of Atonement, he should not confess them again on the following Yom Kippur—and applies to one who does so the verse, "as a dog that returns to his vomit" (Proverbs 26:11). These are strong words, and they reveal to us the contempt of the Rabbis of the Talmud for the indignity inherent in the loss of privacy—even one's own privacy, and even before his Maker only.

That it should be necessary to exhort people to protect their own privacy may be surprising, yet never was it more relevant than today. For as contemporary society becomes more complex, as people become more intertwined with each other, and with increasing urbanization, privacy becomes more and more precarious.[13]

---

[12] Psalms 32:1, according to rabbinic interpretation.

[13] Perceptive observers have seen in the characteristic impersonality and anonymity of apartment house dwellers in our great urban centers a vital defense mechanism against the encroachments on their privacy. See, for instance, the discussion in Harvey Cox, *The Secular City* (New York: Macmillan, 1965), pp. 29–46.

Electronic intrusion has now been developed to a high art and constitutes a grave menace to society. Technologically, man now has the ability to destroy privacy completely and forever.

The Halakhah's legal and moral doctrines of privacy can be shown to be based upon certain fundamental theological considerations. The Bible teaches that man was created in the image of God (Genesis 1:26, 27), by which is meant that the creature in some measure resembles the Creator, and which implies the need by man to imitate God: "as He is compassionate and gracious, so must you be compassionate and gracious." [14] Both the Jewish philosophic and mystical traditions speak of two aspects of the divinity: one is the relatedness of God to man, His knowability; and second, His essence and absoluteness in which He infinitely transcends and remains forever unknown to man. These two areas of "light" and "darkness," the two zones of disclosure and concealment, of revelation and mystery, coexist within God without contradiction. The unknowable Essence or Absoluteness is the inner boundary of God's privacy. In His resistance to and limitation of man's theological curiosity and metaphysical incursions, God asserts His exclusive divine privacy. Even Moses may not gaze upon the Source of the voice that addresses him (Exodus 3:6). The Mishnah declares that one who is disrespectful of the divine dignity by seeking to penetrate into divine mysteries beyond his ken, it were better had he not been born.[15] "Dignity" (*kavod*) is thus a correlative of privacy.

But if this is true of the Creator, it is true of His human creature as well. As God reveals and conceals, so man discloses and withholds. As concealment is an aspect of divine privacy, so is it the expression of human privacy: the desire to remain in part unknown, an enigma, a mystery. Judaism does not absolutize privacy; taken to an extreme, it results in the total isolation of man and transforms him into a closed monad. Without any communication

[14] *Mekhilta to Beshalaḥ,* 3; *Shabbat* 133b. Most of Jewish ethics is predicated on this idea of *imitatio Dei.*
[15] *Ḥagigah* 2:1, according to Jerusalem Talmud (*Ḥagigah* 2:1–8b), which considers the two items in the Mishnah, theosophic overreaching and offense against the dignity of God, as one.

or self-revelation, he must suffer veritable social, psychological, and spiritual death. But the other extreme, unlimited communication and the end of privacy, leaves man totally depleted of self—again death.[16] For both God and man, therefore, in that they share the character of personality, there must be a tension and balance between privacy and communication, between concealment and disclosure, between self-revelation and self-restraint.

This sense of privacy may be referred to as the ethical quality of *tzeni'ut,* which usually is translated as "modesty." But *tzeni'ut* means more than modesty in the moral or sexual sense. By extension, the term comprehends respect for the inviolability of the personal privacy of an individual, whether oneself or another, which is another way of saying respect for the integrity of the self. Man is fundamentally inscrutable in that, according to Judaism, he is more than just *natura* but also *persona:* he is possessed of a mysterious, vital center of personality which transcends the sum of his natural physiological and psychological properties. But not only *is* he mysterious, he also *should* be, and the extension of this free and undetermined center of personality constitutes the boundaries of his selfhood and hence his privacy. It is this privacy which we are called upon to acknowledge as an act of *tzeni'ut.*

"It has been told you, O man," says the prophet Micah (Micah 6:8) "what is good and what the Lord does require of you: only to do justly, and to love mercy, and to walk *humbly* with your God." The Hebrew for "walk humbly" is *hatznei'a lekhet,* the first word deriving from the same root as *tzeni'ut.* Man must tread the path of reverent privacy "with your God"—for it is from Him that we learn this form of conduct and whom we imitate in practicing it.

So sacred is this center of privacy in man that even God does not permit Himself to tamper with it; that is the meaning of the freedom of the will, the moral autonomy of man. And that is why

[16] The same holds true, *mutatis mutandis,* of our conception of God. Denial of either of these poles results in a denial of personality to God. Belief in an uncommunicative God is, as Schopenhauer put it, a polite atheism. And the assertion of a God who has dispossessed Himself of His transcendence, who has exhausted and dissipated His privacy, is a rather impolite atheism—the atheology of those who proclaim that His life has come to an end.

God's "hardening of Pharaoh's heart" (Exodus 4:21, 7:3, *et passim*) became an ethical and philosophical problem for rabbinic exegesis of the Bible. Certainly, then, it is criminal for man to attempt thought-control, even if benevolent.

Indeed, it is personality itself which is at stake. *Persona* meant, originally, a mask. We change masks as we react to different stimuli and encounters, and the sum of these poses and postures is our personality. The *persona* or mask is the mode of our self-disclosure, the highly meaningful medium of our communication to the outside world. Without it we are both naked and dumb. In the absence of privacy we are stripped of such masks, and this process leads, ultimately, to the extinction of personality.

In sum, we have seen that Judaism asserts that man, in imitation of God, possesses an inviolate core of personality, and that privacy constitutes the protection of this personality core from the inroads of society and the state. The earliest legislation on privacy goes back to the Bible. In the Halakhah, which underwent its most creative development between 2000 and 1500 years ago, the right of privacy was legally secured in a manner more advanced than that which prevailed until very recently in contemporary constitutional law; non-physical intrusion was considered the equivalent of actual trespass. The Halakhah's concept of privacy covers both intrusion and disclosure, visual and aural surveillance, tampering with the mails, and, to the largest extent, the use of the polygraph. It is undestood that in all these instances, the right to privacy is not absolute; for instance, such rights would automatically be suspended where there exists a grave threat to national security. But privacy is more than a legal right; there is also a moral duty for man to protect his own privacy.

There Shall Be No Poor

RICHARD G. HIRSCH

When you have eaten your fill and have built fine houses to live in, and your herds and flocks have multiplied, and your silver and gold have increased, and everything you own has prospered, beware lest your heart grow haughty and you forget the Lord your God, who freed you from the land of Egypt, the house of bondage . . . and you say to yourselves, "My own power and the might of my hand have won this wealth for me." Remember that it is the Lord your God who gives you power to get wealth . . . (Deuteronomy 8:12–18).

Wealth can be a blessing; it can also be a curse. Wealth can be a creative influence; it can also be a destructive force. The history of nations and the biographies of men attest to both. The attitude toward material possessions and the use to which they are put determine whether wealth is good or evil. A society can be judged by the way it treats its disadvantaged. The affluent society that tolerates poverty misuses and abuses its wealth.

Judaism has something to contribute here, not in offering pat solutions to complex problems, but in projecting a system of values directing man to serve God by serving his fellow man. These values, an integral part of Jewish life through the ages, evolved under varying social, economic and political conditions. Judaism does not advocate any economic or political ideology, but it is an advocate of a specific response to life's problems. It speaks to our day in the voice of the past, but in a language which is universal in time and place.

234

"The earth is the Lord's and the fulness thereof; the world and they that dwell therein" (Psalms 24:1). No man and no society are "self-made," declares Judaism. Both the resources of nature and the ingenuity of man are divinely bestowed. Every society builds upon the creativity of previous generations. The wealth of today is the fruition of the accumulated efforts of countless individuals. "Yours, O Lord, is the greatness and the power and the glory and the victory and the majesty, for all that is in the heaven and earth is Yours; . . . Both riches and honor come of You" (I Chronicles 29:11, 12). Since wealth comes from God, it must be used to fulfill God's purposes. "Give unto Him what is His, for you and yours are His" (*Avot* 3:8).

Judaism rejects the concept of "survival of the fittest." Man is not engaged in a struggle for survival against his fellow man. Our sages formulated a philosophy which could be called "survival of the sustainers," succinctly expressed in the saying, "Not only does man sustain man, but all nature does so. The stars and the planets, and even the angels sustain each other." [1]

Human life is sacred, so sacred that each person is considered as important as the entire universe. . . . These two emphases—all wealth comes from God; human life is sacred—became the foundation stones for Jewish treatment of the less privileged members of society. Biblical ethics are permeated with laws assuring protection of the poor. These laws relate largely to agriculture, having been developed in an agrarian society. The Bible prescribes that when a field is harvested, the corners are to be left uncut; the field is not to be gone over to pick up the produce which has been overlooked. The gleanings of orchard and vineyard are to be left untouched. All that remains is for the poor, the stranger, the fatherless, and the widow.

Every seventh year was a Sabbatical year, during which the land was to lie fallow, and that which grew of itself belonged to all, "that the poor of your people may eat" (Exodus 23:11). All debts were to be cancelled (Deuteronomy 15:1, 2). Every fiftieth year was a Jubilee year, during which all lands were to be returned to the families to whom they were originally allocated.

[1] *Tikkune Zohar*, 122, T.43 quoted in Louis I. Newman, *The Talmudic Anthology* (New York: Behrman House, 1945), p. 60.

The law of the fiftieth year was too complex to be observed and fell into disuse early in Jewish history, but the spirit behind the law was preserved. Our forefathers realized that an unrestricted pursuit of individual economic interest would result in massive concentrations of wealth for the few, and oppressive poverty for the many. They sanctioned competition, but they rejected "rugged individualism." The intent of the law was to restore the balance, to give those who had fallen an opportunity to lift themselves up again. Land was not the permanent possession of any man. "The land shall not be sold in perpetuity; for the land is Mine; for you are strangers and settlers with Me" (Leviticus 25:23).

Jewish ethics sanction the institution of private property. "Let the property of your fellow man be as dear to you as your own" (*Avot* 2:17). However, Jewish tradition never asserted that property rights take precedence over human rights. Nor did Judaism accept the Puritan emphasis on the acquisition of property and worldly goods as a sign of virtue. On the contrary, for the Jew, human rights have priority over property rights. The tithe prescribed in Biblical law was not a voluntary contribution, but an obligation imposed on all, in order that "the stranger and the fatherless and the widow shall come and shall eat and be satisfied" (Deuteronomy 14:29). Any man who was hungry could help himself to the produce in a field at any time, without asking permission of the owner, so long as he did not carry away food to be sold for his own profit (*Ibid.* 23:25, 26).

No man had absolute control over his own property. The person who cut down young trees in his own garden was to be punished, because he had wasted that which did not belong to him. The man who owned a well in a field had to make the water available to the inhabitants of a nearby community. Such requirements evolved out of the fundamental Jewish conviction that material possessions are gifts from God, to be used for the benefit of all men. Wealth, properly used, is a means of preserving and sanctifying life. Improperly used, it is a profanation of the name of God and of the being created in His image.

The poor man, as much the child of God as the rich man, has been disinherited from his Father's wealth. He has been deprived of his patrimony, of his share of the earth's bounty. Unlike some religions, Judaism does not encourage the ascetic life. Poverty is not the way to piety. Scarcity does not lead to sanctity. The search for holiness is not made easier by insufficiency of basic necessities. Without the necessary material goods of life, man cannot attain the personal growth and satisfaction essential to human fulfillment. "All the days of the poor are evil" (Proverbs 15:15).

The common saying "Poverty is no disgrace" may offer consolation—to those who are well off. As a statement of morality, an ethical imperative, it would have much to commend it—"Poverty *should* be no disgrace." As a statement of fact, however, it is totally inaccurate. Poverty *is* a disgrace—for those who are poor. Poverty is destructive to the human personality. "The ruin of the poor is their poverty" (Proverbs 10:15).

The sages taught that poverty was the worst catastrophe that could happen to a person. "If all afflictions in the world were assembled on one side of the scale and poverty on the other, poverty would outweigh them all" (*Exodus Rabba, Mishpatim* 31:14). The poor man is the lowliest of God's creatures, not only in the eyes of others, but in his own eyes as well. "When a man needs his fellow men, his face changes color from embarrassment" (*Berakhot* 6).

Humiliation leads to dehumanization. The poor man is not a complete man. "Even his life is not a life," said one teacher (*Betzah* 32). The afflictions of poverty are so severe that Jewish tradition makes the seemingly radical statement that "the poor man is considered as a dead man" (*Nedarim* 64b). Poverty is spiritual death. The poor man looks at life from another perspective. Like a space ship circling the moon, he sees only the dark side, while others may see only the bright side. As one sage declared, "The world is darkened for him who has to look forward to the table of others [for sustenance]" (*Betzah* 32). The poor man's outlook is altered. "The sufferings of poverty cause a person to disregard his own sense [of right] and that of his Maker" (*Erubin* 41).

The poor are different. The world asks, "Why are their values not like ours? Why are they so dirty or so sullen or so promiscuous or so indolent or so passive or so uncouth or so uneducated or so unambitious? Why are they not like the rest of us?" The Bible accurately states the consequences of difference: "All the brethren of the poor do hate him; how much more do his friends go far from him" (Proverbs 19:7).

Why are the poor different? Because they are poor. Because material circumstances shape human values. Judaism has never drawn a dichotomy between body and soul as other religions and systems of thought have done. Those who believe that the body is the repository of all evil and the soul of all good cannot see the dependent relationship between spirit and matter. But the Jew knows that a man's values are in great measure shaped by his life experiences. "Where there is no sustenance, there is no learning," declared a teacher of the first century (*Avot* 3:21). Unless a person has the proper environment, learning cannot take place. To feed the mind, the body must also be fed. To nourish the spiritual life, the physical life must be nourished. A Ḥasidic rabbi of the nineteenth century expressed it well when he said, "Take care of your own soul and of another man's body, not of your own body and of another man's soul." [2]

Poverty does not inevitably lead to ruination, just as wealth does not inevitably lead to well-being. But for the most part, the poor man in an affluent society lives in another world. Psychologically, it is a world of humiliation, a world which fails to see that a man cannot pull himself up by his own bootstraps if he has no boots and no straps. The world which callously calls upon the poor to disregard material circumstances asks a man to be more than a man and makes him feel less than a man.

To aid the poor is to "rehumanize" children of God. It is to restore rights which have been denied. The elimination of poverty is not an option, a voluntary decision benevolently made by an individual and a society. It is not charity as thought of in our day. The word "charity" originally derived from the Latin *caritas,* meaning "love," has come to have the connotation of a contribution motivated by sentiment. In our day, a person gives charity not because he feels an obligation, but because he is moved by good will or social pressure. Charity is presumed to come from the goodness of the heart. In the Jewish concept of charity, the heart

[2] Sayings of the Kotzker, quoted in Lewis Browne, *The Wisdom of Israel* (New York: Random House, 1945), p. 588.

plays an indispensable role. But assistance to the poor is more than love. There is no word in the Hebrew vocabulary for "charity" in the modern sense. The word used is *Tzedakah,* which literally means "righteousness." *Tzedakah* is not an act of condescension from one person to another who is in a lower social and economic status. *Tzedakah* is the fulfillment of an obligation to a fellow-being with equal status before God. It is an act of justice to which the recipient is entitled by right, by virtue of being human.

Because God is a God of justice, the beings created in His image must treat each other with justice. Injustice to man is desecration of God. "Whoso mocks the poor blasphemes his Maker" (Proverbs 17:5). On the other hand, "He that is gracious unto the poor lends unto the Lord" (Proverbs 19:17). Jewish tradition went so far as to state that "the poor man does more for the rich man than the rich man for the poor man" (*Ruth Rabba* 5:9; also 19). The poor give the righteous an opportunity to perform good deeds, to sanctify the name of God (*Leviticus Rabba* 34). Refusal to give charity is considered by Jewish tradition to be idolatry (*Tosephta Pe'ah* 4:19).

Only the concept of obligatory justice would have impelled Isaiah to thunder his criticism against the leaders of his time:

> It is you that have eaten up the vineyard;
> The spoil of the poor is in your houses;
> What mean you that you crush My people,
> And grind the face of the poor?
> Says the Lord, the God of Hosts.
>
> (Isaiah 3:14, 15)

Throughout the Bible, injustice is constantly identified as failure to relieve the plight of the poor:

> Wash you, make you clean,
> Put away the evil of your doings
> From before My eyes,
> Cease to do evil;
> Learn to do well;

Seek justice, relieve the oppressed,
Judge the fatherless, plead for the widow.
(Isaiah 1:16, 17).

"Cursed be he that perverts the justice due to the stranger, fatherless, and widow" (Deuteronomy 27:19).

Another frequently used Hebrew term for charity is *mitzvah,* which literally means "a divine commandment." Alleviating poverty is a *duty,* stemming not alone from a man's inner sense of love and justice. It is an obligation ordained by God. Our ancient commentators taught that Abraham was more righteous than Job. According to rabbinical tradition, when great suffering befell Job, he attempted to justify himself by saying, "Lord of the world, have I not fed the hungry and clothed the naked?" God conceded that Job had done much for the poor, but he had always waited until the poor came to him, whereas Abraham had gone out of his way to search out the poor. He not only brought them into his home and gave them better treatment than that to which they were accustomed, but he set up inns on the highway so that the poor and the wayfarer would have access to food and drink in time of need (*Avot de Rabbi Nathan* VII, 17a, b). To fulfill a "divine commandment" is not to watch others struggle through the game of life, but to be an active participant, to take initiative, to seek out those who require assistance, even if they do not request it. True charity is to "run after the poor" (*Shabbat* 104a).

Acts of charity are the means, but not the end. The end is to restore the image of the divine to every man. The essential ingredient is human dignity. The manner in which assistance is given is even more important than the assistance itself. The sensitivities of recipients are to be safeguarded at all times. "Better no giving at all than the giving that humiliates" (*Ḥagigah* 5a). Every effort was made throughout Jewish history to dispense charity anonymously. "He who gives charity in secret is even greater than Moses" (*Bava Batra* 8). In the Temple at Jerusalem, there was a "chamber of secrecy" where the pious placed their gifts and the poor drew for their needs—all in anonymity (*Shekalim* V, 6). The same practice was observed until modern times. In every synagogue, a charity box with a sign *Matan Beseter* (an anonymous gift) was placed.

The Talmud recounts the lengths to which great scholars went in order to protect the self-respect of the poor. A rabbi and his wife, accustomed to giving alms while recipients were asleep, were surprised when one poor man awoke. In order not to offend him, they jumped into a still heated oven, risking serious burns (*Ketuvot* 67b). Another rabbi would tie money in a scarf and when he was near a poor man, would fling the gift over his back, so that the poor man would not have to suffer the embarrassment of facing his benefactor (*Bava Batra* 10b).

Tradition stressed human dignity in declaring that even greater than *Tzedakah* was *gemilut Ḥasadim* or "acts of loving-kindness." "Loving-kindness" entails personal devotion, service, and empathy. "He who gives a coin to a poor man is rewarded with *six* blessings, but he who encourages him with kind words is rewarded with *eleven* blessings" (*ibid.* 9b). The Midrash interprets Isaiah 58:10: "If you draw out your soul to the hungry and satisfy the afflicted soul," to mean "If you have nothing to give a poor man, console him with kind words. Say to him, 'My soul goes out to you, for I have nothing to give you.' " *Gemilut Ḥasadim* was considered superior to almsgiving in three ways: "No gift is needed for it but the giving of oneself; it may be done to the rich as well as to the poor; and it may be done not only to the living, but to the dead" (*Sukkah* 49b).

In connection with funeral practices, an early custom had evolved to bring the deceased into the house of mourning in expensive caskets of silver and gold, whereas the poor were placed in wicker baskets made of willow. The Talmud decreed that everyone should be placed in wicker baskets "in order to give honor to the poor" (*Ta'anit* 27). To this day, Jewish tradition frowns on lavish funeral practices, because "the grave levels all," and the primary emphasis of Jewish burial rituals is to ascribe equal worth to all men.

Jewish tradition wrestled with the problem of how to preserve the dignity of recipients of charity. People vary in their needs. Some have higher standards of living or higher values than others.

If human dignity is the objective of charity, then will not some persons have to be given more than others—and wherein is the justification of such preferential treatment? The Rabbis based much of their discussion on the commandment, "If there be among you a needy man . . . you shall surely open your hand unto him, and shall surely lend him *sufficient for his need in that which he is wanting*" (Deuteronomy 15:7, 8). The phrase "that which he is wanting" was interpreted to mean that if a man did not have sufficient funds to marry, the community should assume responsibility for providing him with the means to support a wife (*Sifre Deuteronomy, Re'eh* 116). The phrase "sufficient for his need" became the peg on which to hang the concept that a man was entitled to be sustained at a standard of living to which he had become accustomed. One Babylonian rabbi sent his son to give a contribution to a poor man on the eve of Yom Kippur. The boy returned to his father and complained that the poor man was not in need since the boy had seen him imbibing precious old wine. Over the protests of his son, the rabbi doubled his normal contribution, on the grounds that the gentleman had been used to a better life than the rabbi had originally thought (*Ketuvot* 67b). The Talmud recounts how the great scholar Hillel, learning of a man of high station who had become poor, gave the man a horse to ride, and when he could not find a servant to run before him, as was the man's custom, Hillel himself ran before him for three miles (*ibid.*).

These incidents, similar to numerous others recounted in rabbinic literature, were undoubtedly exceptional, but they do serve to transmit the underlying spirit of Judaism. Throughout the Bible, the poor man is not called "poor," but "your brother," thus establishing a relationship of equality between poor and rich. The recipient of charity is a "brother" to the donor. The poor man's needs are spiritual as well as material. Because the poor man lacks material blessings, he is likely to feel inferior. Therefore, treat him like a brother. Spare his feelings. Zealously guard his dignity. Respect from others is poverty's most helpful counterbalance. Self-respect is poverty's most effective antidote.

The verse from Deuteronomy quoted above also became the basis for a highly developed system of loans. "You shall surely open your hand . . . and shall surely *lend* him." Throughout rabbinic literature, a loan is emphasized as the finest form of charity. "Greater is he who lends than he who gives, and greater still is he who lends, and with the loan, helps the poor man to help himself" (*Shabbat* 63a). Almost a millennium after this was written, the medieval philosopher Maimonides defined the various types of charity and categorized them into his famous "eight degrees of charity," the highest of which is to enable a man to become self-supporting. Until modern times, every Jewish community had a *Gemilut Ḥesed* society, whose primary purpose was to grant loans to the needy without interest or security.

Our tradition recognized that an outright gift, no matter how well-intentioned, still might instill feelings of inferiority in the receiver. However, a loan is a transaction between equals. Sometimes the loan was a delicate fiction. In those instances where a poor man is too proud to accept a gift, one should offer a loan, even though one might never expect to have the money returned, and then subsequently the loan could be considered as a gift (*Ketuvot* 67b).

The Rabbis dealt in a direct fashion with those who in our day would be called "freeloaders," the poor who exploit the system of welfare. They looked askance at beggars who went from door to door. Instead, the Rabbis favored the "silent sufferers." A man should exert every effort not to be dependent on others. "Skin the carcass of a dead beast in the market place, receive your wages, and do not say, 'I am a great man, and it is beneath my dignity to do such work'" (*Bava Batra* 110a). A person should esteem his independence more than his dignity, even more than his piety (*Berakhot* 8a). Nevertheless, even though the Rabbis maintained a severely critical attitude toward imposters, they were generally liberal in offering them assistance. They realized that even those who made false claims served some purpose. "Be good to imposters. Without them our stinginess would lack its chief excuse" (*Ketuvot* 68a). No man is beyond human concern. No man is beyond repentance and rehabilitation. No man is so bad that the community may be absolved of responsibility. The response to those who would eliminate or diminish welfare programs because of occasional abuse is to be found in the midrashic comment on a

Biblical verse: "If your brother be waxen poor, you shall not suffer him to fall. He is like a load resting on a wall; one man can then hold it, and prevent it from falling, but if it has once fallen to the ground, five men cannot raise it up again. And even if you have strengthened him four or five times, you must (if he needs it) strengthen him yet again" (*Sifra* 109b). The task is never finished until "your brother" is raised from a condition of dependence to the state of self-reliance and self-support.

In the Talmudic period, it became clear that the amelioration of poverty was too complex a task to be left to individuals or to privately organized charity groups. Personal charity alone was too haphazard and spasmodic. The Jewish community supplemented the obligations of private charity with an elaborate system of public welfare—the first in history. Jewish tradition has always been nurtured in and through the community. Hillel's famous "Do not separate yourself from the community" sets the pattern (*Avot* 2:5). Even Jewish worship is a communal experience. Almost all the prayers, including those recited by an individual in private, are written in the plural. So it was only natural for the Jew to look upon poverty as the responsibility of the entire community. The existence of the poor was an indication of social inequity which had to be rectified by society itself. The system of social welfare became the means of restoring integrity to the community.

The practices and theories of Jewish philanthropy anticipated many of the most advanced concepts of modern social work and became the basis for the excellent programs and high standards of American Jewish welfare agencies. The organization of Jewish welfare evolved through the centuries, but the principles were established during the second century.

Every Jewish community had two basic funds. The first was called *Kuppah,* or "box," and served the local poor only. The indigent were given funds to supply their needs for an entire week. The second fund was called *Tamḥui,* or "bowl," and consisted of a daily distribution of food to both itinerants and residents. The administrators of the funds were selected from among the leaders of the community and were expected to be persons of the highest integrity. The *Kuppah* was administered by three trustees who acted as a *Bet Din,* or "court," to determine the merit of applicants and the amounts to be given. The fund was operated under the strictest regulations. Collections were never made by one person, but always by two, in order to avoid suspicion. The collectors were authorized to tax all members of the community according to their capacity to pay, and if necessary, to seize property until the assessed amount was forthcoming. All members of the community were expected to contribute, even those who were themselves recipients of charity—testimony to the principle that no man was free of responsibility for the welfare of all. "He who does not accept his part of the sufferings of the community will not share in the comfort it will receive" (*Ta'anit* 11a).

By the Middle Ages, community responsibility encompassed every aspect of life, as the community fulfilled obligations which its separate members were incapable of fulfilling. The Jewish community regulated market prices so that the poor could purchase food and other basic commodities at cost. Wayfarers were issued tickets, good for meals and lodging at homes of members of the community who took turns in offering hospitality. Both these practices anticipated "meal-tickets" and modern food-stamp plans. Jewish communities even established "rent control," directing that the poor be given housing at rates they could afford. In Lithuania, local trade barriers were relaxed for poor refugees. When poor young immigrants came from other places, the community would support them until they completed their education or learned a trade.

The organization of charity became so specialized that numerous societies were established in order to keep pace with all the needs. Each of the following functions was assumed by a different society in behalf of the community at large: visiting the sick, burying the dead, furnishing doweries to poor girls, providing clothing, ransoming captives, supplying maternity needs, and providing special foods and ritual objects for holidays. A host of other miscellaneous societies were formed to cover every possible area of need. In addition, there were public inns for travellers, homes for the aged, orphanages, and free medical care. As early as the eleventh century, a *Hekdesh* or "hospital" was established by the Jewish community of Cologne—primarily for the poor. Many of the activities centered in and around the synagogue, which in some communities was the only building of a public character.

Caring for the poor became a matter of civic pride. Scholars were warned not to live in a community which did not have an adequate system of public welfare (*Sanhedrin* 17b). A community was judged by the extent to which it became the agent for guaranteeing just treatment to all its inhabitants.

PART VI

The Earth Is the Lord's

Editor's Note

In the immediately preceding section we found an emphasis on the belief that while "the heavens are the heavens of the Lord," "the earth He has given to man." Chapter 1 of Genesis relates that as soon as man was created, God gave him the mandate to "subdue the earth" and to have "dominion" over "every living thing that moves upon the earth."

But there always exists the danger that, as Lord Acton noted, "power tends to corrupt and absolute power corrupts absolutely." Man's "dominion" over the earth and over other living things cannot therefore be absolute. There must be a countervailing principle, and Judaism finds it in the belief that the earth, being the creation of God, belongs to the Creator and not to man.

> The earth is the Lord's and the fulness thereof,
>> The world and those who dwell therein;
> for He has founded it upon the seas,
>> and established it upon the rivers.
>
> (Psalms 24:1–2)

Man's "dominion" is therefore only a stewardship, a tenancy. Ownership is retained by the Creator, to whom the tenant is accountable. "Behold, to the Lord your God belong heaven and the heaven of heavens, the earth with all that is in it" (Deuteronomy 10:14). Man is constantly reminded that although he has been given the power and the right to till the earth and keep it (Genesis 2:15), what the earth brings forth is ultimately dependent upon God; and so it is that God has the right to prohibit His tenants from destroying or abusing what has been placed in their charge.

When man abuses the earth, as we know to our sorrow, punishment comes in due course. There have been other floods since Noah, and they came in many forms: the flood of polluted air; the flood of garbage and litter; the flood of polluted water in seas, rivers, and lakes; the flood of polluted landscapes. It is only in a manner of speaking that it is God who visits the iniquity of the fathers upon the third and fourth generations (Deuteronomy 5:9); for as we look upon the world, we see that it is the natural order of events that the fathers visit their iniquities upon their children to the third and fourth generation. As long as men and women marry and have families and live in social groups, what a man does to and in his environment affects all who share it and all who will come after him, for good or ill, for life or death. "Behold, I set before you this day a blessing and a curse: the blessing, if you obey the commandments of the Lord your God . . . and the curse, if you do not obey the commandments . . ." (Deuteronomy 11:26).

Man has his rights, but so have his children and his grandchildren; and so have the forests and waterways, the prairies and hillsides; the birds, fishes, and beasts in their infinite variety—whooping cranes, polar bears, redwood trees, and whales. We must be ever mindful of what God answered Job out of the whirlwind:

> Behold, Behemoth [the hippopotamus],
> *which I made as I made you;* . . .
> He is the first of the works of God;
> *let him who made him bring near his sword!*
>   (Job 40:15, 19)

Man as Temporary Tenant

SAMUEL BELKIN

When a Jew fufills the positive and negative commandments of the Torah he is, in a sense, making the following pronouncement: "I am not the complete master of the world or of myself; I do not possess unlimited authority over the things of creation, and, therefore, whatever I do or fail to do with the things of creation depends on the will of the owner of creation—God Himself." This attitude, translated into action through the fulfillment of *mitzvot*, reaffirms a man's belief in the governorship of God and in the sanctity of creation. It indirectly brings him to a state of holiness.

This concept is not limited to material things only, as is indicated by the comment of the sages on the verses, "But the soul that does aught with a high hand . . . the same blasphemes the Lord . . . because he has despised the word of the Lord" (Numbers 15:30–1). The Torah does not here specify the particular offence committed. One sage, Rabbi Ishmael, interprets the verse as applying to one who worships idols, but another, Rabbi Meir, says that the law is aimed at a person who is learned in the Torah but refuses to pass his knowledge on to others (*Sifre,* Numbers 112). Such a man is arrogant, he despises God, rules Rabbi Meir. Rabbi Meir's intent is obvious. He teaches us that even one's knowledge must not be considered a personal acquisition and attainment. It, too, is but a gift of God; to refuse to share knowledge with others is, in effect, to despise God to whom all things belong. Philo Judaeus, who often records in his writings ancient Jewish traditions, similarly recognized in this Biblical verse

251

prohibitions against arrogance—which leads to self-deification—
and against selfishness, which leads man to regard all his en-
dowments, intellectual and physical, as personal possessions, instead of as temporary gifts from God.

This concept is the key to a true understanding of the laws
which require man to pronounce a benediction before using the
fruits of creation. The Talmud states:

> Man is forbidden to enjoy anything without pronouncing a benedic-
> tion, and whoever enjoys anything in this world without a bene-
> diction commits a trespass against sacred things [and] . . . is as
> guilty as if he would have derived enjoyment from the things
> dedicated to Heaven, for it is written, "The earth is the Lord's
> and the fulness thereof" (Psalms 24:1). Rabbi Levi raised the
> question: In one place it is written, "The earth is the Lord's and
> the fulness thereof," and in another place it is written, "The
> heavens are the heavens of the Lord but the earth He has given
> to the children of man" (Psalms 115:16). The answer is that the
> former verse applies to the status prior to man's pronouncing the
> benediction; the latter verse applies after one pronounces the
> benediction (*Berakhot* 35a, b).

In other words, for the sages all of creation is as sacred as are
things dedicated to heaven, for creation belongs to the Creator.
A man must, therefore, before enjoying those things which are
permitted him for his sustenance and pleasure, pronounce a
berakhah (blessing) over them to acknowledge that all things
belong to God and are used only by His permission.

This concept is further developed by Philo. More than any other
Jewish philosopher, he voiced the view that creation belongs to
the Creator and that whatever dominion man enjoys over creation
is limited and dependent upon the will of God. In fact, the greater
part of his treatise *De Cherubim* is devoted to this concept. In it he
writes:

> No mortal can in solid reality be lord of anything. . . . God alone
> can rightly claim that all things are His possession. . . . To this
> sovereignty of the Absolutely Existent, the oracle is a true witness
> in these words: "And the land is not to be sold in perpetuity, for

all land is Mine, because you are strangers and sojourners before Me" (Leviticus 25:23). A clear proof surely that in possession all things are God's, and only as a loan do they belong to created beings. . . . Yet he who has the use does not thereby become possessor, because there is one Lord and Master of all who will most rightly say, "All the land is Mine," (which is the same as "All creation is Mine"), "but you are strangers and sojourners before me." [1]

Hence, the Torah regulates what we may enjoy and what we may not, and under what conditions enjoyment of the things of this world becomes permissible to us. Commenting on the same verse quoted by Philo in the above passage, the sages taught:

"And the land shall not be sold in perpetuity"—absolutely, ir-revocably—"for unto Me is the land"—look not sorely upon it, "for you are strangers and sojourners." Do not make yourself prime, for thus it is written, "For we are strangers before you and sojourners like all our forefathers" (I Chronicles 29:15). And so does David declare, "For I am a stranger with you, a sojourner like all my forefathers" (Psalms 39:13)—to teach us that it is sufficient for a slave that he is like his master; "when it will be mine, it is yours" (*Sifra* on Leviticus 25:23).

Both sage and philosopher recognized man's temporal tenancy of God's creation.

How pervasive this concept is in Judaism is indicated by the reasons given by the sages for the law of the Sabbatical year. The Torah states: "Six years shall you sow your field, and six years shall you prune your vineyard, and gather in the produce thereof. But on the seventh year shall be a Sabbath of solemn rest, a Sabbath unto the Lord, you shall neither sow your field, nor prune your vineyard" (Leviticus 25:3–4).

The sages refuse to assign purely economic, agricultural or social motives to this law. Rabbi Abahu answers the question: What is the reason for the law of the Sabbatical year? "The Holy One blessed be He said to the children of Israel: 'Sow for six years and leave the land at rest for the seventh year, so that you may

[1] Philo, vol. 2, Loeb Classical Library, pp. 83, 119.

know that the land is Mine!' " (*Sanhedrin* 39a). Indeed, a careful reading of Leviticus 25 clearly reveals that underlying all the laws of the Sabbatical year and the Jubilee year (during which property is returned to its original owners and slaves are emancipated) is the concept that creation belongs to the Creator, and that man cannot acquire permanent possession of either property or of human beings.

Rooted in this religious concept, such laws must of themselves insure justice for the poor, the slave, the vendor and the community in its totality. But that is not their chief end. Animating these laws is the religious belief that man does not acquire permanent possession of anything in this world because the world is the property of God. Hence by observing such laws, the Jew, by means of his actions, reaffirms one of the root principles of the Torah.

Philo, too, understood this true significance of the laws pertaining to the Jubilee. He writes: "Do not pay the price of complete ownership, but only for a fixed number of years and a lower limit than fifty. For the sale should represent not real property, but fruits . . . [because] the whole country is called God's property and it is against piety to have anything that is God's property registered under other masters." [2]

The Mishnah likewise expresses the idea that all things of creation are the possession of God: "Rabbi Elazar of Bertotha said: Give unto Him from His own, for you and what you possess are His. This was also expressed by David: 'For all things come of You and of Your own have we given You' " (I Chronicles 29:14) (*Avot* 3:7).

This concept is applied to human life too. Reflected in many Midrashic passages, it finds particular and striking application in the story of Rabbi Meir's personal tragedy. Two of Rabbi Meir's sons died on the Sabbath while he was occupied in the Beth Midrash with his studies. When the sage returned to his home Saturday evening, his wife Beruria, who was famous for her scholarship and piety, did not inform him immediately of the great tragedy. Instead she asked a pointed question: "Yesterday, a man gave me a deposit: now he demands that I return the deposit. Should I do so?" Rabbi Meir answered: "What an amazing ques-

[2] *Op. cit.,* vol. 7, p. 113.

tion. Surely the depositary must return the deposit." But when Rabbi Meir saw his two sons lying dead before him, he became hysterical. Beruria then consoled him: "Did you not say that the depositary must return the deposit to its owner? Well, God gave and God took away. May the name of the Lord be blessed." [3]

Apparently it was standard practice to console mourners by reminding them that life is merely a divine deposit held by man and that God, the Depositor, can at any time demand the return of His deposit. For Philo, the most consoling thought possible in cases of tragedy is that life is merely a loan given us by God. In the same vein he records the Jewish tradition that one must not overindulge in grief. To mourn more than necessary for the dead is a sign of selfishness, an indirect declaration that human life, particularly that of close relatives, is one's own possession, and not the property of God.

How fundamental this attitude is toward divine ownership in Judaism is further demonstrated by some features of the Temple service. Tradition records that every day a special chapter of the Psalms was recited in the Temple. The great sage, Rabbi Akiba, reported that on the first day of the week the Levites read, as Jews do today in their prayers, Psalm 24: "The earth is the Lord's and the fulness thereof." This was chosen because it declares that "God acquired possession of the world and apportioned it to mankind, but He always remains the Master of His world" (*Rosh Hashanah* 31a).

Nor is the concept that creation belongs to the Creator an isolated principle in Judaism. Indeed, the entire structure of Judaism rests on it. The moral code of the Torah, its ritual pronouncements and man's obligation to observe the laws whether he knows the reason for them or not, all stem from this principle. By means of revelation, God has instructed man concerning what he is permitted to do or prohibited from doing with His creation. If man were to possess irrevocably the things of creation, were his life his own possession, then his own reason could dictate to him how to use it; he would even be permitted to abuse it. Since, however, creation belongs to God, He alone dictates the terms of man's tenancy in this world. . . .

[3] Midrash *Mishle* 31 on *Eshet Ḥaytl*.

Judaism lays particular stress on *mitzvot ma'asiot,* or religious action. Though we are forbidden to worship created things, the use of created things for the worship of the Uncreated One is regarded as the noblest form of worshipping God. This view lies behind Maimonides' declaration that man must fulfill those *mitzvot* for whose observance no rational explanation is apparent:

> For even wood, stone, dust and ashes become sanctified by mere word of mouth, as soon as the name of the Master of the universe is pronounced upon them, and if one treats them as things common, he commits a trespass against God; and even if it were done inadvertently, it requires expiation. How much more is it with the commandments inscribed for us by the Holy One, blessed be He, that a man should not spurn them because he cannot divine the reason for their observance (*Hilkhot Meilah* 8:7).

Maimonides declares that when one dedicates a material object to the Temple it becomes holy and the property of the Most High; because we pronounce the name of its real Master over it, and since we proclaim that all things of creation belong to the Creator, no formal act of transaction is required to make an object Temple property. How much more sacred then, argues Maimonides, are the laws themselves over which the Master Himself pronounced His Name.

It would appear then that the purposes of sacrifices and monetary donations to the Temple were to actively proclaim, by the act of surrendering something to Him, that all things are God's. The sacrifice was merely a sign of gratitude to God, who permitted man to use all things of creation which, in themselves, as the property of God, are vested with a certain degree of sanctity. The same principle applies to the laws of tithes, first fruits, the tithe of the poor, and the many other ordinances concerning gifts to the priests, the Levites and the poor. Man was not permitted to enjoy any of his fruits until he had separated the necessary tithes. Every acquisition, even that which a man acquires by the labor of his own hands, is holy and must be redeemed; a share must be set aside for a godly purpose, to support the priest, the Levite and the poor man. By such acts man proclaims that the land and the produce thereof are not, in any sense of the word, his own. They belong primarily to God, who demands a share of them not because He has need of them but to ensure that the needy and those who are dedicated to His service may also benefit from His possessions.

Philo, speaking about the bringing of the *bikkurim,* the first fruits, follows a parallel line of thought:

> It is no doubt just and a religious duty that those who have received freely a generous supply of substance so necessary and wholesome and also palatable in the highest degree should not enjoy or taste it at all until they have brought a sample offering to the Donor, not indeed as a gift, for all things and possessions and gifts are His, but as a token, however small, by which they show a disposition of thankfulness and loyalty to Him who, while He needs no favors, sends the showers of His favors in never failing constancy.[4]

Similarly, the Midrash states that it is the custom of the world that when a man turns over his estate to be managed by a supervisor, he gives the supervisor a half, a third or a fourth of his produce, but God, who supervises all of creation and causes the earth to produce, demands only one tenth of the produce.

Commenting on the Biblical verse, "You shall surely tithe all the increase of your seed, which is brought forth in the field every year" (Deuteronomy 14:22), the Midrash declares:

> The Holy One blessed be He said: I have commanded you to honor Me, but not from your own. Give Me what is already Mine, honor the Lord from the substance with which He graced you. . . . If you should say that I asked you to give of your own, see what I have written for you: "When a bullock, or a sheep or a goat, is brought forth" (Leviticus 22:27). When shall you offer a sacrifice? When I will first give you (*Pesikhta Rabbiti* 26:2).

This Midrash, enunciating the meaningfulness of the ancient sacrifices and tithes, repeats the basic principle in the religious philosophy of Judaism: man must at all times recognize that the things of this world belong to God. When a man offers a sacrifice

[4] Philo, *De Specialibus Legibus,* vol. 8, p. 180.

or gives his tithes in full awareness that he is returning to God that which belongs to Him, he performs a genuinely religious act. If, however, he believes that he gives his own, his act is, in a sense, sacrilegious. The offering of an individual who regards creation as man's permanent possession and not as a mere deposit from the Almighty is in effect a form of bribery and an act of superstition.

Similarly, commenting on the stress given to the pronoun "Me" in such phrases as "take Me a heifer" (Genesis 15:9), and "that they take for Me an offering" (Exodus 22:2), Philo remarks:

> It says to us: You have no good thing of your own, but whatever you think you have, Another has provided. Hence, we infer that all things are the possession of Him who gives, [and] not of creation, the beggar, who ever holds out her hands to take. . . . Even if you take, take not for yourself, but count that which is given a loan or trust and render it back to Him who entrusted and leased it to you, thus, as is fit and just, requiting good will with good will. . . . And so in the text He says, "Take you 'for Me,' " thus giving to Himself what is His due and bidding us not to adulterate the gifts but guard them in a way worthy of the Giver. . . . He "takes" in order to train us to piety and to implant a zeal of holiness, and to spur us to His service.[5]

Understanding this concept of God's ownership gives us an insight into the Jewish conception of man's obligations in this world.

5 Vol. 4, pp. 103–23.

Do Not Destroy!

SAMSON RAPHAEL HIRSCH *

When you besiege a city many days to bring it into your power by making war against it, you shall not destroy the trees thereof by swinging an axe against them; for from them may you eat but not destroy them, for the tree of the field is man's life . . . (Deuteronomy 20: 19–20).

The Oral Law explains this as follows: Although you are laying siege to a city, and you are thus about to do harm to man and therefore certainly need not respect the property belonging to man's personality more than man himself, nevertheless you may not destroy this property without reason or purpose. If you have to cut down trees be wise in your choice: do not cut down fruit-trees for the purpose of wood when you have timber-trees at your disposal, as the trunk of the former has a higher purpose to fulfil, while the latter is given to you for the purpose of wood. And from this you should hear the warning of God: "Do not destroy anything," and apply it to your whole life and to every being which is subordinated to you, from the earth which bears them all up to the garment which you have already transformed into your own cover.

"Do not destroy anything!" is the first and most general call of God, which comes to you, man, when you realize yourself as master of the earth. All round you you perceive earth and plant and animal; yea, earth and plant and animal already bearing

* Translation of I. Grunfeld.

your imprint from your technical human skill; they have been transformed by your human hand for your human purposes, into dwelling-place and clothing, food and instruments, and you have taken them as your property. Thus do you stand in the midst of your earthly kingdom, and they are all servants of your might. If you should now raise your hand to play a childish game, to indulge in senseless rage, wishing to destroy that which you should only use, wishing to exterminate that which you should only exploit; if you should regard the beings beneath you as being objects without rights, not perceiving God who created them, and therefore desire that they feel the might of your presumptuous mood, instead of using them only as the means of wise human activity—then God's call proclaims to you, "Do not destroy anything! Be a man! Only if you use the things around you for wise human purposes, sanctified by the word of My teaching, only then are you a man and have the right over them which I have given you as man. However, if you destroy, if you ruin—at that moment you are not a man, you are an animal, and have no right to the things around you. I lent them to you for wise use only; never forget that I lent them to you. As soon as you use them unwisely, be it the greatest or the smallest, you commit treachery against My world, you commit murder and robbery against My property, you sin against Me!" This is what God calls unto you, and with this call does He represent the greatest and the smallest against you and grants the smallest as also the greatest a right against your presumptuousness.

Therefore the sages say: he who in his wrath tears his clothes, breaks his vessels to pieces, or scatters his money, should in your eyes be as one who has worshipped idols. For this is the way of passion—today it says: "Do this," tomorrow it says: "Do that," until it also leads him who has become its slave to idol-worship. And, in truth, there is no one nearer to idolatry than he who can disregard the fact that things are the creatures and property of God, and who presumes also to have the right, since he has the might, to destroy them according to his presumptuous will. Yes, he is already serving the most powerful idol in his inward self— anger, pride, above all his ego, which in its passion regards itself as the master of things.

1. The first prohibition of creation is thus not to destroy anything large or small if it may still be of use, from the fruit-tree which may still refresh the latest grandchild with its fruits down to the smallest piece of thread—in short, anything which can still serve some purpose or other.

2. But destruction does not only mean making something purposelessly unfit for its designated use; it also means trying to attain a certain aim by making use of more things and more valuable things when fewer and less valuable ones would suffice; or if this aim is not really worth the means expended for its attainment. Examples of such destruction are: cutting down a fruit-tree in order to use its wood for planks, when there are enough other trees available; cutting down a fruit-tree merely in order to prettify the garden; similarly, burning a tool for the sake of the heat, or kindling something which is still fit for other purposes, for the sake of light; burning more than is necessary; wearing down something more than is necessary, and similar actions; consuming more than is necessary, and similar deeds.

3. On the other hand, if the destruction is necessary for a higher and more worthy aim, then it ceases to be destruction and itself becomes wise creating. Examples include: cutting down a fruit-tree which is doing harm to other more valuable plants; or the trunk of which, when used for wood, is worth more than the fruits which are to be expected. Therefore, also, a withering fruit-tree, which bears very little fruit, is to be regarded as a tree for wood. Burning a vessel when there is a scarcity of wood in order to protect one's weakened self from catching cold, cutting down fruit-trees in order to use the space for house-building, and similar practices. . . .

There is a lesser degree of destruction which must nevertheless be avoided; wasting—i.e., discarding the means at your disposal in a manner whereby the desired aim does not correspond to the extent of the divestment. This is an offence of lesser degree, as the things in themselves are not destroyed but are passed to others for their use: nevertheless, it is still destruction, since for you they have been destroyed. Every small or large possession which God grants you brings you the duty to make proper use of it, which also includes parting with it for wise purposes. But if you part with it for unwise purposes, or if for purposes which are praiseworthy in themselves but in greater quantity than suits the purposes, then you destroy your means unnecessarily; for they cannot then be used by you more wisely or for other wise purposes. Since every means at your disposal imposes upon you the duty of using it wisely, wasting can in no way be justified by the argument that others to whom your means have now passed will use them wisely—a possible event which in any case you can never guarantee.

What comes far nearer to destruction, however, is avarice. This means regarding things as though possession was their whole purpose, and not just means; and using them for unwise purposes which are not demanded by duty. For that which the miser keeps buried and unused in his coffers is destroyed for all mankind, at least for the duration of his life. Add to this that the guilt of our unfulfilled duty rests upon every unused bit of property.

This, then, is the first law which is opposed to your presumption against things: Regard things as God's property and use them with a sense of responsibility for wise human purposes. Destroy nothing! Waste nothing! Do not be avaricious! Be wisely economical with all the means which God grants you, and transform them into as large a sum of fulfilments of duty as possible. . . .

> If you see the ass of him that hates you lying under its burden, you shall forbear to pass by him; you shall surely release it with him (Exodus 23:5).

> You shall not muzzle the ox when he treads out the corn (Deuteronomy 25:4).

There are probably no creatures that require more the protective divine word against the presumption of man than the animals, which, like man, have sensations and instincts, but whose body and powers are nevertheless subservient to man. In relation to them man so easily forgets that injured animal muscle twitches just like human muscle, that the maltreated nerves of an animal sicken like human nerves, that the animal being is just as sensitive to cuts, blows and beating as man. Thus man becomes the torturer of the animal soul, which has been subjected to him only for the fulfilment of humane and wise purposes; sometimes out of self-interest, at other times in order to satisfy a whim, sometimes out of thoughtlessness—yes, even for the satisfaction of crude satanic desire.

Here you are faced with God's teaching, which obliges you not only to refrain from inflicting unnecessary pain on any animal, but to help and, when you can, to lessen the pain whenever you see an animal suffering even through no fault of yours. As the Oral Law explains, to release an animal of its burden is not only a duty of love towards the distressed owner of the animal, but above all a duty towards the suffering animal. Even without the owner, or where the latter has himself caused the collapse of the animal by overburdening, yes, even if he wants to sit down passively by the side of the fallen animal, you have an obligation towards the animal to release it of its burden. The law also sets a suffering animal on the same level as a non-seriously ill person as far as work on Sabbath and Festivals is concerned, in that certain types of work are permitted in order to help them. It goes without saying, therefore, that you may hurt the animal and strain its powers only for sensible human purposes, and then only in the least painful manner. You may not burden the animal which serves you with excessive loads, you may not make it work constantly without rest, or deny it the fodder it needs.

Above all, those to whom the care of young minds has been entrusted, see to it that they respect both the smallest and the largest animals as beings which, like man, have been summoned to the joy of life and have been granted sensitivity. And do not forget that the boy who, in crude joy, finds delight in the convulsions of an injured beetle or the anxiety of a suffering animal will soon also be dumb towards human pain.

In the Second Law,[1] God demands, as its right, that the animal which works in the cultivation of the field may be allowed to eat of the fruits undisturbed, at the time when it is working there. This applies before the fruits have reached their last ripening in your possession . . . i.e., before the product of the ground belongs to you completely. The law applies to threshing, the bearing of burdens, or any other work. This prohibition gives the animal, which helps you in taking possession of the fruits of the earth, a right

[1] "You shall not muzzle the ox when he treads out the corn."

upon the fruits during its service; and you sin against it by whichever means you prevent it from eating, even if it be by calling to it, or indirectly by instilling fear, or thirst, or by unnecessary separation from the fruits. You may only prevent the animal from eating if the fruits might harm it.

Ecology and the
Jewish Tradition

ERIC G. FREUDENSTEIN

When you besiege a city many days to bring it into your power by making war against it, you shall not destroy the trees thereof by swinging an axe against them; for from them may you eat but not destroy them, for the tree of the field is man's life. . . . (Deuteronomy 20:19–20)

In this Biblical legislation we find a concept that is uppermost in thoughtful men's minds these days: Conservation of the environment, prevention of the destruction of plants and livestock, and limitations on the pollution of air and of fresh water and oceans, in order to protect the ecosystem that makes life possible.[1] Samson Raphael Hirsch, the nineteenth-century commentator, analyzes the passage in Deuteronomy cited above and points out that "the purposeless destruction of anything at all is taken to be forbidden." This is the authoritative traditional viewpoint.[2] Yet it is specifically the despoliation of trees which is prohibited by the Scriptural text. By placing the emphasis on the environment, the Bible seems to speak directly to contemporary man, for whom the environment is high on the scale of priorities.

We may raise the question why the general prohibition against

---

[1] Ever since the Talmudic period this law is referred to in both literary as well as popular usage as *bal tashḥit,* "Do not destroy."
[2] See the preceding essay for the full text of Hirsch's commentary.]

destroying the environment was formulated in a law dealing with a specific situation limited to wartime. One answer seems to be in the well-known Talmudic rule: "Scripture speaks of a common occurrence." Warfare has always been the most destructive of all human activities, from the time of Avimelekh, who "beat down the city [Shekhem], and sowed it with salt" (Judges 9:45), to our own days. . . . For this reason, the case of the beleagured city is a valid example with which to demonstrate the Torah's standards of conduct for safeguarding the environment.

A second answer may also be appropriate. According to Hirsch, the Torah will select a particular law for inclusion in its codes in order to demonstrate the validity of a fundamental principle by showing how that principle must apply even under extraordinary conditions. Thus, for example, the code of law in the twenty-first chapter of Exodus starts with legislation regulating the treatment of slaves, to show the respect to be given all human beings, by demanding dignified treatment for the one on the lowest end of the social scale in antiquity. Applying Hirsch's criterion to Deuteronomy 20:19, the necessity for regard of the environment is shown to be a vital concern of the Torah because it is demanded even under the emergency conditions of a war.

According to Umberto Cassuto, late professor of Bible at the Hebrew University in Jerusalem, the legal cases recorded in the Torah have been selected to show important points in which Israel's conduct was to be different, and superior to the contemporary Middle Eastern legal tradition. Following Cassuto's line of reasoning, the law in Deuteronomy 20:19 was picked to emphasize the importance of the protection of the environment in a civilization where such considerations were not accepted.

The *Sifre,* one of the oldest collections of rabbinic traditions (quoted by *Yalkut* to this passage), specifically extends the legislation of Deuteronomy 20:19 to prohibit interferences with water resources: "From where do we know that one may not divert the arm of a river? Because it is said 'You shall not destroy [the city's] trees' by any means whatever. It is said, 'by swinging an axe against them.' This would seem to prohibit only the use of iron tools. From where do we know then not to divert the flow of water?

Since it is said 'You shall not destroy its trees,' this includes all methods of destruction."

Maimonides spells out the reason thus: "One may not prevent the water supply from reaching the trees of the beleaguered city lest they dry up and wither" (*Code, Laws of Kings* 6:8). Other authorities interpret the *Sifre* in a larger sense, saying that one may not divert the flow of water from the city in order not to cut off the supply of drinking water from man and beast. This extension of the law is involved in the following story from the Second Book of Chronicles:

> And when Hezekiah saw that Sennacherib king of Assyria was come, and that he was purposed to fight against Jerusalem, he took counsel with his princes and his mighty men to stop the waters of the fountains which were without the city; and they helped him. So there was gathered much people together, and they stopped all the fountains, and the brook that flowed through the midst of the land, saying: "Why should the kings of Assyria come, and find much water?". . . This same Hezekiah also stopped the upper spring of the waters of Gihon, and brought them straight down on the west side of the city of David (II Chronicles 32:2–4; 32:30).

The Talmudic sages (in a Baraita in the Babylonian Talmud *Pesaḥim* 56a) strongly disapproved of Hezekiah's action. Stopping the water supply of Jerusalem was contrary to the spirit of the law of *bal tashḥit:* "The Rabbis taught: King Hezekiah stopped the upper spring of the waters of Gihon and the sages did not approve of this action."

Another instance of the Torah's concern not to upset the ecological balance as a result of warfare is the passage in Exodus 23:29–30: "Not in one year will I drive them [the Canaanites] out before you, lest the land become desolate and the beasts of the field multiply against you. By little and little I will drive them out before you until you be increased and can occupy the land."

A second important body of Torah laws on environment are the passages in Leviticus 25:34 and in Numbers 35. In this legislation concerning the land grants given the Levites, the law says: "The fields of the common land surrounding their cities shall not be sold, for it is a possession for them for all time." The traditional Jewish interpretation is clearly stated by Samson Raphael Hirsch:

> The cities which were to be given to the Levites were to be surrounded by a "green belt" which extended 2,000 cubits in every direction, of which the inner 1,000 cubits were called *migrash ha-ir.* This "common," the immediate surrounding of the city, was an open space reserved for the animals, moveable possessions and for the other amenities of the lives of the citizens, e.g., public laundries. The outer 1,000 cubits (according to Maimonides 2,000 cubits) were fields and vineyards. The whole domain of a city consisted, therefore, of 1) inner city, 2) common, and 3) fields. Now here it says: "The field of the common land surrounding their cities shall not be sold." The Talmud (*Arakhin* 33b) takes these words in their widest sense: The land is not to be transferred for another use. Not only is the property not to be estranged from its original owner but also not from its original status. The field may not be converted to a free open space or common; the common not, by being plowed and sown, into a field, or by being built upon into a city; and equally so, not the city into a field or open space (*Arakhin,* last Mishnah). "For it is a possession for them for all time." Because it was given to them as their possession for all time, therefore, at no particular contemporary time has anyone the right to make any alteration to it. No present moment has the sole disposition to it, all future times have equal claim to it, and in the same condition that it has been received from the past is it to be handed on to the future.

An important aspect of pollution abatement—sewage disposal— is regulated in Deuteronomy 23:13–15, even in wartime. Disposal of sewage by burial in the ground, not by dumping into rivers or littering the countryside, is required by this law: "And you shall have a place outside the (military) camp, thither shall you go out, and a spade shall you have with your accoutrements, so that when you sit down outside you shall dig therewith, and turn back and cover over again that which comes from you." Maimonides incorporated this Biblical law into his Code:

> It is forbidden to relieve oneself inside the camp or anywhere on a field. It is a positive commandment to prepare a special path for

easing oneself there. For it is said: "You shall have a place outside the camp." Furthermore, it is a positive commandment for everyone to carry a spade as part of his war gear. One shall go out by that path and dig, ease oneself and cover up. As it is said: "A spade shall be with your gear." Regardless whether or not the Holy Ark travels with the troops, this must be the procedure to be followed. For it is said: "Your camp shall be holy" (*Laws of Kings*, 6:14–15).

Professor Dov Zlotnick, of the Jewish Theological Seminary, feels that one of the ancillary purposes of this law is the maintenance of a cleaner environment, and related to this matter is the fact that the waste disposal of the city of Jerusalem was subject to rabbinic ordinance, and no dunghills or garbage piles were permitted within the city limits because of vermin (*Bava Kama* 82b). The ashes from the Temple offerings were taken outside the city, based on Leviticus 6:4, deposited in a place where they were protected from being scattered by wind and animals (Maimonides *Code, Laws of Tamid and Musaf Offerings* 2:15) or from being washed away by floods (*Meiri, Peshahim* 27b).

Air pollution was controlled by legislation of the early Talmudic period (Mishnah *Bava Batra* 2:8–9; in Talmud editions 24b, 25a). These regulations prohibit the establishment of a permanent threshing floor within 50 cubits of the city limits lest the chaff be carried by the wind and jeopardize the health of the city dwellers. Similarly, animal carcasses, tanneries and cemeteries are not permitted within 50 cubits of the city limits and no furnaces were to be erected in the city of Jerusalem because of the fumes (*Bava Kama* 82b).

The protection of the world's animal species from extinction is an important element in the narrative of Noah's ark. In the Holiness Code of Leviticus, the Torah proclaims the sacredness of each species and its inviolability: "You shall keep My laws: You shall not breed your animal in a mixture of species" (Leviticus 19:19). The Talmud explains the opening sentence of this verse with the statement: "You shall keep My laws: The laws I engraved in My world" (Jerusalem Talmud *Kilayim* 1:7 and Babylonian Talmud *Kiddushin* 39a). Hirsch paraphrases this dictum as follows: "Keep My laws, the laws of nature which I established long before these laws which I am giving you now." Based on this

Talmudic exegesis, Maimonides rules that the cross-breeding of animals is a prohibition of universal relevance and applicable to non-Jews as well as to Jews (*Code, Laws of Kings* 10:6).[3]

The protection of important plant varieties is legislated in the Talmud (Mishnah *Tamid* 2:3; Talmud editions 29a, b). It was forbidden to burn any wood of the olive, the vine, the datepalm or the fig on the altar of the Temple in order to protect the environment of the Holy Land.[4] A modern extrapolation of this thinking is the Nature Reserve Authority of the modern State of Israel.

Even the protection of mineral resources is touched upon briefly in the Talmud as being within the domain of the law of *bal tashḥit*. Thus, it is prohibited to cause a naphtha lamp to burn too quickly, as a wasteful destruction of a valuable natural asset (Babylonian Talmud *Shabbat* 67b).

Preservation specifically of the Palestinian countryside [5] is the objective of an early Talmudic law which states: "One may not raise goats or sheep in the cultivated areas of Palestine," because of the damage these animals will cause to fields of young plants (*Bava Kama,* last Mishnah, chap. 7; in Talmud editions 79b). The depredations of such flocks are still a serious problem in the Arab states and the gravity with which offences against despoiling the countryside were considered is illustrated in this graphic story related in the Talmud:

> The Rabbis taught: It happened that a pious man had a heart ailment. He consulted the physicians and they told him there was only one remedy, namely to take fresh milk every morning. The doctors

[3] The unwarranted killing of any animal or feeding it harmful matter is included by the Talmud in the provisions of *bal tashḥit* (*Ḥullin* 7b, *Avodah Zarah* 30b).

[4] This is the view of R. Aḥa bar Yaakov, which is accepted by Maimonides and others. However, according to R. Papa, the reason for the prohibition against burning vine and olive must be looked for in the fact that these branches give off excessive smoke. We have here, then, another ordinance against air pollution. R. Eliezer adds to the list of forbidden trees the oak, the sycamore, the carob and the unidentified *mayish* because of the smoke and their being, therefore, potential pollutants.

[5] Not included in this essay are the laws of the Sabbatical year (Leviticus 25:1–7), since their primary purposes were religious symbolism and social doctrine and not agricultural technique. However, it may be presumed that soil conservation was an intended ancillary function of these laws.

brought him a goat, tied her to the posts of his bed, and he used the milk every morning. Several days later his colleagues came to visit him. When they saw the she-goat tied to the posts of the bed they turned back saying: "There is an armed bandit in this person's house [the goat] and we should pay a visit here!" Upon further investigation they found that there was no blame attached to that man except for the transgression of the she-goat. On his death-bed he confessed: "I know that I have committed no crime except for the matter of that goat, in which I transgressed the regulations of my colleagues" (*Bava Kama* 80a).

The Spanish medieval commentator, Rabbi Menaḥem ben Shelomo ha-Meiri (quoted in the anthology *Shitah Mekubbetzet*) raises the question as to why the pious man in the story was ostracized by his friends. "May not even the Sabbath be violated for reasons of health, in case the safety of life and limb is at stake?" Meiri answers that the pious scholar should not have relied on his own judgment, even though that judgment was correct. What was involved in this case constituted a decision against the public welfare in his own favor and a dispensation should have been obtained from another qualified authority. . . .

Sensitivity to nature can be found by a careful reading of the creation story. Adam, the first man, is placed in his world, in the garden of Eden, "to work it and to guard it" (Genesis 2:15). This supervision and maintenance can be taken as the duty to protect the natural environment. Benno Jacob, in his commentary on Genesis, says the following:

> Adam's relation to the Owner of the garden in the terminology of Halakhah, Jewish law, is that of a guardian. To guard may simply mean careful treatment and protection against damage. Primarily, however, this term is meant to characterize the garden as someone else's property. It is a garden that belongs to God, not to man.[6]

In other words, man is the trusted steward appointed to guard and maintain the garden, i.e., the setting into which he has been placed by divine providence.

[6] B. Jacob, *Das erste Buch der Tora, Genesis* (Schocken Verlag, 1934), p. 91.

No discussion of ecology in the Jewish tradition would be complete without a mention of the passages—too frequent to enumerate—in the Torah, Psalms and Prophets, in which the messianic age is described as an era of peace between man and nature. The following passages from Joel and Amos must suffice:

> Fear not, O earth,
> Jubilate and be glad. . . .
> Fear not, you beast of the field,
> For the pastures of the desert grow verdant;
> For the tree bears its fruit again,
> Fig tree and vine yield their strength . . .
> For He gives you the former rain in just measure,
> And He causes to come down for you the rain,
> The former rain and the latter rain, at the proper time.
> And the floors shall be full of corn.
> And the vats shall overflow with wine and oil.
> And I will restore to you the years that the locust has eaten,
> The canker-worm, and the caterpillar, and the palmer-worm,
> My great army which I sent among you.
> And you shall eat in plenty and be satisfied,
> And shall praise the name of the Lord your God,
> That has dealt wondrously with you.
>
> (Joel 2:21–26)

> Behold, the days come, says the Lord,
> That the plowman shall overtake the reaper,
> And the treader of grapes him that sows seed;
> And the mountains shall drop sweet wine,
> And all the hills shall melt.
> And I will turn the captivity of My people Israel,
> And they shall build the waste cities, and inhabit them;
> And they shall plant vineyards, and drink the wine thereof;
> They shall also make gardens, and eat the fruit of them.
> And I will plant them upon their land,
> And they shall no more be plucked up
> Out of their land which I have given them,
> Says the Lord your God.
>
> (Amos 9:13–15)

The prophetic metaphor "and I will plant them upon their land" is unmatched in the literary power with which it depicts the organic harmony of man and his natural environment. The first use of this metaphor for the human condition in the messianic age is found in the Song of Moses: "You shall plant them in the mountain of Your inheritance" (Exodus 15:17). The inspired phrase of the "planting of man" is so laden with layers of meaning that the sages of the Talmud commented: "They prophesied but they were not aware of all the implications of their message" (*Bava Batra* 119b). Our generation may discern here a new relevance which was not apparent to Jews of an earlier age. To a generation which finds its existence darkened by the threat to the human environment, the Torah's imagery has acquired an added dimension of meaning. Thus, the Torah's word for the origin of man is that man was "placed in the garden." As yet, no intimate relationship to his surroundings is indicated. But in Moses' song of the messianic fulfillment of the destiny of Israel, of mankind, Moses prays that man shall be "planted in God's mountain," harmoniously integrated into his terrestrial environment. Thus the development of the relationship between man and nature is forcefully described by these contrasting metaphors, one at the outset, the other at the goal, of man's journey.

The passages cited here from the Bible and the Talmud disprove the repeated statements in the popular press that the "Judeo-Christian concept" of Genesis 1:28 is the cause of the destruction of our environment by Western civilization. Rather it is man's misunderstanding of this Scriptural concept and his insensitivity to the Holy Writ's concern for God's nature that should be accused. The concern for the "guarding of the garden" in which man has been placed by providence is implicit in the Scriptural message. It has been made explicit in the Jewish tradition as formulated in the Biblical exegesis of the Rabbis and in the legal ordinances of the Talmud. One observation, however, may be in order. Franz Oppenheimer, the social scientist, once remarked that it is not important for history to record who said something first, but rather who said something first in such a way that the world paid attention. Ancient Jewish tradition stressed the maintenance of the biosphere over three and one half thousand years ago, but during the centuries of the Diaspora, divorced from the land, that message of our venerable tradition became weak. Jews were often cooped up in urban ghettos, their energies absorbed by the struggle for survival in a hostile world which they were powerless to influence. Nor was the destruction of the world's natural assets as yet a threat to human existence. In modern times, the active participation of Jews in the Diaspora, in all phases of the public welfare, the reclamation of the land in the State of Israel and a general awareness of the problems of ecology, have created a new climate for a deeper understanding and acceptance of the concern for the environment evinced by the Jewish tradition. Conditions are now propitious for the ancient Jewish message of *bal tashḥit* to be once again proclaimed loud and clear to all men of goodwill.

PART VII

Pursuit of Peace

Editor's Note

We often think of peace as simply the absence of war—and in this imperfect world we must be grateful even for this mercy. But peace —*shalom*—to the prophets of the Hebrew Bible meant much more than this merely negative state. It meant unity and concord; it meant minds and hearts bound together. It meant almost what we mean by love: such a state of harmony, of trust—of what the Greeks called *homonoia*—that wars or quarrels would be impossible, unthinkable.

It was peace in this sense of wholeness, of total reconciliation, of which the prophets dreamed and which they actively sought. In such a state of peace, "the wolf will dwell with the lamb, the leopard will lie down with the kid" (Isaiah 11:6). In such a state of peace, "men will beat their swords into plowshares and their spears into pruning-hooks" (Micah 4:3).

But it is not the peace of death or sleep or dullness; it is the peace of strength, peace won by mastery over evil, by harnessing the force of the so-called "evil inclination" to serve the interests of the good. Such peace, to be durable and endurable, must be founded on truth and justice: "Speak the truth to one another, render in your gates judgments that are true and make for peace, do not devise evil in your hearts against one another . . . love truth and peace" (Zechariah 8:16, 19). The ideal of Judaism is not peace alone. It is peace and truth and justice. Without peace, there is little room or hope for truth or justice to be effective. Without truth and justice, peace can mean only oppression and suppression. This is why in the Jewish classics truth, justice, and peace are often mentioned together—because they are inseparable and interdependent.

The Vision of Micah

ROBERT GORDIS

Two centuries ago, Voltaire mockingly complained that "the Bible is better known than read." The situation has surely not improved with the passage of time. On the other hand, when reverence for the Bible is matched by knowledge of its contents, a new problem arises. For all too often, familiarity with the great classics of the past blunts their revolutionary impact. In proportion as their words and ideas have become the accepted heritage of the race, later generations find them self-evident, if not downright platitudinous.

This state of affairs is highly deplorable. It means perpetrating a historic injustice, even if unconsciously, against the great teachers and leaders of mankind. It causes men to overlook the struggles and sacrifices which have created the civilization that they have inherited, with the result that they take for granted the values that society has achieved and preserved at so great a cost. Not a little of the spiritual barbarism which is so widespread a phenomenon of our time is due to this factor, for, as Santayana has remarked, he who does not know the past is doomed to repeat it.

The most disastrous aspect of this tendency concerns not the past but the present and future. It deprives men of the unexplored implications and life-giving insights which are still to be found in these classics of the human spirit and which can prove particularly valuable in a confused age sadly in need of guidance and direction.

Among the many outstanding Biblical passages, the Vision of the End-Time in Micah (4:1–5) occupies a unique place. This prophecy, which occurs with some verbal changes in the Book of Isaiah (2:1–5), has raised important critical questions regarding date and authorship. There have been scholars who have regarded Isaiah as the author and Micah as the borrower, while others have held Micah to be the original author and Isaiah the borrower. Other critics have held the passage in both books to be as an interpolation and assigned the Vision to the period of the Second Temple, some even as late as the Hellenistic age. . . . We accept as the most plausible the view proposed as long ago as 1779 by Koppe. He considered the prophecy to be an old, anonymous oracle, which both Isaiah and Micah incorporated into their own thinking and then utilized as a basis for their prophetic activity. These critical problems are interesting to the specialist, but they do not affect our appreciation of the profundity and grandeur of the Vision.

Since no summary or commentary can rival the eloquence of the original text, it is well to repeat these few lines which, so early in human history, adumbrated the concept of human freedom in its widest significance:

> In the end of days it shall come to pass,
> That the mountain of the Lord's house shall be
>   established on the top of the mountains,
> And it shall be exalted above the hills.
> Peoples shall flow unto it,
> And many nations shall come and say,
> "Come, let us go up to the mountain of the Lord,
> To the house of the God of Jacob;
> So that he may teach us of his ways,
> And we will walk in his paths;
> For the law shall go forth from Zion,
> And the word of the Lord from Jerusalem."
> And He shall judge among many peoples,
> And rebuke strong nations afar off;
> They shall beat their swords into plowshares
> And their spears into pruning-hooks;
> Nation shall not lift up sword against nation,
> Neither shall they learn war any more.

They shall sit every man under his vine and under his fig tree;
And none shall make them afraid;
For the mouth of the Lord of hosts has spoken it.
For as all the peoples walk every one in the name of his god,
We will walk in the name of the Lord our God for ever.

(Micah 4:1–5)

At the very outset, the true meaning of the opening phrase, *aḥarit hayamim,* "end of days," should be noted. In spite of their apparent literal meaning, the words are not to be construed as referring to the last climactic act of the human drama before the dissolution of the natural order. That the idiom is very ancient is clear from the Akkadian parallel and from its use in some of the oldest Biblical poems, such as the *Blessing of Jacob* and the *Prophecies of Balaam.* It is used relatively rather than absolutely of the future. Thus it refers to such varied periods as the occupation of Canaan by the Israelite tribes after the Conquest (Genesis 49:1), to the future conquest of Moab and Ammon during the First Temple (Numbers 24:14), to the anticipated early restoration of the Kingdom of Ephraim (Hosea 3:5), to the imagined age of Gog's attack upon a restored Israel (Ezekiel 38:16), and to the age of Antiochus Epiphanes (Daniel 10:14). In other Biblical passages, it is also applied to the ideal or messianic age belonging to the indeterminate future (Jeremiah 23:20; 30:24; 48:47; 49:30, Daniel 2:28). In sum, as Driver has put it, the phrase, "end of days," refers to the final period within the speaker's perspective, whatever that may be.

Undoubtedly, the author of the *Vision of Micah* was thinking of the future, even of the distant future, but it is significant that *there is no indication that he envisaged the establishment of the new world order as a result of a great cataclysm or of a special divine intervention.* For him, the nations of the earth, constituted as at present, would surrender their present attitude of mutual hatred and lawlessness, in favor of a new outlook based on brotherhood and justice.

Therein lies the basic difference between Hebrew prophecy at its highest and the apocalyptists, who emerged after the Babylonian Exile. The Return under Cyrus (538 B.C.E.) proved far less glorious than had been anticipated. The reconstituted Jewish community of the Second Commonwealth, slight in numbers and influence, was beset by countless internal difficulties and dominated by a succession of foreign overlords, Persian, Ptolemaic, Seleucide, and Roman. The historic function of prophecy was now at an end, and so it drew to a close.

In the place of the prophets, the apocalyptists, the "revealers of hidden things," now arose. Despairing of the natural capacities of man, and yet cleaving fast to the prophetic faith in a God of justice, these latter day seers were driven to the conception of a catastrophe as the prelude to the salvation of Israel and the world. As world conditions continued to deteriorate and the possibility of human redemption through natural means became ever more remote, especially in the Hellenistic and Roman periods, this tendency gained in strength and intensity. Apocalypse is represented in the Hebrew Bible only by the Book of Daniel and perhaps a few passages in the prophetic books (Isaiah 24–27; 33–34; Zechariah 12–14). It finds manifold expression, however, in the non-canonical Pseudepigrapha, the New Testament, and rabbinic literature.

Today, the crisis theology, with its emphasis on man's sinfulness, which is popular in many theological circles, reflects the same mood of despair over man's nature, having been elicited by the tragic world-situation confronting our age. Whatever one's attitude toward these spiritual currents of our own day, it is important to note that for our prophet, the End-Time would come to pass without any dramatic catastrophe, but rather as a result of the free conviction of men, voluntarily accepting the law of God as the norm for conduct. The prophet does not look forward to a Utopia into which men will have been driven either by an upheaval of natural forces or by the scarcely gentler compulsions of human power, whether embodied in *pax Romana, Rule Britannia, Deutschland Ueber Alles, the American Century,* or "the dictatorship of the proletariat." His vision rests on a faith in man's capacity to achieve the ideal by the free exercise of his reason and will.

This End-Time is strikingly distinguished from the reality of the present order by the existence of universal peace, and it is in this connection that the passage is generally cited. Here, too, an excess of familiarity with its phrases has dulled men's perception of the novelty and originality of its ideas. Thus, even today, it is far from universally conceded that peace is more than a beautiful ideal, being the inevitable goal of human history, and, by that token, a practical program for human relations. In the ancient world, universal peace was beyond the ken even of a Plato. In *The Republic,* which embodies his vision of the End-Time, the great philosopher makes provision for a standing army to protect his ideal city-state against the barbarian hordes. For him, mankind was forever divided into Greek and barbarian, with the sword as the arbiter of human destiny.

Centuries after Plato, another world figure writing in Greek declared: "There is neither Jew nor Greek, there is neither bond nor free, there is neither male nor female, for you are all one in Christ Jesus" (Galatians 3:28), but for Paul a Hellenistic environment had only been superimposed on a Hebrew heredity. Even closer to the prophetic standpoint, because it is unqualified by any theological doctrine, is the rabbinic statement: "I call Heaven and earth to witness that whether one be Gentile or Jew, man or woman, slave or free, the divine spirit rests on each in accordance with his deeds" (*Yalkut Shimeoni on Judges,* sec. 42). Though he may have lacked the dialectic skill of the Greek sage, it was the Hebrew prophet who enunciated the ideal of peace which entered the mainstream of Jewish thought and which, through the Scriptures, sacred to Christianity as well, became part of the world view of Western man.

The extent to which this ideal has penetrated the soul of mankind is illustrated by one observation. Men often develop a sense of bitterness and frustration at the failure of world organization to achieve lasting peace, but rarely, if ever, does the feeling arise that the goal itself had best be abandoned as chimerical. On the contrary, peace is today regarded as an inalienable human right, the rightful heritage of the race, and those who, rightly or wrongly, are considered as depriving men of this boon are stigmatized as the arch-villains of our day.

The contribution of the Vision of Micah to the formulation of human rights is not exhausted by its enunciation of the ideal of peace, nor even by its faith in the destined attainment of this goal. The prophet goes further and points out the road to peace, through the creation of a binding international law, centered in a recognized authority. He does not depend on goodwill or on love to guard the peace, nor does he expect that all differences of outlook and all conflicts of interest will miraculously disappear in the End-Time. Before peace can be a reality, there must be a law that shall go forth from Zion, which will be accepted as binding among the nations and be enforced among the peoples. The prophet would have denied the doctrine of national sovereignty, when defined to mean "my country, may she always be in the right, but my country, right or wrong." If government means an agency capable of imposing its will upon its members, the prophet emphatically believed in world government.

It is noteworthy that he speaks of judging between nations. Judgment means the enforcement of justice. For the prophet, this Law emanated from the God of Jacob, who, as all the prophets taught, is the one God of humanity. But irrespective of its source, the character of this international covenant is not legalistic, but moral, rooted in justice and truth and therefore capable of supporting the structure of peace. A Talmudic utterance makes this idea explicit: "Upon three things the world rests, upon justice, upon truth, and upon peace. And the three are one, for when justice is done, truth prevails and peace is established" (Jerusalem Talmud, *Ta'anit* 4:2; *Megilla* 3:5).

Unquestionably, however, for our age the most significant contribution to be found in the prophet's vision of the End-Time is one that has been generally overlooked—his conception of nationalism. Within five short verses, the words for "people" and "nation" occur no less than seven times, striking testimony to his belief that national groups will remain as permanent features of human society even in its ideal phase. The bearing of his thought on our age is obvious, for today nationalism has reached the acme of its power and the nadir of its degradation. It is the basic ill of our age, aside from its economic chaos, to which indeed nationalism has largely contributed. No greater peril threatens the survival of the race than nationalism, man's total absorption in his own ethnic or political group, which recognizes no morality beyond it and regards its interests at all costs as the highest good.

It is sufficient to recall the intimate bond between nationalism and Nazi and Fascist dictatorship. But even Bolshevism, which began with the slogan of internationalism and the world proletariat, has adopted with mounting fervor the gospel of the "Communist fatherland," whose "rights" to expansion and buffer states are indistinguishable from the "legitimate interests" of Czarist Russia of several decades ago, except that they are pursued with greater efficiency and skill. The Second World War was the result of unbridled national ambition that wiped out every vestige of fair play and pity in the hearts of otherwise moral men. Should a Third World War eventuate, it would be another colossal and horrible burnt offering on the altar of exclusive national loyalty.

What is the remedy? Some advanced circles have proposed the ideal of cosmopolitanism, the merging and disappearance of all national groupings. Instead of being Frenchmen, Germans, or Americans, men would become citizens of a world state. One nationality, one language, one culture, and, if religion is to survive at all, one faith: this would constitute the common heritage of mankind.

At first such an ideal has an undeniable grandeur and nobility. Upon sober examination, however, it becomes clear that if current versions of nationalism are a nightmare, this type of internationalism would prove an impractical dream.

The history of mankind, both recent and remote, discloses no signs that nations are disappearing, or are seeking to sink their differences in a common world patriotism. On the contrary, the past twenty years have seen the creation of a score of new nations, who struggle desperately for their place in the sun. The First World War created many independent states in Central Europe. . . . The past decade has seen the emergence of nationalism as a dynamic factor in the Arab world, in India, China, Burma, and Indonesia. In sum, all signs point, not to a diminution of nationalist loyalty, but to its intensification, or at least to its retention for decades to come.

Nationalism will endure, not merely because of propaganda or the innate corruption of man, but because it draws upon roots deep in the soul of man. It is normal that a man be attached to the soil where he was born, and where he spent the pleasant years of his childhood; that he be drawn to his own people, with whom he is most familiar. The songs one's mother sang, the language she spoke, the festivals of one's childhood—these have an appeal beyond words and beyond reason, an appeal which no reasonable man will lightly dismiss.

The goal of a uniform mass of human beings seems therefore to fly in the face of reality. But, aside from being impractical, this concept of internationalism would prove disastrous for the human spirit. National loyalty is the matrix in which all culture is formed. Every cultural achievement of which we have record is particularistic in origin, however universal its goal. Culture is always rooted in a given milieu, drawing its substance from a specific tradition, expressing itself in a given language, and deriving its power from a sense of kinship with a definite people. It is true that Hebrew prophecy, Greek art, Italian opera, German poetry, and English drama belong to the world. But in every instance, they reflect their ethnic sources and environmental influences, without which they are inconceivable. If, contrary to all indications, national loyalties were to dissolve, it would spell cultural anemia for the world. To borrow a distinction employed by some thinkers, civilization, the science and technology of the world, may be conceivable without nationalism, but not culture, the literature, art, music, and philosophy of the age. . . .

But if nationalism is, on the one hand, natural and even essential to the growth of culture, and, on the other, constitutes a potential menace to human survival, tragic alternatives seem to face the human race—either stagnation or death. Must mankind be condemned to choose between the Scylla of a sterile, colorless cosmopolitanism and the Charybdis of a mad, bloodthirsty nationalism?

Merely to castigate nationalism as evil may offer some psychological relief, but as a practical program it is quixotic and doomed to failure. In this area of human conflict, as in others, another solution, at once more practical and more ideal, may be discovered in the prophets of Israel. In the literal sense of the term, the Hebrew prophets were the true internationalists, believers in the creation of proper relations among nations.

The author of the Vision of the End-Time looked forward, not to the elimination but to the moralization of national loyalties. As authority would be vested in the World Law, the nexus binding the members of a people together would not be force but a common cultural heritage, the voluntary association of men and women for the preservation and cultivation of a cherished body of ideals, practices, and values. This ideal of nationalism as exclusively a cultural ethnic loyalty has scarcely penetrated the thinking of most men, but it offers the only road to survival for mankind.

It is noteworthy that the only group, which however imperfectly, embodies this prophetic conception of nationalism is the Jewish people, which is united the world over by no central political allegiance, military power, or geographical contiguity. This unique group is best described by the Hebrew term, *am* or people. Possessing an unbroken history of the thirty-five centuries, it feels itself bound by a sense of kinship from the past, and claims Abraham, Isaac, and Jacob as its ancestors, while welcoming those who voluntarily seek to join its ranks from without. Its members share a common religio-cultural tradition in the present, which they feel free to interpret in accordance with their own attitudes and insights. Finally, they look forward to a common destiny in the future, however much their status may differ under varying political, social, and economic conditions across the globe.

The preservation of Jewish group loyalty, which has been so signally advanced in our day by the creation of the State of Israel, does not represent a retrogression from the prophetic ideal, as is sometimes erroneously supposed. The State of Israel will make possible a full national life for those members of the Jewish people who will accept Israeli citizenship and take up residence within its borders. For the majority of Jews, who will continue to live throughout the world, cherishing their political and civic allegiance to their native lands, the cultural and spiritual influence of the land of Israel will prove a regenerative force of incalculable value.

For the author of the Vision, as for all the Hebrew prophets, the establishment of the people of Israel in its homeland was a necessary prelude to the redemption of the world, for the future of humanity was inconceivable without the survival of Israel as a recognizable entity. It is to "the house of the God of Jacob" on Mount Zion that the world will turn for guidance and government.

As the frequent repetition of the terms, "nation" and "people," indicates, however, not only Israel must survive in the End-Time.

The future has room for other national groups on the same terms, a national loyalty cultural in essence and moral in function. In Santayana's words, "a man's feet must be firmly planted in his own country, but his eyes must survey the world." The prophets went further, their hearts embraced the world. . . .

. . . The Vision of Micah is a farsighted interpretation of nationalism, in which love of one's own people and loyalty to humanity represent two concentric circles. The bugbear of dual allegiance, which exercises little minds to the present day, would never have troubled the prophets, because for them all loyalties, national as well as international, were peaceful in expression and subject to the moral law. Hence every Hebrew prophet, from Amos and Hosea to Deutero-Isaiah and Malachi, exemplifies both nationalism and internationalism. Modern religious thinkers, who deplore nationalism or at best seek to ignore or dismiss it as irrelevant, in their conception of the good life of society, would do well to be instructed by the prophets of Israel. For their lives and careers are grounded on the conviction that nationalism is not necessarily evil, and, what is more, can prove a source of spiritual enrichment in the life of man. . . .

Appendices

Bill of Rights in the United States Constitution

First Ten Amendments

Amendment I

Congress shall make no law respecting an establishment of religion, or prohibiting the free exercise thereof; or abridging the freedom of speech, or of the press; or the right of the people peaceably to assemble and to petition the Government for a redress of grievances.

Amendment II

A well regulated Militia, being necessary to the security of a free State, the right of the people to keep and bear Arms, shall not be infringed.

Amendment III

No Soldier shall in time of peace be quartered in any house, without the consent of the Owner, nor in time of war, but in a manner to be prescribed by law.

Amendment IV

The right of the people to be secure in their persons, houses, papers, and effects, against unreasonable searches and seizures, shall not be violated, and no Warrants shall issue, but upon probable cause, supported by Oath or affirmation, and particularly describing the place to be searched, and the persons or things to be seized.

Amendment V

No person shall be held to answer for a capital, or otherwise infamous crime, unless on a presentment or indictment of a Grand Jury, except in cases arising in the land or naval forces, or in the Militia, when in actual service in time of War or public danger; nor shall any person be subject for the same offence to be twice put in jeopardy of life or limb; nor shall be compelled in any criminal case to be a witness against himself, nor be deprived of life, liberty, or property, without due process of law; nor shall private property be taken for public use, without just compensation.

Amendment VI

In all criminal prosecutions, the accused shall enjoy the right to a speedy and public trial, by an impartial jury of the State and district wherein the crime shall have been committed, which district shall have been previously ascertained by law, and to be informed of the nature and cause of the accusation; to be confronted with the witnesses against him; to have compulsory process for obtaining witnesses in his favor, and to have the Assistance of Counsel for his defence.

Amendment VII

In suits at common law, where the value in controversy shall exceed twenty dollars, the right of trial by jury shall be preserved, and no fact tried by a jury, shall be otherwise re-examined in any

Court of the United States, than according to the rules of the common law.

Amendment VIII

Excessive bail shall not be required, nor excessive fines imposed, nor cruel and unusual punishments inflicted.

Amendment IX

The enumeration in the Constitution, of certain rights, shall not be construed to deny or disparage others retained by the people.

Amendment X

The powers not delegated to the United States by the Constitution, nor prohibited by it to the States, are reserved to the States respectively, or to the people.

Other Amendments

Amendment XIII

Section 1. Neither slavery nor involuntary servitude, except as a punishment for crime whereof the party shall have been duly convicted, shall exist within the United States, or any place subject to their jurisdiction.

Section 2. Congress shall have power to enforce this article by appropriate legislation.

Amendment XIV

Section 1. All persons born or naturalized in the United States, and subject to the jurisdiction thereof, are citizens of the United

States and of the State wherein they reside. No State shall make or enforce any law which shall abridge the privileges or immunities of citizens of the United States; nor shall any State deprive any person of life, liberty, or property, without due process of law; nor deny to any person within its jurisdiction the equal protection of the laws. . . .

Section 5. The Congress shall have power to enforce, by appropriate legislation, the provisions of this article.

Amendment XV

Section 1. The right of citizens of the United States to vote shall not be denied or abridged by the United States or by any State on account of race, color, or previous condition of servitude.

Section 2. The Congress shall have power to enforce this article by appropriate legislation.

Amendment XIX

The right of citizens of the United States to vote shall not be denied or abridged by the United States or by any State on account of sex.

Congress shall have power, by appropriate legislation, to enforce the provisions of this article.

Amendment XXIV

Section 1. The right of citizens of the United States to vote in any primary or other election for President or Vice President, for electors for President or Vice President, or for Senator or Representative in Congress, shall not be denied or abridged by the United States or any State by reason of failure to pay any poll tax or other tax.

Section 2. The Congress shall have the power to enforce this article by appropriate legislation.

Provisions from Original Constitution

Article I

Section 9. . . . The Privilege of the Writ of Habeas Corpus shall not be suspended, unless when in Cases of Rebellion or Invasion the public Safety may require it.

No Bill of Attainder or ex post facto Law shall be passed.

Section 10. No State shall . . . pass any Bill of Attainder, ex post facto Law, or Law impairing the Obligation of Contracts. . . .

Article III

Section 2. The trial of all Crimes, except in cases of Impeachment, shall be by Jury. . . .

Article IV

Section 2. The Citizens of each State shall be entitled to all Privileges and Immunities of citizens in the several States.

Article VI

. . . No religious Test shall ever be required as a Qualification to any Office or public Trust under the United States.

Universal Declaration of Human Rights

[On December 10, 1948, the General Assembly of the United Nations adopted and proclaimed the Universal Declaration of Human Rights. Following this historic act, the Assembly called upon all member countries to publicize the text of the Declaration and "to cause it to be disseminated, displayed, read and expounded, principally in schools and other educational institutions, without distinction based on the political status of countries or territories." The United States and forty-seven other member nations voted for the Declaration; none voted against, but eight nations—the U.S.S.R. and five other East European nations, and Saudi Arabia and the Union of South Africa abstained. Implementation waits upon a covenant that would need to be adopted, signed, and ratified.]

Preamble

Whereas recognition of the inherent dignity and of the equal and inalienable rights of all members of the human family is the foundation of freedom, justice and peace in the world,

Whereas disregard and contempt for human rights have resulted in barbarous acts which have outraged the conscience of mankind, and the advent of a world in which human beings shall enjoy freedom of speech and belief and freedom from fear and want has been proclaimed as the highest aspiration of the common people,

Whereas it is essential, if man is not to be compelled to have recourse, as a last resort, to rebellion against tyranny and oppression, that human rights should be protected by the rule of law,

Whereas it is essential to promote the development of friendly relations between nations,

Whereas the peoples of the United Nations have in the Charter reaffirmed their faith in fundamental human rights, in the dignity and worth of the human person and in the equal rights of men and women and have determined to promote social progress and better standards of life in larger freedom,

Whereas Member States have pledged themselves to achieve, in cooperation with the United Nations, the promotion of universal respect for and observance of human rights and fundamental freedoms,

Whereas a common understanding of these rights and freedoms is of the greatest importance for the full realization of this pledge,

Now, Therefore,

The General Assembly proclaims

This Universal Declaration of Human Rights as a common standard of achievement for all peoples and all nations, to the end that every individual and every organ of society, keeping this Declaration constantly in mind, shall strive by teaching and education to promote respect for these rights and freedoms and by progressive measures, national and international, to secure their universal and effective recognition and observance, both among the peoples of Member States themselves and among the peoples of territories under their jurisdiction.

Article 1

All human beings are born free and equal in dignity and rights. They are endowed with reason and conscience and should act towards one another in a spirit of brotherhood.

Article 2

Everyone is entitled to all the rights and freedoms set forth in this Declaration, without distinction of any kind, such as race, color, sex, language, religion, political or other opinion, national or social origin, property, birth or other status.

Furthermore, no distinction shall be made on the basis of the political, jurisdictional or international status of the country or territory to which a person belongs, whether it be independent, trust, non-self-governing or under any other limitation of sovereignty.

Article 3

Everyone has the right to life, liberty and security of person.

Article 4

No one shall be held in slavery or servitude; slavery and the slave trade shall be prohibited in all their forms.

Article 5

No one shall be subjected to torture or to cruel, inhuman or degrading treatment or punishment.

Article 6

Everyone has the right to recognition everywhere as a person before the law.

Article 7

All are equal before the law and are entitled without any discrimination to equal protection of the law. All are entitled to equal protection against any discrimination in violation of this Declaration and against any incitement to such discrimination.

Article 8

Everyone has the right to an effective remedy by the competent national tribunals for acts violating the fundamental rights granted him by the constitution or by law.

Article 9

No one shall be subjected to arbitrary arrest, detention or exile.

Article 10

Everyone is entitled in full equality to a fair and public hearing by an independent and impartial tribunal, in the determination of his rights and obligations and of any criminal charge against him.

Article 11

(1) Everyone charged with a penal offence has the right to be presumed innocent until proved guilty according to law in a public trial at which he has had all the guarantees necessary for his defence. (2) No one shall be held guilty of any penal offence on account of any act or omission which did not constitute a penal offence, under national or international law, at the time when it was committed. Nor shall a heavier penalty be imposed than the one that was applicable at the time the penal offence was committed.

Article 12

No one shall be subjected to arbitrary interference with his privacy, family, home or correspondence, nor to attacks upon his honor and reputation. Everyone has the right to the protection of the law against such interference or attacks.

Article 13

(1) Everyone has the right to freedom of movement and residence within the borders of each state.
(2) Everyone has the right to leave any country, including his own, and to return to his country.

Article 14

(1) Everyone has the right to seek and to enjoy in other countries asylum from persecution.
(2) This right may not be invoked in the case of prosecutions genuinely arising from non-political crimes or from acts contrary to the purposes and principles of the United Nations.

Article 15

(1) Everyone has the right to a nationality.
(2) No one shall be arbitrarily deprived of his nationality nor denied the right to change his nationality.

Article 16

(1) Men and women of full age, without any limitation due to race, nationality or religion, have the right to marry and to found a family. They are entitled to equal rights as to marriage, during marriage and at its dissolution.
(2) Marriage shall be entered into only with the free and full consent of the intending spouses.
(3) The family is the natural and fundamental group unit of society and is entitled to protection by society and the State.

Article 17

(1) Everyone has the right to own property alone as well as in association with others.

(2) No one shall be arbitrarily deprived of his property.

Article 18

Everyone has the right to freedom of thought, conscience and religion; this right includes freedom to change his religion or belief, and freedom, either alone or in community with others and in public or private, to manifest his religion or belief in teaching, practice, worship and observance.

Article 19

Everyone has the right to freedom of opinion and expression; this right includes freedom to hold opinions without interference and to seek, receive and impart information and ideas through any media and regardless of frontiers.

Article 20

(1) Everyone has the right to freedom of peaceful assembly and association.

(2) No one may be compelled to belong to an association.

Article 21

(1) Everyone has the right to take part in the government of his country, directly or through freely chosen representatives.

(2) Everyone has the right of equal access to public service in his country.

(3) The will of the people shall be the basis of the authority of

government; this will shall be expressed in periodic and genuine elections which shall be by universal and equal suffrage and shall be held by secret vote or by equivalent free voting procedures.

Article 22

Everyone, as a member of society, has the right to social security and is entitled to realization, through national effort and international co-operation and in accordance with the organization and resources of each State, of the economic, social and cultural rights indispensable for his dignity and the free development of his personality.

Article 23

(1) Everyone has the right to work, to free choice of employment, to just and favorable conditions of work and to protection against unemployment.
(2) Everyone, without any discrimination, has the right to equal pay for equal work.
(3) Everyone who works has the right to just and favorable remuneration ensuring for himself and his family an existence worthy of human dignity, and supplemented, if necessary, by other means of social protection.
(4) Everyone has the right to form and to join trade unions for the protection of his interests.

Article 24

Everyone has the right to rest and leisure, including reasonable limitation of working hours and periodic holidays with pay.

Article 25

(1) Everyone has the right to a standard of living adequate for the health and well-being of himself and of his family, including food, clothing, housing and medical care and necessary social services,

and the right to security in the event of unemployment, sickness, disability, widowhood, old age or other lack of livelihood in circumstances beyond his control.

(2) Motherhood and childhood are entitled to special care and assistance. All children, whether born in or out of wedlock, shall enjoy the same social protection.

Article 26

(1) Everyone has the right to education. Education shall be free, at least in the elementary and fundamental stages. Elementary education shall be compulsory. Technical and professional education shall be made generally available and higher education shall be equally accessible to all on the basis of merit.

(2) Education shall be directed to the full development of the human personality and to the strengthening of respect for human rights and fundamental freedoms. It shall promote understanding, tolerance and friendship among all nations, racial or religious groups, and shall further the activities of the United Nations for the maintenance of peace.

(3) Parents have a prior right to choose the kind of education that shall be given to their children.

Article 27

(1) Everyone has the right freely to participate in the cultural life of the community, to enjoy the arts and to share in scientific advancement and its benefits.

(2) Everyone has the right to the protection of the moral and material interests resulting from any scientific, literary or artistic production of which he is the author.

Article 28

Everyone is entitled to a social and international order in which the rights and freedoms set forth in this Declaration can be fully realized.

Article 29

(1) Everyone has duties to the community in which alone the free and full development of his personality is possible.

(2) In the exercise of his rights and freedoms, everyone shall be subject only to such limitations as are determined by law solely for the purpose of securing due recognition and respect for the rights and freedoms of others and of meeting the just requirements of morality, public order and the general welfare in a democratic society.

(3) These rights and freedoms may in no case be exercised contrary to the purposes and principles of the United Nations.

Article 30

Nothing in this Declaration may be interpreted as implying for any State, group or person any right to engage in any activity or to perform any act aimed at the destruction of any of the rights and freedoms set forth herein.

Contributors

Lord Acton (John Emerich Edward Dalberg Acton), 1834–1902. Historian. Regius Professor of Modern History at Cambridge University. Planned and edited the *Cambridge Modern History*. Among his works, all published posthumously, are *Lectures on Modern History* (1906) and *The History of Freedom* (1907).

Samuel Belkin. Scholar and educator. President of Yeshiva University of America since 1943. Author of *Philo and the Oral Law* (1940), *Alexandrian Halakhah in Apologetic Literature* (1936), *In His Image* (1961), and other writings.

Ben Zion Bokser. Rabbi and scholar. Since 1933, Rabbi of the Forest Hills (N.Y.) Jewish Center. Author of *Judaism: Profile of a Faith* (1963), *Judaism and the Christian Predicament* (1966), and other works.

Louis Finkelstein. Scholar and educator. President of Jewish Theological Seminary 1940–51 and chancellor since 1951. Author of numerous works, including *The Pharisees: The Sociological Background of Their Faith* (1962); editor of *The Jews: Their History, Culture and Religion* (1949).

Henri Frankfort, 1897–1954. Archaeologist. Born in Amsterdam; came to the United States in 1938. Director of the Warburg Institute and professor of archaeology at the University of London, 1949–54. Author of *Kingship and the Gods* (1947), *The Birth of Civilization in the Ancient Near East* (1951), and other works.

Eric G. Freudenstein. Born in Germany, and educated in Europe and the United States.

Robert Gordis. Biblical scholar and rabbi. Professor of religion at Temple University. Rabbi emeritus of Rockaway Park (N.Y.) Hebrew Congregation. Professor of Bible at Jewish Theological Seminary. Editor of *Judaism*. Author of *The Book of God and*

305

Man—A Study of Job (1965), *Koheleth, The Man and His World* (1951), *The Song of Songs* (1954), and other works.

Richard G. Hirsch. Rabbi and director, Religious Action Center, Union of American Hebrew Congregations.

Samson Raphael Hirsch, 1808–88. Founder of neo-Orthodoxy at Frankfurt-am-Main, where he became rabbi in 1851. Noted for his commentaries on the Pentateuch (1867–78), the Psalms (1882), and the Prayerbook (published posthumously, 1895); author of *Horeb* (1837), *Nineteen Letters* (1836), and other works. All of the aforementioned commentaries and books have been translated into English.

William A. Irwin, 1884–1967. Professor of Old Testament languages and literature at Southern Methodist University and at the University of Chicago.

Milton R. Konvitz. Professor of industrial and labor relations and professor of law at Cornell University. Author of numerous works, including *Religious Liberty and Conscience* (1968), *Expanding Liberties* (1966), and *Fundamental Liberties of a Free People* (1957). Co-editor of *Jewish Social Studies;* contributing editor of *Midstream;* co-founder and member of the editorial board of *Judaism.*

Norman Lamm. Rabbi and scholar. Erna Michael Professor of Jewish Philosophy at Yeshiva University and a rabbi of the Jewish Center of New York.

Moses Mendelssohn, 1729–86. While recognized by his contemporaries for his philosophical writings, and while he served as the model for the hero in *Nathan the Wise* by Gotthold Lessing (1779), he is chiefly important for his work on Judaism and on behalf of Jewish emancipation. Translated the Pentateuch into German, 1780–83. Wrote *Jerusalem* (1783) to show that the power of excommunication is not part of Judaism and that the right to use force for the control of thought belongs neither to the state nor to the church or synagogue. His collected works in seven volumes were published 1843–45.

Emanuel Rackman. Rabbi and educator. Rabbi of the Fifth Avenue Synagogue, New York. Provost of Yeshiva University of America. Associate editor of *Tradition.*

Further Readings

Brownlie, Ian, ed. *Basic Documents on Human Rights*. Oxford: Clarendon Press, 1971.

Chafee, Zechariah, Jr. *Three Human Rights in the Constitution*. Lawrence, Ks.: University of Kansas Press, 1956.

Cranston, Maurice. *Human Rights To-day*. London: Ampersand Books, 1962.

Holcombe, Arthur N. *Human Rights in the Modern World*. New York: New York University Press, 1948.

"International Human Rights: Part I," *Law and Contemporary Problems*, Vol. 14, no. 3 (1949).

"International Human Rights: Part II," *Law and Contemporary Problems*, Vol. 14, no. 4 (1949).

Lauterpacht, H. *An International Bill of the Rights of Man*. New York: Columbia University Press, 1944.

Luard, Evan, ed. *The International Protection of Human Rights*. London: Thames and Hudson, 1967.

Melden, A. I., ed. *Human Rights*. Belmont, Calif.: Wadsworth Publishing, 1970.

Moskowitz, Moses. *Human Rights and World Order*. New York: Oceana Publications, 1958.

Robertson, A. H. *Human Rights in Europe*. London: Manchester University Press, 1963; New York: Oceana Publications, 1963.

Robertson, A. H., ed. *Human Rights in National and International Law*. London: Manchester University Press, 1968; New York: Oceana Publications, 1968.

Schwelb, Egon. *Human Rights and the International Community*. Chicago: Quadrangle Books, 1964.

UNESO. *Birthright of Man*. New York: Unipub, 1969.

United Kingdom Committee for Human Rights Year. *Human Rights*. London: Heinemann Educational Books, 1967.

VanDyke, Vernon. *Human Rights, The United States and World Community*. New York: Oxford University Press, 1970.

Index